Heidi

Rethinking the Rise and Fall of Apartheid

Rethinking World Politics

General Editor: Professor Michael Cox, *London School of Economics*

In an age of increased academic specialization where more and more books about smaller and smaller topics are becoming the norm, this major new series is designed to provide a forum and a stimulus for leading scholars to address big issues in world politics in an accessible but original manner. A key aim is to transcend the intellectual and disciplinary boundaries which have so often served to limit rather than enhance our understanding of the modern world. In the best tradition of engaged scholarship, it aims to provide clear new perspectives to help make sense of a world in flux.

Each book addresses a major issue or event that has had a formative influence on the twentieth century or the twenty-first century world which is now emerging. Each makes its own distinctive contribution as well as providing an original but accessible guide to competing lines of interpretation.

Taken as a whole, the series will rethink contemporary international politics in ways that are lively, informed and – above all – provocative.

Rethinking the Rise and Fall of Apartheid

South Africa and World Politics

Adrian Guelke

First published 2005 by
PALGRAVE MACMILLAN
Houndmills, Basingstoke, Hampshire RG21 6XS and
175 Fifth Avenue, New York, N.Y. 10010
Companies and representatives throughout the world

PALGRAVE MACMILLAN is the global academic imprint of the Palgrave
Macmillan division of St. Martin's Press, LLC and of Palgrave Macmillan Ltd.
Macmillan® is a registered trademark in the United States, United Kingdom
and other countries. Palgrave is a registered trademark in the European
Union and other countries.

ISBN 0–333–98122–7 hardback
ISBN 0–333–98123–5 paperback

This book is printed on paper suitable for recycling and made from fully
managed and sustained forest sources.

A catalogue record for this book is available from the British Library.

A catalog record for this book is available from the Library of Congress.

10   9   8   7   6   5   4   3   2   1
14   13   12   11   10   09   08   07   06   05

Printed in China

Contents

List of Tables

List of Abbreviations

ANC	African National Congress
APLA	Azanian People's Liberation Army
AWB	Afrikaner Weerstands Beweging – resistance movement
CAAA	Comprehensive Anti-Apartheid Act
CODESA	Convention for a Democratic South Africa
COSATU	Congress of South African Trade Unions
DP	Democratic Party
DTA	Democratic Turnhalle Alliance
EC	European Community
EPG	Eminent Persons Group
ESAP	Economic Structural Adjustment Programme
FAK	Federation of Afrikaans Cultural Organisations
FDI	foreign direct investment
Frelimo	Front for the Liberation of Mozambique
GM	General Motors
HNP	Herenigde Nasionale Party (–1951)
HNP	Herstigte Nasionale Party (1969–)
ICJ	International Committee of Jurists
ICU	Industrial and Commercial Workers Union
IFP	Inkatha Freedom Party
IOC	International Olympic Committee
ITTF	International Table Tennis Federation
MK	Umkhonto we Sizwe
MPLA	Popular Movement for the Liberation of Angola
MPNP	Multi-party Negotiating Process
NGOs	non-governmental organisations
NRC	Native Representative Council
NSC	National Security Council
OAU	Organisation of African Unity
OB	Oxwagon Sentinels
PAC	Pan-African Congress
PFP	Progressive Federal Party

PWV	Pretoria–Witwatersrand–Vereeniging
RSA	Republic of South Africa
SACOS	South African Council on Sport
SACP	South African Communist Party
SAIC	South African Indian Congress
SAIRR	South African Institute of Race Relations
SANNC	South African Native National Congress
SANROC	South African Non-Racial Olympic Committee
SASA	South African Sports Association
SAONGA	South African Olympic and National Games Association
SATTB	South African Table Tennis Board
SWAPO	South West African People's Organisation
TEC	Transitional Executive Council
TRC	Truth and Reconciliation Commission
UDF	United Democratic Front
UDI	Unilateral Declaration of Independence
ULPP	Urban Labour Preference Policy

Brief Chronology of South Africa since the Discovery of Diamonds

1867	Discovery of diamonds in the interior
1871	British annexation of the diamond fields (as Griqualand West)
1872	Cape Colony granted responsible government
1877	British annexation of the Transvaal in the context of the promotion of South African Confederation
1879	Anglo-Zulu War
1880–1	First Anglo-Boer War ends British rule over the Transvaal
1886	Discovery of the main gold reef on the Witwatersrand and founding of Johannesburg
1895	Jameson Raid aimed at the overthrow of President Kruger
1899	Outbreak of the Second Anglo-Boer War
1902	Peace Treaty of Vereeniging ends Second Anglo-Boer War
1905	Report of South African Native Affairs Commission
1910	Union of South Africa comes into being
1911	Passage of Mines and Works Act
1912	Formation of South African Native National Congress (changing name to the ANC in 1923)
1913	Passage of Natives Land Act
1914	Formation of National Party
1915	South Africa conquers German South West Africa
1922	Rand revolt by white miners
1923	Passage of Natives (Urban Areas) Act establishing control over movement into towns
1924	Election of National Party–Labour coalition
1934	Formation of United Party out of fusion of National Party and South African Party
1936	Passage of Representation of Natives Act removing Africans from the voters' roll in the Cape

1939	House of Assembly votes in favour of South African participation in the Second World War by narrow majority. J.C. Smuts becomes Prime Minister
1944	Formation of the ANC Youth League
1948	Smuts defeated and Afrikaner nationalist government elected on platform of apartheid
1949	Passage of Mixed Marriages Act
1950	Passage of Population Registration Act and of Group Areas Act
1952	Defiance Campaign, involving civil disobedience and mass protests against apartheid laws
1955	Congress of the People adopts Freedom Charter
1959	Formation of the PAC
1960	Macmillan's 'Wind of Change' speech (February). Sharpeville massacre (March). ANC and PAC banned (April)
1961	South Africa becomes a Republic outside the British Commonwealth
1963	Transkei homeland gets self-government
1964	Nelson Mandela sentenced to life imprisonment
1966	H.F. Verwoerd assassinated in the House of Assembly
1968	Cancellation of English cricket tour of South Africa over D'Oliviera affair
1970	Passage of the Bantu Homelands Citizenship Act
1971	Advisory Opinion of the International Court of Justice that South Africa's rule over South West Africa is illegal
1973	Wave of strikes by African workers
1975	Formation of Inkatha
1976	Soweto uprising originating in protests against the imposition of the use of Afrikaans in African secondary schools (June). Independence of Transkei (October)
1977	Death in detention of Black Consciousness activist Steve Biko (September). UN Security Council imposes mandatory arms embargo on South Africa (November). Independence of Bophuthatswana (December)
1978	P.W. Botha replaces B.J. Vorster as Prime Minister
1979	Independence of Venda
1981	Independence of Ciskei
1983	Formation of the United Democratic Front (UDF)
1984	Low turn-out in elections for (Coloured) House of Representatives and the (Indian) House of Delegates

undermines political credibility of new tricameral constitution

1985   Langa (Uitenhage) massacre (March). Botha's 'Rubicon' speech prompts loss of confidence (August)

1986   Mission of Eminent Persons Group is ended by SAAF bombing raids on Botswana, Zambia and Zimbabwe (May). Congress overrides President Reagan's veto on sanctions legislation (October)

1987   Meeting takes place between ANC and Afrikaner intellectuals in Dakar, Senegal (July). A senior ANC figure, Govan Mbeki, is released from prison (November)

1988   Restrictions placed on 17 anti-apartheid organisations

1989   Meeting takes place between prisoner Nelson Mandela and President P.W. Botha (July). P.W. Botha resigns and is succeeded by F.W. de Klerk (August). Senior ANC leaders, including Walter Sisulu, are released (October)

1990   Ban on ANC, PAC and the SACP lifted and Mandela released (February). Agreement between government and ANC in Pretoria Minute as a result of which ANC suspends all armed actions (August)

1991   Signing of National Peace Accord (September). Start of formal multi-party talks in CODESA (December)

1992   Whites vote by large majority (69 per cent 'Yes') to support continuation of reform process in referendum on negotiations (March). Boipatong massacre (June). Record of Understanding between government and ANC (September)

1993   The SACP leader, Chris Hani is assassinated (April). Transitional Executive Council is installed (December)

1994   Voting takes place in country's first non-racial general election (April). Nelson Mandela is inaugurated as President of South Africa (May)

1995   Truth and Reconciliation Commission is convened (December)

1996   National Party withdraws from the Government of National Unity (June)

1997   Final constitution comes into force (February)

1999   ANC wins landslide victory in second non-racial general election. Thabo Mbeki is inaugurated as President (June)

Preface

The subject of this book is the rise and fall of apartheid, the system of racial discrimination that made South Africa a pariah in international society in the second half of the twentieth century. The book forms part of a series on rethinking major issues in world politics designed to challenge received opinion and thereby stimulate fresh consideration of the nature of the world we live in. The most obvious sense in which apartheid justifies consideration in such a project is that South Africa's domestic racial policy became a matter of global controversy, especially after the Sharpeville massacre in 1960. However, this only scratches the surface of apartheid's global significance. The continuing resonance of the very term, apartheid, more than a decade after its demise shows how deeply the world has been affected by apartheid. It is the contention of this book that apartheid was interconnected with the politics of the rest of the world in a much more profound manner than is simply indicated by the unpopularity of South African racial policy at the United Nations.

One of the objectives of this book is to explore apartheid's international links during the rise of the system, as well as during its fall. In order to explain the genesis of the system, this book delves into the history of South Africa during the nineteenth century. It argues that the region, which then encompassed a number of different political entities, was transformed by mineral discoveries that fundamentally altered the balance of forces between natives and settlers, so paving the way for white minority rule over a unified country in the twentieth century. It then explains how segregation became the basis of the racial policy of the new country, disputing a long-standing interpretation that regarded segregation as a product of the triumph of the influence of the racial attitudes of the frontier. On the contrary, it argues that segregation was primarily the product of imperialism.

This book does not set out to present a condensed account of South African politics from Union through the apartheid years to the arrival of democratic government in 1994. Nevertheless, the reader will be able to follow the broad course of events that took place in South Africa through the twentieth century. This historical narrative is interwoven with reinterpretation. But it also seeks to do much more than simply reinterpret the history of South African racial policy in the light of the most recent scholarship. The heart of the book is a re-examination of debates about the nature of South African society that took place before, during and after the apartheid years. It is a re-examination that involves analysing present-day debates about South Africa's past as well as past debates about South Africa's present. It involves a re-evaluation of the significance of these debates themselves since the book is not an exercise in intellectual history for its own sake. Thus, it is no part of the aim of this book to revisit debates that have long lost their relevance to an understanding of either South Africa today or the wider world in which the concept of apartheid still resonates. In short, the focus is on the debates that still matter both to South Africa and the world.

During the 1970s and 1980s, the study of South Africa was dominated by a debate between liberals and radicals about the relationship between capitalism and apartheid. Liberals contended that apartheid ran against the grain of capitalist economic development and that in the long run apartheid would be eroded by the operation of market forces. By contrast, radicals argued that apartheid and capitalism were interdependent, different sides of the same coin. The impressive growth rate of the South African economy during the 1960s lent verisimilitude to the radical contention that cheap labour under apartheid contributed to the huge profits of capitalist enterprises and to the system's capacity to attract foreign investment. However, the stagnation of the South African economy after the Soweto uprising of 1976 revived the credibility of the liberal case. In the event, far-reaching political change came to South Africa in a manner and in a time frame neither the liberals nor the radicals had expected.

But the fact that members of the business community took the lead in pressing the government to enter into negotiations with the African National Congress (ANC) and that capitalism emphatically survived the transition to democracy in South Africa could be interpreted as vindication of the liberal interpretation. Indeed, in a wide variety of ways, the manner of South Africa's democratisation through a negotiated settlement represented a triumph for liberalism. Yet, paradoxically, liberals themselves had much less influence in the new political dispensation than their radical counterparts, many of whom had a place within the ANC. An example of the continued influence of the radical perspective was the holding of hearings by the Truth and Reconciliation Commission on corporate responsibility on the assumption that capitalist enterprises had benefited from the system of apartheid and ought to be held to account for their actions during those years.

One way in which the radical assumption that the fates of capitalism and apartheid were conjoined could be reconciled with the South African transition would be to assert that what exists today in South Africa does not represent a fundamental break with the past. From this perspective, the new order amounts to a kind of neo-apartheid. However, despite the persistence of a very high level of inequality in both incomes and wealth, though no longer as racially skewed as in the past, this point of view has attracted surprisingly few adherents. The main reason is the domination of the political system by the ANC with an ideology of non-racialism that is the complete antithesis of apartheid. Indeed, so complete has the triumph of the ANC proved to be that for most contemporary analysts of South Africa, the old liberal–radical debate has been displaced by a new puzzle. This is to explain the sudden demise of apartheid. Almost as striking has been the withering away of the party that ruled the country continuously for nearly half a century. In its own way, the course of events in South Africa in the 1990s was just as surprising as the collapse of Communism in Eastern Europe and the disintegration of the Soviet Union.

The approach of this book is not merely to look again at the fall of apartheid, but also to re-examine both the circumstances of its rise and the nature of the system itself. These issues are addressed through the posing of a series of questions. The answers have been sought not merely in the writings of scholars of present-day South Africa, but also in such classic texts as Hannah Arendt's *Origins of Totalitarianism* and J.A. Hobson's *Imperialism: A Study*. Throughout the book, use is made of works written close to the time of the events being analysed since they provide a means to overcome one of the greatest obstacles to understanding the past. This is the difficulty of recapturing the spirit of earlier eras. This is especially important in the case of apartheid. One of the factors that has given a measure of credibility to an isolationist interpretation of South African history that disconnects the country's political development from trends in world politics is the assumption that belief in white racial supremacy was virtually unique to South Africa. It fits in with a naïve tendency within the West to translate current values, including the commitment to racial equality, back in time when examining the West's role in world history.

The distorting effect of this sanitising of history was evident in the debate that occurred after the end of apartheid as to whether the nature of the system was totalitarian. The controversy was notable for the polarisation it revealed between scholars who had lived in South Africa throughout the apartheid era and writers whose view of the system had been forged in exile. While the former readily accepted that apartheid was outmoded, few of their number were inclined to accept the judgement of international society that apartheid was a crime against humanity, which formed a starting point of the latter. While insiders claimed closer experience of the actual functioning of the system, outsiders argued that their view of the system had not been limited by the operation of censorship. The emotive touchstone of the debate was whether apartheid was in any way comparable to the totalitarian system established in Nazi Germany. Not even the most radical critic of apartheid claimed that horrors on the scale of those in Nazi Germany had occurred in South Africa. Consequently, the issue hinged on whether, making due allowance for this massive difference in scale, there was any basis for comparing the two systems at an ideological level.

An argument advanced in contradiction of the claim that the nature of apartheid was totalitarian was that the system belonged to the colonial era. The implication was that apartheid had more in common with the practices of imperialism than with those of totalitarianism, as if that actually exculpated the authors of apartheid. Another difficulty with this view was that it disregarded the connections between imperialism and totalitarianism, in particular, the claims made by Hannah Arendt in her seminal work on the subject that the origins of totalitarianism lay in imperialism. Be that as it may, it remains entirely reasonable to question whether apartheid was sufficiently radical in its aims to bear any comparison with National Socialism. Two other issues are connected to this question. Firstly, how different was apartheid to the policy of segregation, a policy that indubitably belonged to the colonial era? Secondly, was apartheid implemented on the basis of a blueprint or does that present a misleading picture of the coherence of the policies pursued by the National Party during the 1950s?

It becomes even more difficult to characterise the system after the assassination of the system's principal architect, Hendrik Verwoerd, in 1966. Was the system being eroded or modernised under Vorster? Did 'reform apartheid' under Botha constitute a new departure or were its most significant aspects the rise of the security state and the involvement of the military in political decision-making? Answering these questions brings us to the greatest challenge of all, explaining the South African miracle. How did South Africa escape the racial bloodbath so confidently, if mournfully, predicted by writers and analysts before the country's transition? The simple answer to the question is that the National Party government and the ANC negotiated a deal that saved the country from this fate. And, in fact, a considerable number of books have been written on how the deal was done. However, there was far more to the transition than the negotiation of an interim constitution providing a framework for the holding of the country's first democratic elections. The nature of the deal, or even whether there was a deal at all, cannot be explained without reference to the shift in the balance of power between the parties that occurred during the transition. The penultimate chapters of the book examine the internal and external sources of the shift towards the ANC that made a political settlement possible.

The last chapter of the book analyses the demise of apartheid in a longer historical perspective, examining or recapping the role of demographic, economic, normative, international and domestic political factors in the country's transformation from minority to majority rule. Perhaps the most remarkable aspect of all of that transformation was that there was legal and constitutional continuity between the old order and the new. That is to say, the institutions of apartheid voted themselves out of existence by enacting the interim constitution. Admittedly, the final shape of the new order was determined by the outcome of the 1994 general election. Nonetheless, it is striking how much South Africa's constitutional continuity owes to the flexibility of the Westminster system which allowed both apartheid and majority rule to be put into effect without a constitutional revolution.

This book was long in its gestation. In fact, since my days at the University of Cape Town in the late 1960s, I have always wanted to write a book criticising what has long seemed to me to be a myth, that South Africa's political development has primarily been a product of the country's isolation. During the years of apartheid, that appeared to many to be a rather quixotic ambition. The country's pariah status made the distinction between being isolated and being isolationist appear moot to many people. South Africa's transition to democracy has made it a lot easier to argue the case that the country's development is best viewed in a wider international context, though it has not made the task redundant since isolationist interpretations of South Africa's history continue to be written. My views have been influenced by conversations over the years with very many people. They include Jack Spence, Merle Lipton, James Mayall, Rupert Taylor, Keith Gottschalk, Adam Habib, Kenneth Hughes, Michael Popham, Richard Hopgood, Stan Siebert, Debbie Gaitskell, Christopher Saunders, Greg Mills, Noam Pines, Chris Alden, Meverett Koetz, James Barber, Heribert Adam, Eddie Webster, Aubrey Lekwane, David Welsh, and John and Judith Kalk, to mention just a few. The usual disclaimer applies that none bears any responsibility for the views I express or for any errors of fact or argument that appear in the book.

I also owe a large debt of gratitude to my family. My wife, Brigid, my son, John, and my daughter, Kate have made a major contribution to the book by forcing me to justify my arguments and sometimes by encouraging me to pursue a line of thought further. They all know South Africa in different ways and that has helped a lot. My thanks are due to an anonymous reader of the proposal and the manuscript for his/her valuable comments. The production team at Palgrave Macmillan, primarily Steven Kennedy and Cecily Wilson, have given me guidance from the inception for which I am most grateful. I am also most grateful to Keith Povey of Keith Povey Editorial Services Ltd who arranged the copy-editing. Finally, I owe a large debt of gratitude to the editor of this series, Michael Cox, an old friend of many years. I very much doubt if I would ever have had the opportunity to write this book without the existence of the series he has created. In addition, he has been of major help to me in finalising the manuscript through his helpful comments and suggestions, as well as his encouragement for the case the book makes.

ADRIAN GUELKE

1

Introduction: Apartheid's Global Significance

Apartheid was labelled a crime against humanity by the United Nations General Assembly as early as 1966. By contrast, a freelance journalist from Cape Town, Andrew Kenny, claimed in an article published in 1999 that apartheid had saved South Africa from Communism.[1] Even after its demise apartheid has continued to be a source of both academic controversy and political contention. The struggle against apartheid produced one of the towering figures of the twentieth century, Nelson Mandela. His standing was a reflection not just of his own extraordinary qualities but also of the significance the world attached to the miracle of South Africa's transition to democracy in 1994. The triumph of liberal-democracy constituted an amazing conclusion to the story of South Africa in the twentieth century. During the long years of Mandela's imprisonment such a development had seemed wildly improbable. There was a broad consensus among analysts that white minority rule could not last for ever on the southern tip of the African continent, but those who predicted its demise rarely predicted such a benign political outcome. Indeed, it had been widely feared that apartheid would end in a racial bloodbath with a profound impact on race relations in the rest of the world.

Before the country's political redemption under President Mandela, South Africa had been a byword for both racism and gross inequality. The stereotypical view prevailing before the South African transition was that the country's white population enjoyed an enviable life-style with a standard of living matching the very richest countries in

1

the world. By contrast, it seemed that the indigenous African majority lived in conditions that were typical of the poorest countries in the Third World. The reality was slightly more complicated than this picture of polarisation suggested. In particular, whites were not the only racial minority in South Africa. Coloureds and Indians occupied an intermediate position between whites and Africans. Further, there were significant ethnic divisions within both the white and African communities. Whites were by no means uniformly wealthy. Indeed, the quest of the Afrikaners, who traced their roots back to the original Dutch settlement at the Cape in the seventeenth century, for a place in the sun underpinned Afrikaner nationalism for much of the twentieth century.

The Meaning of Apartheid

Any book on South Africa's modern history must necessarily start by considering what the system of apartheid meant to South Africa and to the world. The term 'apartheid' was in wide usage by the end of the twentieth century as the substantial entry under apartheid in the *New Oxford English Dictionary* (*NOED*) published in 1998 underlines. It defines the term as follows:

> historical (in South Africa) a policy or system of segregation or discrimination on the grounds of race.
> • segregation in other contexts – sexual apartheid.
> Origins 1940s from Afrikaans literally 'separateness', from Dutch *apart* 'separate' + -*heid* (equivalent of – **HOOD**).

The dictionary also provides this brief account of the history of apartheid:

> Adopted by the successful Afrikaner National Party as a slogan in the 1948 election, apartheid extended and institutionalized existing racial segregation. Despite rioting and terrorism at home and isolation abroad from the 1960s onwards, the white regime maintained the apartheid system with only minor relaxation until February 1991.[2]

This entry is worth examining in some depth, not just as a guide to the word's current usage but also as a distillation of British, if not Western, opinion on the subject of apartheid. However, it should be noted at the outset that the entry does not fully convey the notoriety attached to the word. An implication of apartheid's disrepute is that when the term is used in other contexts, it is generally for the purposes of condemnation, denunciation and delegitimisation.

Some aspects of the entry are not contentious. It is basically correct on the term's origins. The political columnist, Louis Louw, claimed that the word was first used with reference to racial policy in a leading article in the Afrikaans daily, *Die Burger*, on 26 March 1943. The paper used the term again in this sense in an editorial on 9 September 1943. According to Louw, it was first used in the South African parliament in a speech on 25 January 1944 by the leader of the National Party, D.F.Malan. Malan declared that one of the aims of the Republic that Nationalists sought was 'to ensure the safety of the white race and of Christian civilisation by the honest maintenance of the principles of apartheid and guardianship'.[3] However, Louw's research has not proved to be the last word on the issue of the origins of the term. Dan O'Meara accepts that the National Party only started using the term in 1943, but argues that it had been used in its modern meaning years before this: 'The word seems to have been invented in 1935 by the Afrikaner historian P. van Biljon to indicate "an all-embracing racial policy essential to replace the old notion of segregation".'[4] While Van Biljon's notion coincides with the meaning the term was to acquire, the hold of segregation on South Africa in the 1930s gave such an idea little resonance at the time.

Others have gone back even earlier. Hermann Giliomee argues that 'the first printed record of the term "apartheid", used in its modern sense, dates back to 1929'.[5] His example comes from an address given by the Rev. Jan Christoffel du Plessis to a conference of the Dutch Reformed Church, in which Du Plessis referred to the 'spirit of apartheid' that had always underpinned the church's missionary work. While Du Plessis had in mind the separation of white and black congregations when he spoke of 'the spirit of apartheid' in relation to missionary work, it is open to argument as to how far this really constitutes use of the term 'in its modern sense', to quote Giliomee. Giliomee argues that it does in the context of the argument he develops that thinking about apartheid originated in debates about racial policy in the Afrikaans churches. Nevertheless, there remains a considerable difference between the advocacy of separation in one sphere and 'an all-embracing policy'. Further, Du Plessis's words hardly ran counter to the public policy of the period. Giliomee's purpose is to suggest that apartheid was not simply based on racism, but like segregation, which was acknowledged to have well-meaning as well as bigoted supporters, was at least partly motivated by respect for cultural differences among South Africa's communities. Thus, according to Giliomee, 'The church leaders were enthralled by their utopian vision of separate peoples, each with their own mission and would continue to justify the unjustifiable, thus paving the way for the politicians.'[6] However, he acknowledges that they were 'fooling themselves'. But the implication of their good intentions remains. Another significant implication of Giliomee's argument is that there was continuity between segregation and apartheid.

Apartheid and Segregation

The issue of the relationship between apartheid and segregation is a large and important subject, which will be discussed further in Chapter 4. The fact that apartheid and segregation have come to be seen as successive phases in South African racial policy in the course of the twentieth century has inevitably tended to underscore the differences between the two, rather than their similarities or interdependence. Yet part of the inspiration for apartheid was concern that segregation was being eroded by social and economic forces. Indeed, apartheid might fairly be characterised, initially at least, as a programme to ensure the maintenance and reinforcement of segregation in the face of industrialisation and urbanisation. This is well conveyed by the *NOED*'s emphasis that 'apartheid extended and institutionalized existing racial segregation'. Apartheid took off as a political idea during the 1940s precisely because that was a time when the erosion of segregation – in part through the impact of the Second World War – was becoming most evident. The spirit of the times was encapsulated in a widely quoted statement of the South African Prime Minister of the time, J.C.Smuts. He declared in a speech to the South African Institute of Race Relations in February 1942: 'Isolation has gone and segregation has fallen on evil days.'[7]

The National Party (strictly speaking the *Herenigde Nasionale Party* or Reconstituted National Party) adopted apartheid as its official racial policy in 1945. Further flesh was put on the bones of the concept by a commission appointed by the party in 1947. The outside world first became aware of apartheid as a result of the South African general election of May 1948. Apartheid was the National Party's main election slogan. In what was a huge upset the United Party government of General Smuts was defeated by the National Party and its Afrikaner Party electoral ally. The question of how far the idea of apartheid contributed to the National Party's victory continues to be debated in the literature on South African politics (and will be examined further in Chapter 4). Also a matter of debate is the impact of the victory on South Africa's relations with the rest of the world. The election of a government committed to a policy that ran so directly counter to the trend in world opinion at the time was badly received and the negative reaction was compounded by the National Party's association with opposition to South Africa's participation in the war against Nazi Germany. However, it is possible to exaggerate the impact in retrospect by contrasting South Africa's special status during the war with the international reaction in the late 1940s and early 1950s to the unfolding of the policy of apartheid.

In fact, international criticism of South Africa's racial policy preceded the election of the National Party government. Racial policy was the major reason why Smuts failed to persuade the United Nations to support South Africa's request to incorporate South West Africa. India put the spotlight on the issue further by raising the issue of the treatment of the Indian minority in South Africa at the United Nations. The United Party government was put on the defensive and the electoral value to the party of the reputation Smuts had gained as an international statesman during the war was diminished. In his 1973 study of South African foreign policy, James Barber described reaction inside South Africa to the change in the country's standing as follows:

A bitter experience for Smuts was that his Nationalist opponents were able to use his international difficulties as a rod with which to beat him. In the past the attacks on Smuts had been that he spent too much of his time and energy on international affairs. Now the opposition were able to add that he spent this time and energy unsuccessfully.[8]

However, viewed from a longer-term perspective, the change of government in 1948 was indeed a pivotal moment in both the country's internal development and its relations with the rest of the world.

South Africa's Place in the World

The story of South Africa during the twentieth century is usually conceived of as a racial drama. It is typically told as a tale of how a multiracial society forged during the era of European imperialism became the testing ground of theories of the fundamental importance of racial difference. Thus, Frank Welsh summarises South Africa's history in the first half of the century as follows:

> [The nineteenth century] ended with two systems in conflict: the colonial British ideal of progress towards a multiracial society, slowing but still powerful, facing the Dutch republicans' unflinching assertion of white dominance and denial of political rights to all others. The British victory in the Anglo-Boer War of 1899–1902 proved illusory. Within seven years the former Dutch republicans had come to power in a united South Africa and new restrictions on black political rights were gradually enforced, inspiring in turn new black political organizations. After 1948, when the policies of apartheid – separate development – and *baasskap* – frank white domination – were introduced, the fabric of decent society began to disintegrate.[9]

The second half of the century is then told as the story of how the failure of the National Party's experiments in social engineering culminated in the triumph of their opposite, non-racialism. This oversimplified view of South African history has proved very influential. Part of its appeal is that it fits neatly into another common but also contestable narrative of the century, the story of the triumph of Western liberalism over fascism, then Communism and finally racism. What such a characterisation of the West's role in the political dramas of the twentieth century conveniently overlooks is the fact that fascism, Communism and racism were themselves products of the West. It also ignores the racial underpinning of the concept of the West itself, making the West's commitment to racial equality in the course of the second half of the century problematic and ambiguous.

Indeed, it remains problematic. The Janus-faced nature of Western society is reflected in the complexity of the relations that prevailed between the countries of North America and Western Europe and South Africa during the apartheid era.

Further, such a simple geographical characterisation of the West as North America and Western Europe (plus, perhaps, Australia and New Zealand), while very roughly accurate for the period of the Cold War, hardly begins to describe its partially overlapping multiple meanings in all their political, cultural and social complexity. In particular, it was the strong conviction of successive governments in South Africa during the apartheid era and earlier that they were acting as the guardians of Western, Christian civilisation on the continent of Africa. In fact, the view that the whites of South Africa were a fragment of Western society had considerable resonance within both North America and Western Europe. That gave a very special character to the passions which apartheid aroused as it became more and more in conflict with the shift in norms that occurred within Western societies in the 1960s. Further, the campaign against apartheid was implicitly (if not explicitly) linked to the continuing struggles against racism within Western society itself.

Apartheid South Africa tended to be regarded as an erring relative, the black sheep of the family, as it were. Anti-apartheid became *the* liberal cause in Western societies in the last four decades of the twentieth century. However, as discussed further in Chapter 10, the campaign against apartheid was conducted within limits that generally ruled out support for those seeking to bring about the overthrow of the system through violent means. As in the case of family relationships, there was widespread anger at the damage to the family's reputation as a result of South African behaviour, but tempered by the presence of feelings of responsibility for the fate of the errant relative. Such feelings were very evident at the end of the century in the response, particularly in Britain, to the rough treatment of white farmers in Zimbabwe. The *NOED*'s characterisation of the violence directed at the overthrow of white rule as 'terrorism' provides a further illustration that the view within the West of apartheid as illegitimate was not totally straightforward.

The ambivalence of the West towards apartheid South Africa forms part of a much larger contradiction at the centre of world politics, the triumph of political doctrines espousing ideals of human equality at a time when human living conditions in the world have never been more unequal. Paradoxically, the very responsiveness of governments in the rich world to the interests of their citizens virtually precludes substantial action to reduce the gulf between the rich and poor worlds. The relevance of this larger issue of global inequality to South Africa is that through the course of the century the country has held up a mirror to the world of its differences, with the gulf in living standards among the peoples of South Africa resembling those across continents. Further, it is not difficult to suggest equivalents in Western policy to the South African state's construction of barriers to entry of poor blacks to the urban areas, its reliance on military might to counter demands from below, or the white electorate's rallying to such threats. Since the demise of apartheid in South Africa, the term apartheid has been applied by way of analogy to a number of other relationships of inequality, as will be discussed below.

Jack Spence, the scholar who pioneered the study of South Africa's conflict with the rest of the world, described the apartheid regime in a resonant phrase as 'the most popular corpse in history'.[10] This was a reasonable evaluation of the South African government's international isolation in the years immediately before the government formally embarked upon negotiations with the African National Congress in the 1990s. However, it cannot be applied to South Africa's relationship with the West in the heyday of apartheid and even when applied to the 1980s such a judgement understates the extent of sympathy that existed beneath the surface of political rhetoric for whites in South Africa. This was evident on the right of the political spectrum in Europe and North America throughout the apartheid era and beyond. External criticism of apartheid in its early years was relatively muted outside the forum of the United Nations. This first phase lasted to 1960, a watershed year in terms of South Africa's relations with the rest of the world. The Sharpeville massacre on 21 March 1960 was the principal reason for the change.

However, there were also other indications of a parting of the ways between South Africa and Western policymakers. By far the most significant of these was a speech by the British Prime Minister, Harold Macmillan, on 3 February 1960. Macmillan spoke of a 'wind of change' sweeping the African continent, which by implication demanded the abandonment of apartheid. It is worth noting that Macmillan's speech shocked not just the South African government but a section of his own party. These British Conservatives dubbed the day of the speech Black Monday and that provided the inspiration of the formation of a rightwing pressure group, the Monday Club. The completion of the process of decolonisation in most parts of Africa during the 1960s and desegregation in the Southern states of the United States of America as a result of the civil rights movement provided the context for the disavowal within the West of doctrines of racial inequality.

Race in the West

But the new commitment to racial equality did not gain universal acceptance. One indication of that was the response in Britain to a speech by a maverick Conservative MP, Enoch Powell, in which he predicted that Britain might be engulfed in rivers of blood if immigration was not halted. The wave of support for Powell was an indication both of public susceptibility to the argument that Britain was an already overcrowded island, as well as the continuing strength of racial prejudice since the term 'immigrant' was treated as if it were synonymous with non-white. It was evident that Powell's view that Britain had no future as a multiracial society struck a chord with a considerable section of opinion.

Another indication of the relatively shallow roots of the new discourse of equality within Western societies was the size of the vote for the segregationist, George Wallace, in the American Presidential election of 1968. Wallace won 13.5 per cent of the vote nationwide and 46 electoral college votes through victories in a number of Southern states. The Republican Party responded to the challenge that the vote for Wallace represented by the adoption of a Southern strategy in Presidential elections, a formula that assisted the Republican Party to win a majority of Presidential elections in the period between 1968 and 2000. Another indicator of resistance to the new norm of racial equality was the continuing re-election in the Southern states of such unrepentant defenders of segregation as Senator Jesse Helms and Senator Strom Thurmond. The growth of the Front National in France and the rise of a number of anti-immigrant parties in other countries across Western Europe showed that voters' susceptibility to appeals that ran counter to the new norm was by no means confined to Britain and the United States.

With anti-Communism waning as a factor favouring rightwing political parties in elections in the West, the race card became a tempting one for rightwing politicians to play. Thus, the race card was played with devastating effect by Margaret Thatcher in the year-long run-up to the British general election of May 1979, in which she decisively defeated the Labour government led by James Callaghan. However, it had to be played carefully in the context of broad acceptance of the changes that had been ushered in under the banner of racial equality. The issue of race was also one that had the potential to cause division and difficulty on the right. In particular, any association with extreme positions, such as the reimposition of segregation or the compulsory expulsion of immigrants, tended to damage rather than to aid the conservative cause. In this context, ideological identification with apartheid counted as an extreme position. Thus, for the most part, conservative support for South Africa was argued on the basis of *realpolitik* and self-interest through the Verwoerd and more especially the Vorster years. But whether priority was given to strategic or economic reasons for maintaining ties with South Africa varied according to circumstances.

P.W. Botha, with his Total Strategy to counter the 'total Communist onslaught', gave Western politicians reason to focus on South Africa's strategic contribution to Western security in the context of the Cold War. At the same time, his commitment to reform within South Africa, initially at least, made it possible to downplay the issue of apartheid. However, both the failure of the tricameral constitution and the damage done by South African policies of destabilisation within the region of Southern Africa ultimately undermined the basis even for Western conservatives to support his government. In particular, it became evident that Botha's government was incapable of generating political stability either inside South Africa or in the region. With the recognition that a radically new political dispensation was needed, the alternative prospectus of the African National Congress (ANC) for the future of South Africa as a non-racial society began to gain in credibility. Support for this idea was personified by the campaign for the release of the imprisoned ANC leader, Nelson Mandela. From the mid-1980s the campaign attracted broad support among liberals and on the left in Western societies. On the right there were considerable reservations about supporting the ANC, which a number of conservative and rightwing politicians continued to characterise as a terrorist organisation. In the case of student supporters of the British Conservative Party, opposition to the liberal consensus took the highly aggressive form of T-shirts, buttons and posters with the slogan 'hang Mandela', to the embarrassment of Conservative Party leaders.

On the far right of politics, throughout the apartheid era, among political groups alienated from mainstream politics in the West for one reason or another, South Africa had considerable attraction as an alternative model to the welfare state that had emerged in Western Europe. The prowess of South Africa's military forces and the image of South Africa as a country in which the economy had been developed by the pioneering efforts of European settlers formed part of the appeal, as more simply did South Africa's association with racist doctrines of white supremacy. As long as white minority rule continued in South Africa, the country's fortunes could be presented as demonstrating the advantages of an alternative to African majority rule. In particular, there was scope for a contrast to be drawn between South Africa's prosperity and stability and economic and political failure among African states that achieved independence from the European colonial powers in the 1950s, 1960s and 1970s. Admittedly, making out a case in these terms became more difficult in the 1980s as a result of stagnation in the South African economy and of the challenge from below to minority rule. While explicit endorsement of apartheid was rare outside the extreme fringes of opinion, these ideas had considerable influence within sections of the media in an attenuated form that stopped just short of endorsing notions of racial superiority.

Even after 1960 there was a reservoir of sympathy within Western society for white resistance to African majority rule. It explains why South African governments continued to set considerable store by their relations with the West and adopted a variety of stratagems to secure support from Western governments, as will be discussed in Chapters 6 and 7. A legacy of this sympathy is to be found in the expectation on the right within the West of the 'failure' of post-apartheid South Africa. The acknowledgement that however 'failure' is defined in this context, hitherto South Africa's political transition, does not fit such a description provides one of the underpinnings of the characterisation of the transition as a miracle. But the assumption remains that it is a fragile miracle. (It should be noted in parenthesis that different concerns exist on the left that South Africa's transition remains incomplete as long as there are vast disparities of income among the population.)

On the right the debate about the future of South Africa was influenced at the end of the century by developments in Zimbabwe, where Robert Mugabe adopted a populist programme of land redistribution from the country's white farmers in order to stay in power. It was reflected in a commonly posed question at the end of the millennium: would South Africa follow the path of Zimbabwe in future years? As Zimbabwe was itself once seen as a model for the rest of Africa, it was possible to regard South Africa's transition in the 1990s from pariah to paragon as a temporary phase that would be followed by similar economic and political decline. In its most extreme form, this viewpoint presented a vision of the continent of Africa under African majority rule as entailing virtually a return to the conditions that prevailed in pre-colonial times. Giving verisimilitude to such prognostications has been the catastrophic impact of the AIDS epidemic, particularly on life expectancy in the most severely affected societies.

Imperialism and South Africa

From these assumptions a very different narrative of South Africa in the twentieth century to the one presented by Frank Welsh could be developed in terms of the ebb and flow of Western imperialism. The high tide of European imperialism was at the start of the century following in the wake of major mineral discoveries and underscored by the scale of Britain's military commitment during the Anglo-Boer War. Under the impact of two world wars the tide receded. It receded further under the impact of the competition between the United States of America and the Soviet Union, though with the twist that in South Africa's case the end of the Cold War facilitated the final triumph of majority rule. Within this perspective different views existed as to the role of settlers and indigenous peoples, the appropriate relationship between them and the imperial relationship. In part, this reflected the fact that at times European metropoles gave backing to the creation of settler colonies, while at others they acted forcefully to restrain the political ambitions of settlers. The conflict between metropole and settler provides a particularly interesting theme.

In general the metropole acted to curb the activities of settlers because of their propensity to cause conflict with the indigenous population. This aspect of the record of the metropole provides the justification for the presentation of its policies as liberal and pluralist, attempting to accommodate the interests of both settler and native under the imperial umbrella. However, it is arguable that it was the cost of conflict rather than liberal impulses that provided the main motivation behind imperial restraint. Further, at other times settlers were the cutting edge of imperial expansion and the readiness of the metropole to subsidise settler enterprise is hard to reconcile with any notion that imperialism was driven by humanitarian consideration for the interests of indigenous peoples. A complicating factor in assessing the record was that there was often division within the metropole itself as to the value of imperialist enterprises, whether they were based on European settlement, plantation, native peasant production or some combination of these elements. Which of these promised to bring about the greater commercial benefit was an important consideration, from the metropole's perspective. Thus, hostility towards the Afrikaner republics at the end of the nineteenth century owed, in reality, more to their perceived commercial and political failings than to their insistence that there could be no equality in church or state between white and black.

Anti-Apartheid and Anti-Imperialism

From the perspective of the Third World, a further narrative can be developed in which the struggle against apartheid formed an integral part of a much wider struggle against European imperialism. In so far as the very existence of apartheid was an affront to anyone who was not of European origin, opposition to apartheid naturally provided a common point of reference throughout the process of African and Asian decolonisation. While independence created sovereign states that were formally equal in legal status to the former colonial powers, the continuing vast disparity in living conditions between the states of the West and those of the Third World underscored how unequal the world in fact remained. This was further underlined by the fact that apartheid continued in existence long after the independence of most of Europe's former colonies elsewhere in Asia and Africa. Indeed, arguably, the only unfinished business from the era of European imperialism that remained when Mandela became the President of a non-racial South Africa in 1994 was the conflict between Israelis and Palestinians in the Middle East. At the time of Mandela's inauguration, hopes were high that this conflict was in the process of being resolved. Consequently, the unfinished business in the Middle East did little to undermine perceptions of the South African transition as the final culmination of the struggle of the peoples of the Third World for recognition of their political rights.

Admittedly, ethno-nationalist conflicts in the West, in areas of former Communist rule, and in the Third World remained common-place. But few of these conflicts had racial overtones or had an obvious or compelling connection with the struggle of the Third World against domination by the West. Indeed, with the end of apartheid, it was possible to question whether any basis for Third World solidarity still existed. Another reason for questioning the relevance of the concept of the Third World in a post-apartheid world was that with the disintegration of the Soviet Union, non-alignment between the West and the East, which had been one of the defining elements of the concept, no longer had any meaning. It was also clear that the economic agenda that the Third World had pursued at the time of the first oil crisis in the 1970s, when Third World states had given support to the concept of a New International Economic Order, was dead by the 1990s, if not before. Nevertheless, despite the absence of any obvious radical alternative to neoliberal economic policies, global disparities of wealth and power made it possible to argue that the struggle against imperialism was not over after all, particularly in the economic sphere.

Since the demise of apartheid in South Africa itself, a number of politicians and writers have employed the concept of global apartheid both to describe the scale of economic inequalities in the world and to challenge its legitimacy. A speech by the South African President, Thabo Mbeki, at the opening of the World Summit on Sustainable Development in Johannesburg in August 2002 provides a striking example. Mbeki defined global apartheid as 'a world in which a rich minority enjoys unprecedented levels of consumption, comfort and prosperity, while a poor majority endures daily hardship, suffering and dehumanization'.[11] Mbeki reminded the delegates that apartheid had still been in force in South Africa at the time of the previous Earth Summit in Rio de Janeiro in 1992. He attributed its demise to the determination of the peoples of the world that apartheid would not be tolerated. Mbeki argued that it was similarly time to scrap an economic order based on the 'savage principle of the survival of the fittest'. He added that 'a global human society based on poverty for many and prosperity for the few, characterised by islands of wealth, surrounded by a sea of poverty, is unsustainable'.[12]

Mbeki was not deterred from continuing to use the concept by the fact that when he had previously made reference to global apartheid, his government's neoliberal macro-economic strategy had itself been criticised in this context. In particular, a year before the summit Patrick Bond had published a savage attack on the government's economic policies under the title, *Against Global Apartheid: South Africa Meets the World Bank, IMF and International Finance*. Bond accused South Africa's rulers of being 'intent on polishing, not abolishing global apartheid'.[13] However, the concept of global apartheid also resonated outside South Africa. Bond's book was only one of a number of books published after 1994 that used the words 'global apartheid' in its title and none of the others had a specifically South African focus. An early example was Anthony H.Richmond's *Global Apartheid: Refugees, Racism and the New World Order* published in 1995.[14] The subject of Richmond's book was British, Canadian, Australian and American immigration policies. Another example was a book by Titus Alexander entitled *Unravelling Global Apartheid*, which was published in 1996.[15] Alexander's book advocated a series of reforms to international institutions as a way of tackling global economic inequality. Lastly, radical criticism of the international economic system by the Cuban leader, Fidel Castro, was published in English in 2001 under the title, *War, Racism and Economic Justice: Global Apartheid and the World Economic Order*.[16]

While Castro's use of such an analogy might be considered predictable propaganda against Western imperialism, more mainstream International Relations scholars have also been struck by the force of the comparison. An example is Thomas Schelling who soon after the end of the Cold War foresaw the possibility that a new world order might resemble apartheid writ large. Schelling wrote:

> If the US was to contemplate gradually relinquishing some measure of sovereignty in order to form not a more perfect, but a more effective legal structure, what familiar political entity might be the basis for our comparison? I find my own answer stunning and depressing: South Africa. We believe in a world that is one fifth rich, four-fifths poor; the rich are segregated into rich countries,

and the poor into poor countries. The rich are predominantly lighter skinned, the poor darker skinned. Most of the poor live in homelands that are physically remote, often separated by oceans and great distances from the rich. Migration on any scale is impermissible. There is no systematic redistribution of income. While there is ethnic strife throughout the world, the strife is more vicious and destructive among the poor.[17]

Other Meanings

The term 'global apartheid' has also been used in a non-economic context to describe relations between the sexes. An example is the account for the Third World Network of the Beijing Conference by Vandana Shiva. It was subtitled 'Gender Justice and Global Apartheid'.[18] This usage may be compared to that of sexual apartheid, the one example the *NOED* gives of the use of the word 'apartheid' outside the context of South Africa. More commonly these days reference is made to 'gender apartheid', a term that has been applied to social practices in a number of countries including Afghanistan, India, Iran, Israel, Saudi Arabia and the United States of America. From a feminist perspective the intention may be to convey criticism of patriarchy no less strong than that of white supremacy. In so far as the term apartheid conveys the notion of systematic discrimination from the cradle to the grave, gender apartheid fits best the case of the Taliban in Afghanistan. However, the separation of men and women does not always carry such a strong implication of inequality or of systematic discrimination against women. Consequently, the usage of the term 'apartheid' to describe, for example, the separation of men and women on buses for Orthodox Jews in Jerusalem does not have quite the same force as it does in contexts where such practices are regarded as being inseparable from the maintenance of inequality. For that reason, too, use of the term in this context has not engendered the same level of controversy as its use elsewhere.

At the end of the twentieth century and the beginning of the twenty-first century, the most controversial use of the term 'apartheid' was its application to Israeli policies towards the Palestinians. With the breakdown of the peace process in 2000, the use of analogy has mushroomed. By the end of 2003, several books had been published on the conflict between Israelis and Palestinians that contained the word 'apartheid' in their title. Examples include Marwan Bishara's *Palestine/Israel: Peace or Apartheid?* and Uri Davis's *Apartheid Israel*.[19] Its use in this context has engendered a somewhat similar controversy as the earlier contention over a General Assembly resolution that equated Zionism with racism. However, Israel's building of a security wall within the occupied territories has prompted much more widespread acceptance of the validity of the analogy than was ever previously the case.[20] The Middle East is not the only arena in which the analogy has been used. In 1997 Ashgate published a book by George Hicks with the title, *Japan's Hidden Apartheid: The Korean Minority and the Japanese*.[21] However, it is striking that relatively few examples exist of the sustained use of the term apartheid to apply to anywhere other than South Africa prior to 1994.

The End of Apartheid in South Africa

Nineteen ninety-four was the year when Nelson Mandela was inaugurated as the President of a democratic South Africa. His inauguration on 10 May or the elections in April that preceded it are commonly treated as the terminal point of apartheid in South Africa. The logic of this position is that it was only with the full extension of political rights to South Africans of all races in an undivided country that a complete end to apartheid was achieved. However, a case can be made that the demise of apartheid preceded South Africa's transition to democracy. This was because much of the racial discrimination associated with apartheid had been abandoned well before the transfer of political power to a new regime took place. Thus, the *NOED* treats February 1991 as the terminal date of apartheid. This was the month in which De Klerk announced that the remaining legislative pillars of apartheid, the Population Registration Act of 1950, the Group Areas Act of the same year and the Natives Land Act of 1913, would be repealed. The actual process of repeal was completed in June of that year. The *NOED*'s choice might be considered slightly odd since, on the basis of future intentions, it might just as reasonably be argued that De Klerk's announcement of the release of Nelson Mandela in February 1990 spelt the end of apartheid. This initiative clearly entailed a commitment to enter into negotiations to bring about an entirely new political dispensation.

In fairness to the *NOED*, it should be conceded that from an international perspective the repeal of the last legal pillars of apartheid had considerable importance. It was one of the conditions under America's Comprehensive Anti-Apartheid Act of 1986 for the lifting of economic sanctions against South Africa. However, designating any single date for the ending of apartheid presents difficulties for the rather obvious reason that its demise took place in stages. Other significant points in the process were the repeal of the pass laws in 1986, the passage of the Restoration of South African Citizenship Act in the same year, and the release of a senior member of the ANC in 1987, to name but three. There remains plenty of scope for argument about the point at which reform of the system made further change inevitable and the abandonment of apartheid irreversible. What makes this an even more complex question is the debate over whether or not apartheid ever constituted a systematic blueprint for the future of South Africa. The contrary argument is that it was simply a rubric that in practice covered a wide variety of contrasting, and sometimes even conflicting, tendencies in the realm of racial policy. This is an issue that will be discussed in greater depth in both Chapter 2 and Chapter 5.

The prevalence of analogies with apartheid since the demise of apartheid in South Africa itself might be seen as evidence of a greater sensitivity to racial inequality elsewhere and thus perhaps even to point to the triumph of anti-racism as a universal idea. Prior to South Africa's transformation, hopes existed in some quarters that the ending of apartheid would be such a blow to those in the West still drawn to racism that parties espousing racial hatred would be marginalised still further and that the incidence of racial attacks would decline. In fact, contrary to such expectations, neither has happened. While extreme rightwing parties drew inspiration from the example of apartheid in South Africa, they were not so dependent on South Africa as a model as to be affected electorally by the disappearance of apartheid. Further, the increase in the number of people seeking asylum in Western societies, although tiny in absolute terms compared to refugee flows within the Third World, has provided those seeking to promote racial hatred with a potent weapon for doing so. This has been compounded by the popularisation of the notion that many of the claimants are bogus, whatever countries they come from. State failure and economic collapse in the Third World have added to fears of unstoppable waves of migrants seeking to escape such conditions. Post-apartheid South Africa provides an example that runs counter to such prejudices about the Third World, but without overriding a more general picture of decline and decay. A further factor has prompted hostility to newcomers: terrorism, particularly after the events of 11 September 2001. Consequently, sneaking sympathy for apartheid no longer plays the role that it once did in the perpetuation of racism in the West.

Terms of the Debate in South Africa

Less surprisingly the terms of political debate have changed radically in South Africa since the demise of apartheid. In the 1970s and 1980s the study of South Africa was dominated by a debate between liberals and radicals on the relationship between capitalism and apartheid. The primary focus of the debate was economic forces. One consequence of the centrality of this debate was that relatively little attention was paid to South Africa's relations with the rest of the world. Admittedly, the question of the pros and cons of economic sanctions did receive some attention, but almost entirely in terms of the likely *economic* impact of sanctions.

One of the main purposes of this study is to integrate the impact of South Africa's relations with the rest of the world into the story of the rise and fall of apartheid itself. In the process, an enduring myth of the country's development will be challenged, which is that South African racism was a product of the country's isolation. One reason that the story of the rise and fall of apartheid has so much resonance in Western societies is that it is not an account of an alien planet but a chapter in the history of the West itself. Further, just as that story did not begin suddenly in May 1948, it did not end suddenly in May 1994. Apartheid may be dead, but race still matters in South Africa. What is more, as suggested above, South Africa is not alone in that.

The debate on the relationship between capitalism and apartheid started at a time when white rule in South Africa appeared secure. If liberals believed that capitalism would erode apartheid, it was not because they believed that the collapse of apartheid was imminent. Indeed, the case that liberal economists presented was one of the incompatibility of capitalism and apartheid in the long run. To radicals, that seemed a pipe-dream in the light of the country's booming economy in the 1960s at the height of Verwoerd's rule.

A very different kind of debate has been prompted by the demise of apartheid. It can be summarised in the questions: how bad was apartheid? How unique was apartheid? Was apartheid justly labelled a crime against humanity by the international community? Can the racism of the apartheid system be compared to Nazism? Or is the analogy of colonial rule a more appropriate one? These are questions that will be addressed in the next chapter.

2

The Debate on the Nature of South African Racial Policies: Totalitarian or Colonial?

The assertion that the government of South Africa prior to 1994 was totalitarian is generally based on one or other of two grounds. They were the arbitrary behaviour of agents of the state seemingly unconstrained by law or legal principle and the manner in which the country's racial policies affected the lives of its citizenry in all aspects from the cradle to the grave. Admittedly, in some accounts a clear distinction was not made between these two aspects of the governance of South Africa. Consequently, it became relatively common for both the racial policies adopted by the country's white minority regime and the security measures it took to defend itself to be identified with the single word apartheid. This issue did not arise in the context of segregation, but what made it part of the debate on the nature of white minority rule in South Africa was the question as to whether it was qualitatively different from apartheid or not. Since segregation tended to be associated with the European colonial era, one implication of the assertion that apartheid was not qualitatively different from segregation was that colonial was a more appropriate label for South African racial policies than totalitarian.

From the formation of the Union of South Africa to the eve of the country's first democratic elections in April 1994, when the interim constitution agreed by the parties in the negotiations came into force, South Africa was governed under a political system modelled on Westminster. The Westminster system was a legacy of British rule over the units that made up the Union, as well as of Britain's victory in the Anglo-Boer War of 1899 to 1902. British legislation, the South Africa Act of 1909, established a constitution for the Union of South Africa that enshrined white minority rule. During the first fifty years of South Africa's existence as a political entity, the most important changes to the constitution were changes to the franchise. They entailed the expunging of the last remnants of nineteenth-century Cape liberalism from the constitution. African voters were removed from the common roll in the Cape in the 1930s while Coloured voters were removed from the common roll in the Cape in the 1950s. The overall structure of government remained little changed.

In 1961 South Africa became a Republic but the only substantive constitutional change was the replacement of the Governor-General with the State President as head of state. The policy of granting independence to ethnically based African homelands brought much more far-reaching constitutional change to the way the country was governed in the 1970s and 1980s. Further change was made to the structure of government in the 1980s with the adoption of a tricameral system of government. The Republic of South Africa Constitution Act of 1983 established a House of Representatives to be elected by Coloured voters and a House of Delegates to be elected by the country's Indian minority. At the same time the presidency was transformed into an executive post.

Competitive Party System

As in the British system, from Union onwards general elections were regularly held on the basis of a competitive party system. The electoral system employed was first past the post in single-member constituencies. The party or parties commanding an overall majority in the House of Assembly formed the government. Up to the adoption of the tricameral constitution in the 1980s, the Prime Minister was the head of government, while the head of state had a largely ceremonial role. South Africa was governed according to the Westminster doctrine of the sovereignty of parliament. Consequently, a government with a majority in the House of Assembly could enact laws in the confident expectation that they would be enforced by the courts and not rejected on the grounds that they conflicted with any basic constitutional principles. The enormous latitude the Westminster model accorded to the executive meant that the most far-reaching restrictions on the lives of the population could be imposed by fully constitutional means.

It can be argued that in the 1950s the means used to secure the removal of the Coloureds from the common roll in the Cape stretched constitutionality close to breaking point. Further, from the 1960s South African governments authorised the security forces to act outside the law in suppressing extra-parliamentary opposition to the government. Cover for such action was provided by frequent proclamations of a state of emergency. However, significant though some of thc breaches of the law were, they did not amount to the complete abandonment of constitutional government. The courts retained their independence and on occasion their decisions hampered the government's implementation of apartheid or the methods used by the security forces. Further, although legislation restricted the freedom of the press in a multitude of ways, the press still provided a significant platform for opposition to the government throughout the period of National Party rule after 1948.

A political factor of very considerable importance in creating space for opposition to the government after 1948 was the persistence of ethnic divisions among whites. The gulf between Afrikaners and the English-speaking white community remained a formidable barrier to the government's establishing political conformity among whites. That prevented the government from achieving complete political hegemony over the society as it was much more difficult for the government to take action against white opponents than opponents who came from communities without the vote. In terms of the expression of political opinion, even at the worst of times South Africa under apartheid was a freer society than Ian Smith's Rhodesia. The English–Afrikaner ethnic divide also provided a more reliable obstacle to the National Party government's totalitarian tendencies than the opposition of Western governments to its policies. The strength of their protests waxed and waned according to circumstances.

History of Racial Policy

The second ground for considering South Africa to be totalitarian is somewhat more substantial. To consider it fully, an account of the evolution of South African racial policy is necessary. Apartheid developed out of the policy of segregation that preceded it. Segregation began to be used as a term for racial policy at the beginning of the twentieth century. However, discrimination on the basis of race went back much further to the very origins of white settlement in the seventeenth century. Writers such as the economic historian De Kiewiet attributed the hold of race-thinking on the societies of Southern Africa to the role of the frontier as underlined by the racial attitudes championed by the independent Boer republics during the nineteenth century. However, another interpretation was that the approach taken to the incorporation of the Zulus in the British colony of Natal by Theophilus Shepstone laid the basis for the development of the policy of segregation.[1] More recent scholarship has emphasised the role played by scientific racism in the development of the idea of segregation, as well as the influence on South Africa of racial practices in America's Deep South.

From 1910 to 1948, South Africa was led by three generals who had fought against the British during the Anglo-Boer war of 1899–1902. The three were Louis Botha, Jan Christiaan Smuts and J.B.M. Hertzog. They headed a variety of administrations, each of which enacted significant segregationist legislation. The Native Labour Regulation Act of 1911, one of the so-called Master and Servant laws, made a breach of contract by African mineworkers a criminal offence. The Mines and Works Act of the same year prevented the promotion of African workers to skilled work by denying Africans the possibility of acquiring blasting certificates that provided entry into positions of responsibility. The Natives Land Act of 1913 made it illegal for Africans to purchase land outside areas designated as native reserves, though this provision was not applied to the Cape because in that province there existed a non-racial property qualification for the exercise of the franchise. However, this came to an end in 1936 under the Native Trust and Land Act and the Representation of Natives Act, which removed Africans from the common roll in the Cape while adding land to the existing reserves so that they totalled 13 per cent of the country.

The Apprenticeship Act of 1922 provided that Africans could not be apprenticed. The report of the Transvaal Local Government Commission, the Stallard Commission, asserted that towns were 'the White man's creation' and that 'the masterless Native in urban areas is a source of danger and a cause of degradation to both Black and White'.[2] In its wake influx control was introduced under the Native Urban Areas Act of 1923. This provided for the removal from the urban areas of 'idle' or 'undesirable' Africans. The Industrial Conciliation Act of 1924 prevented African workers from engaging in collective bargaining. It did so through the simple device of excluding them from the definition of employees under the Act. This was one of the first of the so-called 'civilised labour' measures intended to enhance the position of white workers, while protecting them against competition from African workers. The Immorality Act of 1927 outlawed extramarital sex between whites and Africans. In short, racial discrimination was deeply entrenched in the laws of South Africa well before 1948.

Systematic Apartheid

Where apartheid differed from segregation was in its much more systematic character. Segregation for many purposes depended on local custom and practice. That had permitted its erosion, a process the National Party was determined to reverse. An important pillar of apartheid was the Population Registration Act of 1950. This provided for the racial classification of the entire population, initially under three headings: Native (which subsequently became Bantu and then Black), White and Coloured. In 1959 the Coloured category was sub-divided into seven sub-groups: Cape Coloured, Malay, Griqua, Chinese, Indian, Other Asiatic, and Other Coloured. Under the Act, an individual could appeal against his or her classification to the Race Relations Board. The results of these appeals provide a striking illustration of the racial hierarchy that prevailed under apartheid. Those for the year 1986 are given in Table 2.1.

In a debate in the Coloured House of Representatives in 1988 on the Population Registration Act, one of the members cited as evidence of the absurdity of the legislation the fact that while he was classified as Malay, two of his brothers were classified as Cape Coloured, a third as white. At the same time, two of his sisters were classified as

Table 2.1   Reclassifications, 1986[3]

	Applied	Successful	Unsuccessful
White to Cape Coloured	9	8	1
Cape Coloured to White	506	314	192
White to Malay	2	2	0
Malay to White	14	9	5
Indian to White	9	4	5
Chinese to White	7	7	0
Griqua to White	1	1	0
Cape Coloured to Black	40	35	5
Black to Cape Coloured	666	387	279
Cape Coloured to Indian	87	81	6
Indian to Cape Coloured	65	63	2
Cape Coloured to Malay	26	25	1
Malay to Cape Coloured	21	21	0
Malay to Indian	50	43	7
Indian to Malay	61	53	8
Cape Coloured to Griqua	4	4	0
Griqua to Cape Coloured	4	2	2
Griqua to Black	2	2	0
Black to Griqua	18	16	2
Cape Coloured to Chinese	12	10	2
Black to Indian	10	9	1
Black to Malay	2	2	0
Black to Other Asiatic	5	1	4
Indian to Other Coloured	2	2	0
Other Coloured to Indian	1	1	0
TOTAL:	1624	1102	522

Cape Coloured, a third as Indian.[4] Another of the pillars of apartheid was the Group Areas Act of 1950. It was the main basis for the enforcement of residential segregation in urban areas. Further, under the rubric of prohibiting 'occupation' by people of different races in 'white' areas, it became the means for imposing segregation for a variety of other purposes, such as going to the cinema. In 1965 under Proclamation R26 the provision applying to cinemas was extended so that the presence of people of different races at 'any place of public entertainment'[5] required a permit from the government. This followed a tour of South Africa by the pop singer, Dusty Springfield, who was deported from the country in 1964 after she had insisted that she would only perform at venues open to all races.

The Prohibition of Mixed Marriages Act of 1949 made marriages across the colour line illegal; a 1968 amendment extended the law to cover marriages contracted by South African citizens outside the country. The Immorality Act of 1950 made sex across the colour line illegal; a 1957 amendment increased the criminal penalties applicable to offenders. The Reservation of Separate Amenities Act of 1953 reinforced the legal basis for segregation by removing any obligation on the government to ensure equality of provision to people of different races. The Extension of University Education Act of 1959 made it illegal for the University of Cape Town and the University of the Witwatersrand to admit 'non-white' students, except by government permit in individual cases.

Whites-only buses, railway carriages, ambulances, park benches, beaches, swimming pools, libraries, toilets and even lifts in public buildings were a pervasive feature of public amenities in South Africa's towns after 1948. This aspect of National Party policies was often referred to as 'petty apartheid'. By contrast, the term, 'grand apartheid', was applied to Verwoerd's ambitious objective of territorial separation of the races. This involved in the first instance stripping Coloureds and Africans of the last remnants of the rights they enjoyed in the country's central political institutions. Coloureds were removed from the common roll in the Cape in 1956. In compensation Coloured voters were given the right to elect on a separate roll four members in the House of Assembly and two provincial councillors. These representatives had to be white. This separate representation was abolished in 1968 under the Prohibition of Improper Interference Act. Africans taken off the common roll in the 1930s had similarly been compensated. Their representation was abolished under the Promotion of Bantu Self-Government Act of 1959.

However, the main purpose of the 1959 Act was the creation of the homeland system. Henceforth, Africans were expected to exercise any political rights through the homelands, which were created out of the African reserves established in the era of segregation. The African population was allocated on the basis of ethnicity, initially, to one of eight different national units or population groups. They were North Sotho, South Sotho, Tswana, Zulu, Swazi, Xhosa, Shangaan-Tsonga and Venda, while the Ndebele were added later as a ninth national unit or population group. Eventually, there were to be a total of ten homelands, as Xhosas were assigned to one of two homelands, Transkei and Ciskei. There was a gradual devolution of power from Pretoria, the country's administrative capital, to the homelands. This was allied to a process of consolidation, involving the forced removal of Africans from so-called black spots, to make them into viable territorial units. In 1963, the largest of the former reserves, Transkei, was granted self-government.

Ultimately, four homelands, Transkei in 1976, Bophuthatswana in 1977, Venda in 1979 and Ciskei in 1981, achieved full independence. However, they were recognised as independent states only by South Africa. Yet their independence was not without effect. Africans allocated to these four homelands lost their South African citizenship as a consequence. In fact, under Verwoerd's ideological blueprint, which the National Party government only abandoned in the 1980s, the intention was that South Africa would be left with no African citizens. Loss of their South African citizenship through association with a homeland in which some of them had never even set foot was a major grievance of urban Africans affected by the policy. The hostility the policy aroused eventually persuaded the government to pass the Restoration of South African Citizenship Act in 1986.

Another dimension of apartheid linked to the homeland system was labour policy. It entailed extensive control over the movement of African labour, as well as elaborate restrictions on the entry of African workers into skilled and semi-skilled positions. Under the ideology of apartheid as elaborated by Verwoerd, Africans were to be treated as temporary sojourners in white South Africa, the 87 per cent of the country not allocated to the homelands. Verwoerd maintained that the presence of Africans in white South Africa should be dependent on their capacity to serve the needs of white society. Under this nostrum existing controls on the influx of Africans into urban areas were tightened up through the creation under legislation enacted in 1952 of a nationwide system of labour bureaux. With important exceptions applying to the existing urbanised African population, Africans required labour bureau permission to remain in an urban area for longer than 72 hours.

An indication of the effect of the controls on the movement of African labour was the Department of Bantu Administration and Development's boast in 1960 that the greatest contribution to overcoming the shortage of agricultural labour had been made from the urban areas rather than the homelands.[6] When Durban dockers went on strike in 1969, they had been replaced *en masse* by workers supplied from the homelands by labour bureaux. A further indication of the impact of the pass laws on the bargaining power of African workers was the fact that Coloured wages in agriculture in the 1960s were twice those of Africans. Coloureds were not subject to the pass laws, but, under the Coloured labour preference area proclaimed in the Western Cape by the government, farmers did not have the option of employing African workers. The impact of these controls on the African population can be gauged from the scale of prosecutions for offences under the pass laws. At their peak almost 700,000 people a year were prosecuted under the pass laws.[7]

The Industrial Conciliation Act of 1956 empowered the government under a system known as job reservation to lay down by decree what jobs individuals of a particular race could perform. Areas affected by job reservation determinations included the building, clothing, footwear, furniture and motor assembly industries. In 1970 the Bantu Labour Amendment Act empowered the Minister of Bantu Administration and Development to prohibit employment of Africans in specified areas, classes of employment, trades or even by specified employees. This measure was introduced because of concern that employers were becoming increasingly lax in providing separate workplace amenities for white workers. It underscores the point that in a number of fields the extension of apartheid was reactive. That is, it was a defensive response to the perception of the erosion of the existing racial hierarchy in which whites occupied the top position and Africans were at the bottom, with Coloureds and Indians in an intermediate position.

Characterisations of Apartheid

At its height under Verwoerd's premiership, apartheid could reasonably be characterised as a pervasive system that intruded into virtually every aspect of a person's life. This characterisation can be compared with a common description of the totalitarian state as one that 'extends its influence over the whole of life, private as well as public, and exacts full submission of the individual to its demands'.[8] The first half of the definition fits the South African case well. As already mentioned, the English–Afrikaans divide provided one obstacle to the government's control of society and hence its ability to exact 'full submission'. John Kane-Berman identifies another, the strength of civil society.

The totalitarian state – most cogently depicted in George Orwell's prophetic *1984* – tolerates no sphere of life outside state or party control. Though South Africa under National Party rule was an authoritarian state, it was never totalitarian – in part because of the abundance and rich diversity of non-governmental organisations (NGOs) that made up civil society, among them many working in one way or another for the end of apartheid.[9]

However, this picture needs to be qualified in two ways. It is an apt description of only the final phase of apartheid, what Giliomee and Schlemmer characterise as the era of 'reform-apartheid'.[10] NGOs offered relatively feeble opposition to the system prior to the 1980s. Further, those who were active in NGOs working for an end to apartheid in the 1980s often paid a high price for their involvement as a result of covert actions by agents of the state. Ironically, the toll of victims of violence by the state actually increased as the hold of the apartheid system on society diminished in other respects.

Linked to the issue of whether white minority rule during any part of the apartheid era could be characterised as totalitarian is whether National Party rule in South Africa could legitimately be compared to the Nationalist Socialist rule in Germany. The emotive comparison of the Nats (as members of the National Party were colloquially referred to in South Africa) with the Nazis has generated a great deal of debate since 1994, much of it heated. An example was the furore in 1996 over the publication of *Reconciliation through Truth* by Asmal, Asmal and Roberts. The authors pressed the comparison as follows:

> If one leaves aside the systematic and technologically adept extermination of Jewish people that intensified under the Nazis in 1941 and which really has no parallel, there is a striking overlap between early Nazi German solutions to the Jewish Problem and apartheid's ways of dealing with the Black Threat.[11]

They summarised the charges against apartheid as follows:

> Apartheid was a form of colonialism; it was a pariah state, illegitimate in international law; it denied the majority its right to self-determination and thereby triggered that majority's right, in international law, to revolt; it was a criminal system in itself; in

addition, it committed specific crimes of aggression and against peace; it committed crimes against humanity as well as war crimes; and it committed genocide.[12]

Hermann Giliomee wrote a highly critical review of the book in the *Cape Times*. He argued that to bear out the contention that apartheid was a crime against humanity 'it would be necessary to back up such a charge with evidence of deliberate government intent to kill or starve blacks to death'.[13] Population growth and the rise in life expectancy under apartheid were impossible to square with that happening on any large scale. Giliomee also pointed out that the resolutions in the United Nations General Assembly labelling apartheid a crime against humanity were bound up with the Cold War, reflected politicking by the Soviet bloc and had not been supported by the West.

The book by Asmal, Asmal and Roberts was published as the Truth and Reconciliation Commission (TRC) was conducting its hearing into gross human rights violations between 1960 and 1994. After having originally supported a process analogous to the Nuremberg trials that had followed Germany's defeat, Kader Asmal had become a strong supporter of the setting up of the TRC as a means of establishing the accountability of apartheid's rulers. The viewpoint of Kader Asmal and his fellow authors was summarised by Antjie Krog as follows:

The book states very precisely: the Truth Commission will not be able to fulfill its implicit mandate to create a new moral order, if it does not make a distinction between those who fought against Apartheid and those who defended it. This is an old debate, but these writers give it a new dimension. They spell out, that contrary to the claims made by the Commissioners, there is no imperative in the legislation not to make any distinction between the perpetrators and the victims of the two sides. It is not a question of bad apples on both sides, says Kader Asmal, it is a question of a bad tree, a weed, on the one hand, and an apple tree on the other. The book asks: if the Truth Commission cannot distinguish between right and wrong, how can it weave a moral fabric.[14]

By contrast, Giliomee argued in his review that experience elsewhere of political transitions showed that 'setting up a complete dichotomy between a benign present and an evil past' could do very serious damage to the prospects for democratic consolidation.

However, in the event, in spite of the fact that the majority of the Commissioners were sympathetic to the viewpoint of the national liberation movements and interpreted the rise and fall of apartheid accordingly, they insisted on applying the same criteria to their actions as to those of the state. Consequently the national liberation movements, as the ANC and the PAC were described, were held to be accountable for the gross violations of human rights that were committed in the course of their struggles against apartheid. Such an outcome was only partly due to the capacity of the Commissioners to rise above partisan considerations. It was also the inevitable consequence of the nature of South Africa's transition and the fact of legal continuity between the old regime and the new. In legal terms, it would have been hard to sustain the position of ignoring serious transgressions that had taken place in the name of the struggle against apartheid. It would have required the presumption that all the acts of the previous regime were illegitimate and illegal, which would actually have undercut the Commission itself, since it represented the fulfilment of a commitment made in the interim constitution, which had been enacted into law by the tricameral parliament.

Asmal, Asmal and Roberts were by no means the first (or for that matter, the last) writers to draw an analogy between apartheid and Nazism. The elements of racism and grand design lent obvious verisimilitude to such a comparison. A sustained comparison of the two systems was published in the 1960s under the title, *The Rise of the South African Reich*.[15] The author was Brian Bunting, a Communist who had been elected to the House of Assembly in 1952 as a representative of Africans in the Western Cape but had been expelled under the Suppression of Communism Act. He wrote the book in exile. The book was banned in South Africa but as Patrick Laurence notes, 'copies were nevertheless smuggled in and widely read in original and samizdat form'.[16] There were two main strands in Bunting's analysis. First, he detailed the influence of Nazism on Afrikaner nationalism in the 1930s and 1940s. For example, in a chapter entitled 'Followers of Hitler', he examined the Afrikaner nationalist campaign against Jewish immigration to South Africa. In another chapter, he gave an account of a court case in the 1940s in which Verwoerd, then editor of a leading Afrikaans daily newspaper, failed to prove libel over the accusation that his paper had acted as a tool of Nazi propaganda. Secondly, he highlighted similarities between the theory and practice of apartheid and the record of the Nazis, highlighting, for example, points in common between the Nuremberg laws and South African legislation after 1948, particularly the Population Registration Act.

Nazi links with Afrikaner nationalists during the 1930s and 1940s and the similarity of their racial policies prior to the Holocaust have continued to provide the main elements of the comparison. In his most recent book, *The Afrikaners*, Hermann Giliomee discusses both issues. On the subject of links, he discounts the notion that radical rightwing movements 'had anything but a fleeting impact on the Afrikaner nationalist movement or on apartheid as an ideology'.[17] In discussing anti-Semitism among Afrikaner nationalists as reflected in the campaign against Jewish immigration during the 1930s, Giliomee argues that it had local roots and that the National Party's anti-Semitism was 'opportunistic rather than deep-rooted'.[18] On the issue of the similarity between Nazism and apartheid, he argues:

Apartheid was not based on the failed racial ideology of Nazi Germany, but on mainstream Western racism, ranging from a superficial color preference to a pathological abhorrence of race mixing, which was still widespread in both Europe and the USA.[19]

Giliomee's view of the comparison stands in marked contrast to that of the veteran journalist, Allister Sparks. Sparks concludes:

The fact is that the influence of Nazi Germany on the minds of those who fashioned apartheid was very great, especially among key members of the Broederbond secret society, the inner body of Afrikanerdom's new political intelligentsia where the actual ideological groundwork was laid. That is not to say that the two are the same thing. To equate apartheid with Nazism is an overstatement that invites incredulity: its evil is in a different category from the calculated genocide of the death camps. But they are of the same genre. Apartheid and National Socialism both arose from the same witches' cauldron of national grievance and economic depression. Driven by the same sense of cultural despair, the same group hatreds and personal resentments, and feeling much in common with their Germanic kin, the Afrikaner ideologists responded to the national revival that Hitler kindled.[20]

However, despite the differences of viewpoint over the issue of the Nazi comparison in the literature, there is agreement on one central point. It is that for all the horrors that might be attributed to apartheid, they were not of the same order as the destruction wrought by the Nazis. This may seem a very banal point to make, as it is quite obvious that the ultimate consequences of the National Party rule in South Africa were in no way comparable with the impact on the world of Hitler's rise to power. The question – aside from the population and economic weight of the two countries – is why. Was it because the nature of South African racism under apartheid was different from German racism of the Nazi era, as Giliomee argues? In so far as his argument seeks to associate South African racism with settler and colonial racism more generally, it carries the further implication of continuity in racial attitudes from the colonial era through the country's segregationist phase up to apartheid itself. This raises the larger issue of how similar apartheid was to segregation.

Distinguishing Apartheid from Segregation

Two grounds have commonly been advanced for distinguishing between segregation and apartheid. First, it was argued that apartheid was applied with much greater thoroughness and ideological fervour than segregation. For example, in his study of South Africa in the twentieth century, James Barber writes the following:

> Apartheid was both a creed and a set of policies. The policies were in many ways a continuation of those developed under segregation, but now they were applied with a thoroughness not previously envisaged, and they were underpinned by a burning conviction of right. It represented a major step of degree, even of kind, in policy towards blacks.[21]

Secondly, it was argued that it was the different context of the post-war world that primarily distinguished apartheid from segregation. Sparks expresses the point as follows:

White South Africans are genuinely bewildered that they should be treated as an outcast nation when other countries, too, have racial skeletons in their cupboards, when many are more overtly dictatorial and at least a dozen are guilty of more tyrannical behaviour. They fail to understand that whatever other sins there may be in Old Adam's garden, on this issue at least the postwar world reached a consensus: any public declaration of racism is morally objectionable. And at the very moment the consensus was reached, white South Africa declared just that, more emphatically and comprehensively than they had ever done before.[22]

William Beinart in his summary of why apartheid 'gave South African society a distinctive profile and a long shadow', combines the two points:

Although segregationist attitudes in earlier decades may have been more stringent than in many other colonies, or in the USA, they were not vastly different. Apartheid was a more intense system and increasingly jarred in an era of decolonization and majority rule.[23]

Admittedly, there is no necessary coincidence between analytical and moral distinctions. Nevertheless, many writers on apartheid can be placed into one of three broad categories, on the basis of their approach to these issues of comparison. First, there are those who see no contradiction between viewing apartheid as a form of colonialism and comparing it with the practices of Nazism. They regard all three systems as fundamentally illegitimate and entailing gross violation of human rights. One might label it as the Third World perspective, as it would be the position with which many in the Third World would identify. Secondly, there are those who regard white minority rule under apartheid as fundamentally different from cases of totalitarianism, such as Nazism. For these writers the equation of apartheid with colonial practices is not to damn the system but to underscore the elements of paternalism and even trusteeship that were involved in the development of the idea. However, this view also often acknowledges that in practice the results of the implementation of apartheid did not match such relatively benign intentions.

Thirdly, there are writers who draw a clear line between segregation and apartheid, in the process separating it from both mainstream Western racism and colonialism. From this perspective, an important consideration was that apartheid was the product of a radical anti-colonial movement in Afrikaner nationalism.

Arendt and South Africa

Of course, by no means all accounts of apartheid can be fitted neatly into any of the three categories. In any event, none of these perspectives provides a wholly satisfactory account of the evolution of South African racial policy for reasons that were brought out very well in a study published over fifty years ago. The study in question was the seminal work by Hannah Arendt, *The Origins of Totalitarianism*. Arendt treated the emergence of South Africa as a race society, imperialism and the rise of the Nazis as interconnected developments. Arendt integrated South Africa into the history of the West. This was despite her acceptance of the De Kiewiet thesis that the origins of South African racism lay in frontier society. Arendt argued that the roots of Nazism extended well beyond Germany. For example, she devoted a chapter to the *Dreyfus* case in France.

Captain Alfred Dreyfus was a Jewish officer on the French General Staff. In December 1894 he was convicted of espionage for Germany. With the emergence of evidence that the conviction had been a miscarriage of justice, public controversy over the case grew. His sentence was eventually reduced as a result of a retrial in August 1899. This was quickly followed by his being freed under a presidential pardon. The retrial had been preceded by a wave of anti-Semitic demonstrations across France. 'Mobs trampled the streets crying "Death to Jews"' and 'the forces of law and order, badly over-stretched and sometimes indifferent, were often late on the scene'.[24] Yet, in spite of all this, there were no deaths. Given the widespread nature of the demonstrations and the virulence of the hatred expressed towards Jews, this was remarkable. However, for Arendt the significance of these events was not the absence of deaths, but the capacity of the army to mobilise the mob against the Dreyfusards by appealing to anti-Semitism. A legacy of the Dreyfus affair was the survival of racism in France that made the country 'an easy prey to Nazi aggression' as 'Hitler spoke a language long familiar and never quite forgotten.'[25] (In parenthesis it should be noted that a weakness of the thesis of Daniel Goldhagen that focuses on German eliminationist anti-Semitism as an explanation of the Holocaust[26] is the extent of non-German participation in the final solution.)

Arendt argued that a crucial precursor of totalitarianism, both Nazism and Stalinism, was the era of imperialism between 1884 and 1914, which she contended was a product of an alliance between mob and capital. A central figure in her analysis was Cecil John Rhodes, the megalomaniac politician and businessman who played a leading role in the politics of Southern Africa in the 1880s and 1890s. Rhodes's obsession with race was underlined by his unfulfilled plans for a secret society to promote the expansion of the Nordic race after his death. According to Arendt, South Africa developed into the 'culture-bed of Imperialism' with the mineral discoveries of the 1870s and 1880s, just as its role in assuring the maritime road to India had become redundant as a result of the opening of the Suez Canal in 1869:

> Prospectors, adventurers and the scum of the big cities emigrated to the Dark Continent along with capital from industrially developed countries. From now on, the mob, begotten by the monstrous accumulation of capital, accompanied its begetter on those voyages of discovery where nothing was discovered but new possibilities for investment. The owners of superfluous wealth were the only men who could use the superfluous men who came from the four corners of the earth. Together they established the first paradise of parasites whose lifeblood was gold. Imperialism, the product of superfluous money and superfluous men, began its startling career by producing the most superfluous and unreal goods.[27]

Limiting the impact of imperialism on Britain itself was, as Arendt put it, 'the good sense of English statesmen who drew a sharp line between colonial methods and normal domestic politics'.[28] It was precisely this separation that was absent in the case of the totalitarian movements so that the methods used on the peripheries invaded the centre. As to the influence of South Africa on the development of totalitarianism, Arendt wrote the following:

> South Africa became the first example of a phenomenon that occurs whenever the mob becomes the dominant factor in the

alliance between mob and capital. In one respect, the most important one, the Boers remained the undisputed masters of the country: whenever rational labor and production policies came into conflict with race considerations, the latter won. Profit motives were sacrificed time and again to the demands of a race society, frequently at a terrific price.[29]

The lesson for the totalitarian movements was that the normal laws of capitalist development could be suspended:

South Africa's race society taught the mob the great lesson of which it had always had a confused premonition, that through sheer violence an underprivileged group could create a class lower than itself, that for this purpose it did not even need a revolution but could band together with groups of the ruling classes, and that foreign or backward peoples offered the best opportunities for such tactics. The full impact of the African experience was first realized by leaders of the mob, like Carl Peters, who decided that they too had to belong to a master race. African colonial posses- sions become the most fertile soil for the flowering of what later was to become the Nazi elite. Here they had seen with their own eyes how people could be converted into races and how, simply by taking the initiative in this process, one might push one's people into the position of the master race.[30]

Finally, she noted:

Long before the Nazis consciously built up an antisemitic movement in South Africa, the race issue had invaded the conflict between the *uitlander* and the Boers in the form of antisemitism, which is all the more noteworthy since the importance of Jews in the South African gold and diamond economy did not survive the turn of the century.[31]

Arendt emphasised the role that world politics played in the rise of totalitarianism during the twentieth century from within, not out- side, Western civilisation. She was also insistent on the wide appeal of the Nazis' propagation of racism prior to their defeat.

Hitlerism exercised its strong international and inter-European appeal during the thirties because racism, although a state doctrine only in Germany, had been a powerful trend in public opinion everywhere... Racism was neither a new nor a secret weapon, though never before had it been used with this thorough-going consistency.[32]

It may fairly be argued that Arendt's arguments rest on some contentious foundations. Most evident is her treatment of the imperialism of the period prior to the First World War as a special phase of history, a perspective that enjoyed wider support among historians at the beginning of the last century than at its end. But whether Arendt's general argument holds up or not, in the case of South Africa the emphasis she placed on the mineral discoveries as a significant watershed appears justified. This will be discussed more fully in the next chapter.

The International Dimension

It has become a cliché in the age of globalisation that politics any-where is connected in one way or another to politics everywhere. Indeed it can be argued that this was true of most of the world much earlier. In particular, the completion of Africa's conquest at the end of the nineteenth century was an important watershed in ending the continent's relative isolation from world politics up to that point. As a consequence, it was inevitable that South Africa's racial policies of the twentieth century would be connected to both totalitarianism and colonialism, as well as much else besides. The reason the issue of the very existence of such links generates so much controversy is the role that the labels such as Nazi and neo-Nazi still play in political polemic in post-apartheid South Africa. For example, in 2000 the ANC made considerable play of the support for the opposition Democratic Party (DP) from a radical rightwing paramilitary move-ment, the Afrikaner Weerstands Beweging (Afrikaner resistance movement) or AWB. The ANC drew particular attention to the swastika-like, triple-seven emblem of the AWB to damn the DP as having been polluted by neo-Nazis.[33]

Damning the Democratic Party on the basis of such an association might be considered unfair, given the party's espousal of a mix of liberal and libertarian policies. However, there is no escaping the fact that the AWB, which during the 1980s became a significant political movement on the Afrikaner radical right opposed to 'reform-apartheid', quite consciously and deliberately adopted symbols that evoked the era of Nazism. After the release of Mandela in February 1990, the AWB staged a large demonstration in Pretoria at which a Nazi flag was waved along with banners proclaiming 'Hang Mandela – Free Barend'. The second part of the slogan referred to Barend Strydom, a member of the AWB who had been convicted of murdering seven black civilians in a shooting spree in November 1988. Such echoes of European fascism underline the fact that in the twentieth century at least South Africa's development did not occur in isolation from the rest of the world. The question of South African isolation before that is examined next.

3

Origins of Racial Policy: Consequence of an Imperialist War or the Prejudice of the Frontier?

There has been contention over the causes of the Anglo-Boer War of 1899–1902 for more than a hundred years. Even with the establishment of an entirely new political dispensation in South Africa that owes nothing to that conflict and the dawn of a new millennium, the argument has continued to rage over the role that gold played in the war. Radicals going back to John Atkinson Hobson at the outbreak of the conflict have argued that gold was central to a quintessentially imperialist war. Liberals and conservatives have dismissed these claims and have focused on unconnected political and strategic factors as both the ostensible and the real causes of the conflict. For example, Frank Welsh argues:

> The last thing the mine-owners needed was a war. Millions of pounds of investments in plant and equipment, together with all the mine-workings, would be at risk; there was no question of war leading to increased prices or more sales after the fighting was over; the best that could be hoped for would be that production would not stop for too long, and that at least running costs would be reduced, although the considerable expenses of servicing capital and maintenance would remain... In the face of this, the claim made by some Marxists, even such eminent historians as Dr Eric Hobsbawm, that 'the motive for war was gold' hardly deserves serious consideration.[1]

By contrast, Sampie Terreblanche states just as emphatically:

> The growing animosity between the ZAR [Zuid-Afrikaansche Republiek] and Kruger on the one hand and the gold mining industry and Alfred Milner, the British high commissioner for South Africa, on the other eventually led to the Anglo-Boer War (1899–1902). There can be little doubt that this was an imperialist war *par excellence* and, more specifically, a gold war.[2]

Giliomee occupies the middle ground in this particular argument. He writes on the one hand, 'there is no substantial evidence that Britain went to war to control the Transvaal's gold supply' but, on the other, 'it would be quite strange if the war in South Africa had nothing to do at all with gold'.[3]

The controversy over whether gold was a cause of the South African war is not unlike the argument over whether concern over oil supplies in the wake of the attacks on America of 11 September 2001 was a cause of the war against Iraq in 2003. In both cases, the debate was central to the legitimacy of the war itself, so that by and large it was the opponents of the war who underscored the role respectively of gold and oil. Since acknowledgement of the central importance of gold or oil would have undermined the case for war, unsurprisingly, policymakers in each instance seeking to justify war focused on other issues. The fact that in both cases the 'other issues' did not provide altogether compelling arguments for war compounded the suspicion of their opponents that they were pretexts that concealed the policymakers' real motivation. Further complicating historical judgements in the case of the Anglo-Boer War was the disastrous course of the war itself. In particular, it is quite evident that British policymakers did not anticipate the consequences of the conflict.

The Frontier Explanation

Given the gulf between the war's causes and consequences, the dispute over its causes might seem to be one of limited historical significance. What gives it a much wider relevance is its connection to one of the most persistent and dominant interpretations of South African history. This is that South Africa's racial policies, and most particularly apartheid, originated from the prejudices forged on the frontier. According to this view, the isolation of the settlers in the interior both created the Afrikaner people as an ethnic group with no emotional attachment to a European homeland and shaped their attitudes on race, instilling in them an assumption of white racial superiority. Their treatment of the indigenous groups they encountered in their expansion into the interior brought them into conflict with both the missionaries and the British government after the establishment of British rule. The Afrikaners' hostility towards the freeing of the slaves prompted the Great Trek in the 1830s. And race continued to be a factor in the conflicts between the British and the Boer republics through the course of the nineteenth century. From this perspective, the conflict at the end of the century between the Boer republics and the forces of the British Empire was a battle between the perpetuation of feudal relationships and incorporation into the modern world, as well as between racism and multiracialism.

The narrative continues on the following lines. The pyrrhic nature of the British victory in the Anglo-Boer War of 1899 to 1902 meant that although the Boer republics had been defeated, Afrikaners gained the whip hand in the Union of South Africa. Their dominance was reflected in the racial policies of South African governments after 1910. However, political divisions among the Afrikaners and the continuing strength of the Cape liberal tradition acted as a check on governments prior to the Second World War. The election victory of the Nationalists in 1948 marked the beginning of a new and more extreme phase of policy that offended world opinion and led to the country's international isolation. The title of a book by Margaret Ballinger published in 1969, *From Union to Apartheid: A Trek to Isolation*, neatly sums up this interpretation of the development of the country's racial policies after Union. As was the case with authors of other works of this genre, Ballinger conflated the isolation imposed on the country by the international community and what she saw as the disposition Afrikaners inherited from the frontier to live in isolation from the rest of the world.

The myth that racism in South Africa developed as a result of the country's isolation from the rest of the world had a strong hold on South African historiography during the heyday of apartheid. It had obvious appeal when the climax of the story of South African politics appeared to be the triumph of Afrikaner nationalism. An obvious weakness was its assumption of continuity in the attitudes of the Afrikaner community in the twentieth century with those of trekboers (stock farmers) during the seventeenth and eighteenth centuries and voortrekkers in the nineteenth century. This was assumed despite vast economic changes that took place as a consequence of the mineral revolution of the late nineteenth century. In fact, as a consequence, the circumstances faced by predominantly urban Afrikaners in the twentieth century bore very little resemblance to the world their ancestors had inhabited. This was reflected in the fact that their expansive view of the role of government could hardly have been more different from their ancestors' individualism. Another highly contestable dimension of the isolationist perspective was its counterposing of Afrikaner racism to English liberalism. For example, in their 1961 study of British policy, Robinson and Gallagher characterised the conflict between Britain and the Boer republics as a 'clash between a liberal, multi-racial imperialism and a racialist republicanism'.[4]

Hobson's Perspective

Their view can be contrasted with the observations of a contemporary observer, John Atkinson Hobson. Due allowance must be made for the offensive character of some of the terms Hobson used. They reflected the times he lived in:

> With a very few individual exceptions the British Afrikanders have no more belief in the educational and equal political rights of the Kaffirs than have the Dutch. Loyal Natal is quite as unlikely to defer to the influence of the Imperial Government should it ever be exerted in order to procure for black or coloured folk equal political and civil power with that conferred on whites.[5]

It may be objected that Hobson's observations were of the attitude of white English-speaking settlers. However, his description of the character of South African society under British rule was no less critical:

> The entire system of South African society stands upon various modes of coercing Kaffirs into working for the benefit of whites, by invading their territories, goading them to reprisals, depriving them of their land and cattle, tempting them by strong drink and

guns, and in one way or another placing them in such a position of political and economic weakness that they are unable to refuse wage work upon terms offered by white masters.[6]

Hobson was the *Manchester Guardian*'s correspondent in South Africa during the course of the Anglo-Boer War. He was a radical liberal whose writings influenced both Lenin and John Maynard Keynes. His most influential work was a study of imperialism that was first published in 1902. His interpretation of imperialism, which formed one of the building blocks of Hannah Arendt's analysis of the origins of totalitarianism quoted extensively in the last chapter, owed a great deal to his experience of South Africa. It is worth examining in some detail.

In the first chapter of *Imperialism: A Study* Hobson set out to define nationalism, imperialism and colonialism. After a brief exposition of nineteenth-century nationalism, he quoted with approval 'the true nature and limits of nationality' as expounded by J.S.Mill in *Representative Government*. This stated that 'a portion of mankind may be said to constitute a nation if they are united among themselves by common sympathies which do not exist between them and others'.[7] Various causes were held to generate this feeling of nationality including language, religion, geography, political antecedents and race. Hobson then argued:

It is the debasement of this genuine nationalism by attempts to overflow its natural banks and absorb the near or distant territory of reluctant or unassimilable peoples that marks the passage from nationalism to a spurious colonialism on the one hand, imperialism on the other.[8]

Hobson's next step was to draw a distinction between colonialism and imperialism. He defines colonialism as 'the migration of part of a nation to vacant or sparsely peopled foreign lands'.[9] In short, he used the term 'colonialism' in the sense of colonisation. His examples were Australia and Canada. He envisaged in their case the establishment of local self-government on the pattern of the mother country as a transition stage to the development of a separate nationality and identity. However, later in his analysis he discussed ways in which they might be kept within the imperial fold through imperial federation. By contrast, he argued that Britain's tropical and sub-tropical colonies were 'plainly representative of the spirit of imperialism rather than of colonialism'. In these cases, in most instances, a small white minority wielded 'political or economic sway over a majority of alien and subject people, themselves under the despotic political control of the Imperial Government or its local nominees'.[10]

This analysis presented Hobson with a problem that he failed to solve fully, or satisfactorily: how to classify South Africa; for its self-governing colonies fitted neatly into neither category. This led him to treat South Africa as a hybrid in which 'the conflict between the colonial and the imperial ideas has long been present in the forefront of the consciousness of politicians'.[11] In this context he referred to Rhodes's calls for the elimination of the imperial factor and his championing of the rights of the colonists. That Rhodes, the great imperialist, should have objected to the imperial factor seems on the face of it paradoxical. Yet some South African historians found Rhodes's record perplexing on almost directly contrary grounds. For example, D.W.Krüger, commenting on Rhodes's involvement of Chamberlain in the Jameson Raid, stated 'strangely enough, matters had come to the point where the very man [Rhodes] who had always rejected the imperial factor came to invoke that factor to gain his ends'.[12]

In fact, the paradox, whichever way it is looked at, was more apparent than real. It stemmed from the use of the term 'imperial factor', to denote both the policy of expansionist imperialism and to refer to such manifestations of British liberalism as the Cape's qualified but non-racial franchise. It was the imperial factor in the latter sense that Rhodes wanted to eliminate. Essentially the same point has been made by Hannah Arendt in her own characteristic fashion:

> The conscience of the nation, represented by Parliament and a free press, functioned and was resented by colonial administrators, in all European countries with colonial possessions... In England in order to distinguish between the imperial government seated in London and controlled by Parliament and colonial administrators, this influence was called the 'imperial factor', thereby crediting imperialism with the merits and remnants of justice it so eagerly tried to eliminate.[13]

Rhodes's chosen instrument for the colonisation of Rhodesia was the Chartered Company precisely because it excluded the supervision of Parliament.

Hobson's great merit was that he clearly understood that late nineteenth-century imperialism was very different in character from the liberalism of an earlier age. However, the distinction he drew between imperialism and colonialism had the unfortunate result that he was unable to incorporate his analysis of the South African situation into his general theory. The central claims of his general theory are well known so require only the briefest summary here. After he had rejected the view that the nation benefited from the acquisition of new tropical territories through trade or the export of surplus population, he asked 'How is the British nation induced to embark upon such unsound business?' and asserted:

> The only possible answer is that the business interests of the nation as a whole are subordinated to those of certain sectional interests that usurp control of the national resources and use them for their private gain. This is no strange or monstrous charge to bring; it is the commonest disease of all forms of government. The famous words of Sir Thomas More are as true now as when he wrote them: 'Everywhere do I perceive a certain conspiracy of rich men seeking their own advantage under the name and pretext of the commonwealth.'[14]

He went on to argue that the direct outcome of imperialism was:

> more posts for soldiers and sailors and in the diplomatic and consular services; improvement of foreign investments by the substitution of the British flag for a foreign flag, acquisition of markets for certain classes of exports, and some protection and assistance for British trades in these manufactures; employment for engineers, missionaries, speculative miners, ranchers and other emigrants.[15]

He concluded that 'these influences...furnish an interested bias towards Imperialism throughout the educated classes'.[16] A point worth underlining is that Hobson was not arguing that imperialism in general was promoted by a conspiracy in a narrow or literal sense of that term.

A second element in Hobson's analysis, in contrast to but not in conflict with the first, was his well-known theory of under-consumption, what he called 'the economic tap-root of imperialism'.

Under-consumption at home, he argued, led to the generation of surplus capital seeking outlets abroad. Those areas which were politically weakest 'at first penetrated by private business enterprise soon acquire a political significance which grows along a sliding scale from "spheres of legitimate aspiration" to spheres of influence, protectorates, and colonial possessions'.[17] He did not regard this process as inevitable. Surplus capital, he saw, not as a necessary outcome of industrial progress but as the result of 'the maldistribution of consuming power which prevents the absorption of commodities and capital within the country'.[18] In short, he believed in the reform of the capitalist system as a cure for the malady of imperialism. Finally, there was a third, sociological element in Hobson's writings, a belief that the social conditions of rootlessness in Britain's industrial cities provided fertile ground for jingoism and the manipulation of public opinion by imperialism.[19]

The Case Against Hobson

Two of the most common criticisms of Hobson were that the export of capital was greater after the period of ostensible imperialism and that there was little correspondence between territories annexed and areas of capital investment.[20] The first can be met by Hobson's argument that annexation marked 'the beginning of a process of imperialization' and that he envisaged 'the intensive growth of empire'.[21] The second is in part based on a misunderstanding of Hobson's position. It was not his argument that annexation took place where capital investment was greatest but rather where opposition to imperial rule was weakest. Nonetheless, the absence of capital investment in Britain's tropical territories in Africa does need to be explained. Critics have pointed out, for example, that Rhodes's British South Africa Company, which colonised Rhodesia, paid out no dividends between 1890 and 1923.[22] This particular criticism can be quickly disposed of in view of the hopes of the investors and of Rhodes that a second Witwatersrand was to be found in the African interior. Of course, their investment was in the nature of a gamble but to argue that gamblers are not motivated by economic considerations is clearly unsound.

The more general criticism is much harder to meet but it can be partially met if one does not leave out South Africa, which was obviously not characterised by an absence of capital investment. By excluding South Africa from his general analysis for the reasons of definition mentioned earlier, Hobson damaged his case. In particular, he failed to include in his main work the central argument of *The War in South Africa: Its Causes and Effects*. This was that:

> The one all-important object [of the mine owners] is to secure a full, cheap, regular supply of Kaffir and white labour... If the output of gold is to be enlarged on terms which will yield a maximum of profits, a large expansion of the labour market is essential... The sources of native labour in the Republics and the Colonies are quite inadequate... By far the most important supply comes from the Portuguese territories on the east coast, and it is to this quarter and to the lands north of the Zambezi that the mine owners are looking for this increased supply. It is thus manifest that the pressure of the powerful mining interests will continually be used to drive us into interference with countries which lie outside our present possession. By persuasion or coercion labour must be got from Mocambique and from the north. For this reason our international capitalists are expanders of the British Empire.[23]

In short, Hobson was arguing that in some instances a motive for annexation was provided not by the possibility of capital investment in the new territory, but by the need to acquire labour to serve capital investment elsewhere.

In support of his interpretation of the Anglo-Boer War as a war fought to secure cheap labour for the mines, Hobson pointed to the constant complaints of the Chamber of Mines over the shortage of African labour.[24] He highlighted the Chamber's attempts to recruit migrant workers from as far afield as the Gold Coast and Sierra Leone. He quoted speeches by Rhodes, Rudd and others all stressing the high priority they placed on meeting the labour shortage of the mines. Typical of these was a speech by a leading figure of the mining industry and Jameson Raid conspirator, Hays Hammond, in which he declared: 'With good government there will be an abundance of labour and with an abundance of labour there will be no difficulty in cutting down wages'.[25] Hobson also showed that Chamberlain regarded the labour question as important and cited a speech to the House of Commons in 1898 in which Chamberlain stressed 'the need to induce [Africans] to adopt the ordinary means of earning a livelihood by the sweat of their brow'.[26] That after the war Milner's administration introduced Chinese labour and mine wages were reduced provided further circumstantial evidence for Hobson's thesis.

Nevertheless, there remain strong objections to Hobson's interpretation of the causes of the war in South Africa. First, the documentary record did not bear out the existence of a conspiracy between the British government and the mining houses that he appeared to be implying. However, on this point, the research of Thomas Pakenham in uncovering evidence of 'an informal alliance between Sir Alfred Milner, the British High Commissioner and the firm of Wernher-Beit, the dominant mining house'[27] has undermined the emphatic rejection of Hobson by earlier diplomatic historians. Secondly, even if the evidence of 'a thin, golden thread'[28] is acknowledged, Milner seems to have been motivated much more strongly by the strategic objective of establishing British political supremacy in the region. This and the argument over the franchise for the Uitlanders have formed the basis of the interpretation of the causes of the war that has been put forward by most historians.

For example, Leonard Thompson argued that Chamberlain (the Secretary of State for the Colonies) 'misled by jingo rhetoric from the South African League,...came to believe that there was a pan-Afrikaner conspiracy to gain control of the entire region and eliminate British influence', though 'in fact there was no such conspiracy'.[29] For their part, Robinson and Gallagher argue that 'the late-Victorians' imperial instincts, their determination to secure the long route to the East and fear of losing their British allies in South Africa, brought them to restore their supremacy and shape a loyal dominion' though 'restoring imperial supremacy...in the long run...was to prove impossible'. They conclude: 'The empire went to war in 1899 for a concept that was finished, for a cause that was lost, for a grand illusion.'[30]

Why South Africa?

Yet the question that the strategic interpretation begs is why did the British government regard control of the South African interior as a vital interest by the 1890s? The answer to that question cannot be separated from the impact of the mineral discoveries, as the following brief account of the evolution of British policy before the opening up of the Witwatersrand gold fields in the 1880s will underline. In the early 1860s the three colonies of the Cape, Natal and British Kaffraria[31] were neglected outposts of the British Empire. The principal justification for the British presence at the Southern tip of the African continent was the Cape's importance as a port of call on the route to India. Some trade had developed with the colonies themselves that might be seen as providing an additional motive for the maintenance of British rule. However, its value was very small and in the minds of both British policymakers and their parliamentary critics was not sufficient compensation for the financial burden that defence of the colonies imposed on the British treasury.

At this time, the British government was eager not merely *not* to enlarge responsibilities in South Africa, but to reduce them. This policy was maintained in the face of the conflict in the interior between Afrikaner trekboers and African tribes over land, a conflict that continued to give rise to disturbances and movements of population impinging on the security of the colonies. The reason was that a policy of intervention had been tried and had proved a costly failure. In the early 1850s, the Secretary of State for the Colonies, Earl Grey, had toyed with the idea of a British African protectorate in the interior and had backed annexationist policies of the governor of the Cape, Sir Harry Smith, who hoped to solve the Cape's perennial border problems. However, the cost of the Cape-Xhosa wars of 1850 to 1853 prompted a sharp parliamentary backlash against Smith's policy and the abandonment of his annexations in the interior.

As late as 1868, the Secretary of State for the Colonies, the Duke of Buckingham, commented on the Transvaal Republic's quest for a port of its own, 'Why not? This is but fair play'.[32] Admittedly, Buckingham refused to recognise President Pretorius's proclamation purporting to expand the republic's boundaries to Delagoa Bay, but his main reason was that he rightly did not believe that the Transvaal controlled the territory it claimed. Indeed, in so far as there was any pressure to cut off the Boer republic's way to the sea, it can be argued that it came from the colonies rather than from London. After Britain's withdrawal from the interior, the policy of non-intervention became firmly established. It had only one parliamentary critic, Charles Adderley, who championed the cause of the colonists in the House of Commons. He advocated the re-annexation of the abandoned territories and the formation of a self-governing confederation.[33] At first sight this seems paradoxical as it was Adderley who had led the parliamentary onslaught on Earl Grey and Smith. Yet it is not so surprising if the kind of empire Earl Grey envisaged is considered. There was one other supporter of confederation at this time: Sir George Grey, the governor of the Cape Colony from 1854 to 1861.

The initiative he took to this end was opposed by the Colonial Office and led to his recall in disgrace. It is worth examining this episode in a little more detail in view of the regret that some liberal historians have expressed that Sir George Grey was rebuffed. For example, S.H.Frankel argues that 'if his policy had not fallen on deaf ears, it might have altered the political history of South Africa, prevented the South African War and laid the foundations of a truly multi-racial South African Commonwealth'.[34] It seems an extravagant claim. It is based on the fact that Grey was a humanitarian who opposed racial segregation and, in particular, the setting up of African reserves, as well as being a federalist. It is, nonetheless, somewhat ironic that his confederation initiative was, in part, a result of a misunderstanding, though an instructive one.

During 1858, while acting as a mediator in the Orange Free State's war with Basutoland, Sir George Grey had sounded out opinion in Bloemfontein, the republic's capital, on the possibility of a federation with the Cape. In a despatch to London he wrote enthusiastically of the desire for unity.[35] A few months later, the Secretary of State for the Colonies, Sir Edward Bulwer-Lytton, sent a despatch to Grey in which he asked the governor whether South African unity would enable the British Government to reduce its garrisons in the Cape.[36] In reply, Grey proposed the passing of a permissive Act to enable both Britain's colonies in South Africa and the Boer republics in the interior to unite in a federation that would require responsible government.[37] This despatch was very badly received in London. What Bulwer-Lytton had in mind was that a federation of Britain's colonies might enable the government to reduce its expenditure and commitments in South Africa and most certainly not that the policy of non-intervention in the interior should be reversed. Nor was there any support for Grey on humanitarian grounds. Lord Carnarvon, later himself to champion confederation in the 1870s, wrote in a minute on the despatch of the colonies and the republics that their 'present separation and consequently individual sense of weakness is the best safeguard for fairness towards the native tribes'.[38] (His opinion did not change. It was humanitarianism he abandoned when he became converted to confederation.) Grey's recall followed in 1859 when he continued to promote wider confederation.

At the heart of the misunderstanding between the governor and the Colonial Office was Grey's conception of South Africa. In this he was indeed 'in advance of his times'.[39] To the Colonial Office South Africa was no more than a geographical entity. Economically, the foundations of South Africa as a political entity had not yet been laid. By 1860 there were no railways to speak of.[40] The Boer republics whose economies were dominated by largely self-sufficient stock farmers had little in common with the more advanced Cape colony where commercial farming and manufacturing on a limited scale had been established. The opening up of the interior seemed a distant prospect. By the time the British government looked afresh at confederation radical changes were taking place in the economic context.

Discovery of Diamonds

In 1867 diamonds were discovered on the banks of the Orange River. (More important discoveries along the Vaal and Harts Rivers were to follow.) The following year on 12 March the British government renewed its political involvement in the interior by annexing Basutoland. However, the two events were not directly related. The annexation was essentially a response to impact on the Cape Colony of another serious round of war between Basutoland and the Orange Free State. The governor of the Cape Colony, Sir Philip Wodehouse, secured reluctant permission from the British government for the annexation as an expedient to end the fighting on condition that the acquisition did not 'involve any pecuniary liability on the part of the Imperial Government'.[41] The war did end. However, the Colonial Office's efforts to dispose of the territory as had been planned were to prove in the long term less successful.[42] Later that same year, Wodehouse wrote to the Colonial Office of reports of the discovery of 'extraordinarily rich'[43] gold-fields beyond the Limpopo. There were soon further gold discoveries, most notably in the Eastern Transvaal. It was in this context that the Colonial Office began to reformulate Britain's policy towards South Africa. In a minute in November 1868, the Secretary of State for the Colonies, the Duke of

Buckingham, wrote that the proposals for 'an union of the various white settlements and colonies should be examined' in view of 'the material changes [that] have occurred and are occurring'.[44] This minute presaged the reversal of the policy of non-involvement in the interior, a policy under strain but by no means dead as a result of the acquisition of Basutoland. The reversal was rapid. Within a few years increasingly sharp denunciations of the abandonment of the interior in the 1850s appeared in the Colonial Office files.

The impact of the mineral revolution on South Africa was succinctly described by a guide to the country published in 1875.

> The increasing trade of the last few years has done much to promote friendly intercourse between the Cape Colonists and Natalians, who hold possession of the coast, and the Dutch settlers northwards of the Orange River… The opening up of the Northern trade, consequent on the successful prosecution of the diamond industry, has done much to break down political and social divisions. It is not impossible that before many years have elapsed a Federation of the South African Governments and dependencies similar to the Dominion of Canada may be established. Already the Cape Colony and Natal are so associated with the Trans-Orange territory in commercial and social relationships, and the whole life of the country, if we may so say, has flowed so persistently northwards, that the time has passed when a Handbook of South Africa can deal exclusively with the older settlements.[45]

Later John Angove characterised the transformation as follows: 'South Africa, which may be styled the "Cinderella of the British Colonial family", was generally ignored by the rest of the Empire. She, however, like Cinderella, eventually eclipsed her sisters in the brilliancy of her wealth'.[46]

The End of Non-intervention

Economic change was accompanied by a reversal, similar to that in the Colonial Office, in parliamentary attitudes. Debates in the House of Commons in 1871 and 1872 revealed widespread support for resolutions backing confederation of both colonies and republics.

The debates abound in references to the mineral discoveries and the opportunities these opened up for railway construction. Pressing the government to support one of the railway schemes being mooted, one speaker found cause to refer to the smouldering religious controversy surrounding Bishop Colenso. He declared:

> Even the two Bishops, who could not agree in directing the people which road to take to Heaven, could yet agree the best mode of sending them to the gold-fields. The rival Bishops had signed a memorial in favour of this line, and it was probably the only document they had both signed since the signature of the Thirty-nine articles.[47]

It epitomised the spirit of the debates. In the same debate, the Under Secretary for the Colonies, Knatchbull-Hugessen, was congratulated 'on his good fortune in having initiated a change in policy in relation to South Africa'.[48] Knatchbull-Hugessen himself in common with other speakers expressed regret that Smith's annexations in the interior had even been abandoned. Considerable play was made of the barrier the continuing independence of the Boer republics posed to commerce. R.N.Fowler quoted with approval the opinion of *The Friend of the Free State*:

> The pretended freedom of the Free State has already proved, and is proving, a very serious obstacle to progress, and to the advancement of civilisation in South Africa. Does anyone doubt this; we would remind them of the following painful facts: the proposed electric telegraph has been turned aside, and the idea of its passing through the State abandoned; the bridge over the Orange River thwarted; foreign banks expelled; the influx of capital checked; railways not to be thought of; Christian missionaries driven out of Basotholand; educated and enlightened men and capitalists prevented by our wars from settling here.[49]

But perhaps the most significant aspect of the debates was the total absence of any references to the strategic importance of the Cape. With the recent opening of the Suez Canal in 1869, the Cape had lost its importance as the only sea route to India. Similarly, fears that the white settlers might provoke a general African uprising no longer loomed as large. It was implicitly recognised that one consequence of the mineral revolution was that the balance of power within South Africa had moved decisively in favour of the whites. There were few dissenting voices raised against confederation. One member thought the treatment of the BaSotho 'disgraceful' and declared: 'Better give up our colonies than govern them so',[50] but this was not the general opinion. Under Lord Carnarvon, Secretary of State for the Colonies from 1874 to 1878, the policy of confederation was pursued with vigour but met with repeated failure. During this period strategic arguments resurfaced as a justification of policy, though the context was no longer the threat to the Cape and hence to the sea route to India. There was no such threat and the Cape's importance as a sea route had diminished. The new context was the increased importance of the interior. Referring to King Leopold's emerging ambitions in the Congo, Carnarvon wrote:

I should not like anyone to come too near us either on the South towards the Transvaal, which *must* be ours; or on the North too near to Egypt and the country which belongs to Egypt.

In fact, when I speak of geographical limits I am not expressing my real opinion. We cannot admit rivals in the East or even the central parts of Africa: and I do not see why, looking to the experience that we have now of English life within the tropics – the Zambezi should be considered to be without the range of our colonisation. To a considerable extent, if not entirely, we must be prepared to apply a sort of Munro [*sic*] doctrine to much of Africa.[51]

Even before the largest of the mineral discoveries, the Witwatersrand gold-fields, the basis of British engagement with South Africa had changed fundamentally. In particular the British government was no longer preoccupied with a fear that the action of the white settlers would give rise to conflict with the indigenous population that would embroil the British government in costly wars. The mineral discoveries transformed the balance of forces in South Africa in favour of the whites, not least because of the numbers of whites they attracted into the African interior. In the process the prudential arguments in favour of what was called humanitarianism or is labelled liberalism by historians lost much of their force.

The Sub-Imperialism of Rhodes

British policy in the 1880s and 1890s reflected this transformation. The shock of British military defeats by the Zulus at Isandhlwala in 1879 and by the Transvaal Boers at Majuba in 1881 provided temporary discouragement to the advance of British control. However, the mineral discoveries made the pull of the interior irresistible. When the British government ministers could not be persuaded to take the initiative to extend British rule, others did so in their stead. The most important figure in this sub-imperialism was Cecil Rhodes, who was Prime Minister of the Cape Colony from 1890 to the end of 1895, when the Jameson Raid, an attempted coup against the Kruger government in which leading figures in the mining industry were also involved, forced his resignation. John Benyon has argued that the British government's creation of the post of High Commissioner in 1846 to deal with the frontier problems of the Cape Colony ultimately itself also played a part in the logic of expansion. He summarises his argument as follows:

The search for security provided a steady incentive toward the incorporation of trans-frontier polities, both black and white; and the later economic-gravitational pull of mining development drew not only capital and labour, but also the High Commission into a new dimension of conflict. Even when excused from spearheading the major thrusts of imperial expansion, the High Commission was therefore kept busy with the piecemeal absorption of territory – in the trans-Kei, Basutoland, the Diamond Fields, Bechuanaland, and elsewhere. When the auspices on the periphery tended to favour an expansive solution, the imperial agent's knowledge that he, personally, held the great, undefined powers of High Commission in reserve could be *decisive* in provoking the advance: the *mechanics* of British frontier extension had developed a momentum of their own. In the central example of this sub-continent it seems not unreasonable to add to the controversial list of impulses behind imperial expansion the 'self-generated' and 'self-sustaining' powers of the High Commission.[52]

Hobson's contention that the Anglo-Boer War was fought for cheap labour for the gold-mines oversimplified interlocking political, strategic and economic factors. However, he was surely right in his assumption of the centrality of the mineral revolution in South Africa to British imperialism at the end of the nineteenth century and the beginning of the twentieth century. In fact, it can reasonably be contended that the mineral revolution laid the foundations for white minority rule in South Africa for much of the twentieth century, in that it entrenched white supremacy by arming the settlers with Western capital. The British government's policy of 'seeking out local collaborative agents' to advance its control favoured this outcome, since, as Keegan points out, 'the ideal allies and agents of British hegemony at the end of the day were white colonists rather than indigenous peoples'.[53] In this context, Frankel's regret that the British government failed to support Sir George Grey's scheme for confederation amounts to the wish that the political foundations of modern South Africa had been laid under different economic circumstances.

The Isolationist Interpretation

Divisions within the white community between Afrikaners and English-speakers, an important legacy of the Anglo-Boer War, have had the effect of obscuring the political importance of the mineral revolution. Because Afrikaners occupied the top political positions and English-speakers dominated commerce in South Africa from 1910 to 1994, it was possible for historians to assume an almost complete disjunction between the country's political and economic development. That buttressed the isolationist interpretation of South African history that treated Afrikaner nationalist leaders as the ideological descendants of the eighteenth-century trekboer. Writing at the beginning of the 1970s, Heribert Adam described as one of the principal factors accounting for the emergence of South Africa's particular social, political and economic institutions her 'isolation from other Western nations'.[54] Donald Watt in the same period characterised Afrikanerdom as an 'escapist community' and Afrikaner nationalism as a movement to 'hold the clock back'.[55] They reflect a widespread tendency in the historiography after the transformation of the West's own racial attitudes to associate modernity and capitalism with liberalism. Unsurprisingly, Hobson made no such assumption.

In the political section of *Imperialism: A Study*, he considered ways in which self-governing parts of the Empire might be kept within the imperial fold. Hobson suggested that there was one possible inducement, namely: 'to involve them on their own account in imperialism, by encouraging and aiding them in a policy of annexation and the government of the lower races'.[56] This turned out to be more or less how relations between Britain and South Africa developed during the first half of the twentieth century. As Atmore and Marks argued in a piece published in 1975:

> There is little doubt that at least until 1948 and probably even after that (notwithstanding the flutter in Whitehall because of the Nationalist victory in that year's election) Britain has found in South Africa's white governments entirely satisfactory collaborators in safeguarding imperial interests.[57]

There could hardly be a greater contrast between the view of Atmore and Marks and that of Robinson and Gallagher of the war as a grand illusion quoted earlier in this chapter.

Their disagreement underscores the fact that differences in the literature over the long-term consequences of the war have been just as sharp as the argument over its causes. The controversies are related. Historians who emphasise political and strategic factors as causes of the war, while rejecting the notion that gold played any part in this equation, usually argue that the British government failed to achieve its objectives. By contrast, those who accord a central role to gold typically argue that the government achieved its principal aims. (This leaves aside those who recognise that to counterpose strategic and economic explanations is to put forward a false dichotomy.) The point of contention can be put in another way. Was it out of weakness that the British government permitted the establishment of white minority rule in South Africa or was the entrenchment of white supremacy in the Union of South Africa entirely compatible with British interests, as they were conceived at the beginning of the twentieth century? The role that Milner's reconstruction administration played in laying down the foundations of the policy of racial segregation provides a clue as to which is the more plausible interpretation.

There is much less disagreement in the literature on the war's immediate consequences. Britain secured a victory, but at a very high cost. According to Pakenham, there were some 22,000 deaths on the British side in the conflict, 7,000 on the Boer side to which must be added the 18,000 to 28,000 men, women and children who died in British concentration camps.[58] The war did considerable damage to Britain's international reputation as well as prompting divisions at home, two of the factors that have prompted historians to compare these events to America's military intervention in Vietnam in the 1970s and to dub the war, Britain's Vietnam.[59] The domestic political damage to the British government paved the way for a change of government and the Liberal Party's landslide victory in the British general election of 1906. The new Prime Minister's conciliatory policies towards the Afrikaners provided the basis for the subsequent claim that the further consolidation of South Africa as a race society arose out of British magnanimity towards a defeated enemy. However, even before Campbell-Bannerman took office, the outlines of the racial policy that would be adopted by an emerging South African state were discernible in initiatives taken by the Milner administration, as is explained in the next chapter.

4

Segregation: Home-Grown or Imported?

In his seminal comparison of the southern states of the United States of America and South Africa, John W.Cell describes segregation as 'a phase, the highest stage, in the evolution of white supremacy'.[1] According to Cell, usage of the term 'segregation' in its modern meaning of racial discrimination dates from the 1890s in the case of the United States of America and from the 1900s in the case of South Africa. The timing was not coincidental. South African segregationists paid close attention to the American example.[2] Saul Dubow notes that the term was used at the 1902 opening of the parliament of the Cape Colony, as well as in the report in 1905 of the Lagden Commission.[3] However, there were clearly precedents for segregation in practices that date much earlier than the 1890s in the United States of America and the 1900s in South Africa. Complicating the question of origins is that segregation, like apartheid, consisted of a number of different strands. That also makes it difficult to put a definite date to the start of the era of segregation in either country. Thus, in the case of South Africa, some writers attach most importance to the framing of an overall approach to 'native policy' as it was described; others to the actual passage of legislation to enforce segregation.

Reports of commissions have played a central role in formulating the principles of South African racial policy, whether realised or not. Examples are the report of the Stallard Commission in 1922, the report of the Fagan Commission in 1948, the report of the Tomlinson Commission in 1954 and the report of the Theron Commission in

61

1976. What gave added significance to these reports is that they laid down broad principles with applicability beyond their immediate context. The earliest of these commissions, as well as arguably the most important, was the Lagden Commission of 1903–5. The influence of its report was not confined to South Africa. Its principles became the basis of racial policy in Britain's other settler colonies in Africa, Southern Rhodesia and Kenya. This is not to argue that the Lagden Commission provided the only or even main precedent for land apportionment as the foundation for racial discrimination in these colonies. Indeed, in its deliberations the Lagden Commission was strongly influenced by existing practices, most particularly the system that had been established by Theophilus Shepstone in Natal during the nineteenth century. Nevertheless, the report of the Lagden Commission provides an appropriate point of departure for analysing the different strands of policy that were to constitute the system of segregation.

British Rule

The conquest of the Transvaal and the Orange Free State in 1900 ushered in a period of British political control in South Africa that lasted roughly through to the Liberal Party's landslide in the British general election in 1906. The transfer of power to the white minority in the defeated Boer republics followed, paving the way to the creation of the Union of South Africa as an independent white-ruled state within the British Empire. The dominant figure in South Africa in the first years of the century was Sir Alfred Milner, the High Commissioner and administrator of the former Boer republics as Crown Colonies to 1905. Initially, the focus of historians tended to be on his failure either to attract British settlers in sufficient numbers to the Transvaal to overturn the Afrikaner majority within the white community or, through his educational policies, to anglicise the Afrikaners. The result was to obscure Milner's legacy in the realm of racial policy.

Another reason why the war tended to be seen as a pyrrhic victory was the failure of the British government to uphold its promise to replace the racial basis of voting in the two Boer republics by a nominally colour-blind franchise based on ownership of property and educational qualifications. However, Chamberlain's promise on

the franchise had been designed to secure parliamentary approval
for the war and as events were to prove did not reflect any serious
commitment on the issue. Consequently, it was not difficult for
Smuts to secure the agreement of the British government to leave
the question of the franchise until after the grant of self-rule in the
negotiations that preceded the Treaty of Vereeniging of May 1902
ending the war. The significance of this agreement was that it meant
that the vote would be confined to whites when elections were first
held under British rule in the former Boer republics. It also meant
that in any negotiations to bring about political unity among the
British colonies in South Africa, the political representatives of
three of the four colonies would be wedded to the principle of a
whites-only franchise. It would be the proponents of the qualified,
but non-racial franchise in the Cape Colony who would be under
pressure to change. The Treaty of Vereeniging effectively put in
place an important political underpinning of segregation.

Milner raised the 'Native Question' at a conference of all the
colonies of South Africa held in 1903 to discuss the establishment of
a common customs policy. He argued that agreement among the
colonies on the general principles of racial policy would help to legitimise each of the colonies in their implementation of policy. To this
end, a commission was established to consider the principles of 'native
policy' in South Africa, particularly in view of the possibility of a
federation of the colonies. Significantly, it included the High Commission territories of Basutoland, Swaziland and the Bechuanaland
Protectorate, as well as Southern Rhodesia, within its scope. Its
official title was the South African Native Affairs Commission, but
it was commonly referred to as the Lagden Commission after its
chairman, Sir Godfrey Lagden. Lagden had been the Resident
Commissioner in Basutoland before being appointed by Milner to
take charge of Native Affairs in the Transvaal. Lagden also had
experience of the system of indirect rule in British West Africa.

A major preoccupation of the Lagden Commission was how 'native
policy' might be geared to overcome the labour shortages affecting
the South African economy. A solution to this problem was seen as
of vital importance to the revival of the economy after the war. In
response to the pleas of the gold-mining industry after the failure of
attempts to meet the industry's labour shortage through recruitment
from tropical Africa, as far afield as Uganda and Nigeria, Milner had
authorised the importation of indentured Chinese labour. The first

10,000 Chinese labourers arrived in South Africa in May 1904. A further 50,000 came to the Witwatersrand in the course of the next four years. After completing three-year contracts, they were repatriated. The extremely harsh terms of their contracts and their brutal treatment, including flogging, caused a scandal in Britain, damaging the Conservative Party in the 1906 general election and leading the Liberal government to discontinue the scheme.

The Lagden Commission argued that the normal operation of market forces could not be relied upon to increase the supply of labour. Indeed, it argued that raising wages might perversely decrease the supply of labour in so far as it made it possible for African workers to reduce the period they needed to work for the purposes of maintaining a subsistence existence in their reserves. According to the Commission:

> There is a measure of truth in the suggestion, that while increased wages might have the effect of tempting a larger number of labourers into the market, on the other hand, such increased gains would enable them to remain for a longer period at their own homes.[4]

Nevertheless, the Commission rejected the solution to the problem of a backward-sloping supply curve that was favoured by leading figures in the Afrikaans community that the reserves should be broken up.

Indeed, the Commission proposed, on the contrary, that the existing division of land between areas of white settlement and African areas should form the foundation of territorial separation. It recognised that African reserves could serve as labour reservoirs for the white areas, absorbing some of the social costs of African integration into the economy. At the same time, the Commission argued that steps should be taken to prevent the acquisition of land by Africans outside the areas specifically reserved for Africans. These would prevent Africans from earning a living as peasants in competition with white farmers and force them on to the labour market. The most forthright part of the report was its strong attack on the non-racial franchise in the Cape Colony that enabled African voters to exercise a large influence on the outcome of elections in some Eastern Cape constituencies.[5]

While many of the recommendations and attitudes of the Commission seem pernicious by present-day standards, they did not strike
most contemporary observers that way. Indeed, its defence both of
the reserves and of tribalism could be presented as enlightened and
even liberal in the context of what some white leaders were proposing.
For example, in a remarkable exchange of views with Theophilus
Shepstone in 1891–2, the President of the Orange Free State, F.Reitz,
argued for a root and branch attack on tribalism. He advocated the
abolition of chieftainships, the break-up of locations, whether small
or large, and the discouragement of polygamy. But he also simultan-
eously insisted on the steadfast maintenance of the principle 'that
there shall be no "equality" between the aborigines of South Africa
and the people of European descent who have made this land their
home'.[6] Shepstone's response was that what Reitz was proposing
was tantamount to the establishment of a system of slavery. In fact,
Shepstone was no less committed to the doctrine of white supremacy
than Reitz. However, he recognised that the preservation of tribal
society did not pose a threat to white domination. Indeed, it facilitated the subordination of Africans in so far as it operated as a
barrier against African political mobilisation, while also providing
ideological justification for the denial of rights to the African population in a common society.

Julius Lewin in his 1960s study of South African politics took the
findings of the Lagden Commission as his point of departure. He
argued that the most striking feature of South African racial policy
was its continuity and concluded 'public policy never changes'.[7] The
principal recommendation of the Lagden Commission was put into
effect after Union through the passage of the 1913 Natives Land Act.
The Act defined the areas of land reserved for African ownership and
use. Outside these, amounting after some addition to the areas originally scheduled to less than 9 per cent of the country, it provided
that Africans could neither purchase nor rent land. However, because
property was an element in the Cape's franchise provisions, the Act
did not apply to the Cape. The leaders of the newly established South
African Native National Congress (SANNC) campaigned against
the Act but to no avail. (SANNC changed its name to the African
National Congress or ANC in 1923.) According to Terreblanche:

The Land Act was extraordinarily successful in proletarianising
the great majority of Africans and creating large reservoirs of

cheap and docile African labour for white farmers and the mining industry. It was truly the rock on which not only the political alliance between a section of the Afrikaner farming elite and the British/English business elite was built, but also on which the ultra-exploitative system of racial capitalism was built and maintained until the 1970s.[8]

Another substantial contribution that the Milner administration made to the development of South African racial policy was the introduction of a statutory colour bar on the mines through Transvaal Ordinance No.4 of 1904. In an effort to overcome opposition to the introduction of indentured Chinese labour, Milner decreed that the employment of non-whites would be restricted to unskilled labour. What then became a source of conflict between the mine-owners and trade unions representing the white mineworkers was the ratio of skilled to unskilled. It led to a strike in 1907, by which time the Transvaal had responsible government. As Hobart Houghton commented in his 1973 study of the South African economy:

Thus in the Transvaal the two main methods for protecting the white skilled workers had emerged before Union. These were measures designed to reserve certain occupations for whites only, and pressure to resist any attempts by employers to alter the overall ratio of non-white to white workers.[9]

Of course, it may reasonably be argued that Milner's contribution to the establishment of segregation was a product of the circumstances in which he and the British government found themselves. For political and economic reasons they had little choice but to opt for an alliance with the white settlers. Further, the British government was not responsible for how the policy of segregation was implemented. That was the responsibility of successive Union governments, led until the second half of 1948 by former generals of the Boer republics that Britain had defeated. Terreblanche argues that the Afrikaner leadership of Union governments between 1910 and 1948 masked their real character and his chapter on the period from around 1890 to 1948 is headed provocatively 'The systemic period of British imperialism and the political and economic hegemony of the English establishment'.[10] That Terreblanche feels able to make such a claim is itself a reflection of the influence of the research of writers such as Saul Dubow and Paul Rich in emphasising the English or British origins of segregation. It completely turns on its head De Kiewiet's oft-quoted judgement of 1941:

> The Union constitution, in native policy at all events, represented the triumph of the frontier, and into the hands of the frontier was delivered the future of the native peoples. It was the conviction of the frontier that the foundations of society were race and the privileges of race.[11]

An English Establishment?

In justification of his characterisation, Terreblanche argues that the Afrikaans leadership of South African governments between 1910 and 1948 disguised the extent to which they were dependent on the support of the English-speaking white community. He bluntly asserts, 'From 1910 to 1948 South Africa was controlled by the predominantly English establishment, except for the nine years of the Pact government from 1924 to 1933.' To evaluate Terreblanche's claim, some explanation of developments in white politics during the period, as well as their relationship to the implementation of segregation, is necessary. Following the Liberal Party's landslide victory in the 1906 British general election, responsible government was granted to the Transvaal in December 1906 and to the Orange River Colony in February 1907. The key electoral background in the whites-only Legislative Assembly elections in the two colonies in 1907 was the Transvaal. The preponderance of Afrikaners in the Orange Free State made the outcome there a foregone conclusion.

The outcome of the Transvaal election was a triumph for the Afrikaner leaders, Louis Botha and Jan Christiaan Smuts. Their party, Het Volk, won an overall majority of seats in the Transvaal Legislative Assembly. Botha and Smuts propounded a policy of reconciliation between the two white communities. A large part of the appeal of this policy to Afrikaners was that it also addressed the very painful issue of the divisions within Afrikanerdom over the war between *Bittereinders* (who fought to the bitter end) and *Hendsoppers* (those who tended to surrender). There is a parallel to be drawn here with Mandela's advocacy of reconciliation in the 1990s. At the same time, the policy divided the English-speaking community. Consequently, the political heirs of Cecil Rhodes were defeated in both the Transvaal and the Cape Colony, where an alliance between English liberals and the Afrikaner Bond won power in the election of February 1908. The prospect that Afrikaners would provide the leadership for a united South Africa gave Botha and Smuts every incentive to press for unification. At the same time, their imperialist opponents also advocated South African unification. They hoped that the economic benefits of unification would attract foreign investment and with it large numbers of British immigrants which would overturn the Afrikaner majority within the white community.

These hopes proved unfounded and when the Union of South Africa was established it was under the predominantly Afrikaner leadership of the South African Party headed by Louis Botha, with the English-speaking Unionist Party in opposition. (The results of elections from 1910 to 1948 are given in Table 4.1.) However, the white political landscape soon changed with the departure from the government of the Orange Free State leader, J.B.M. Hertzog. That led to the formation of the National Party in January 1914. The outbreak of the First World War in August 1914 caused further division and dissension among Afrikaners. South Africa's status as part of the British Empire automatically meant South Africa's entry into the

Table 4.1   General election results in seats, 1910–48[12]

Party	1910	1915	1920	1921	1924	1929	1933	1938	1943	1948
National Party		27	44	45	63	78	75	27		
Herenigde Nasionale Party									43	70
South African Party	67	59	41	79	53	61	61			
United Party								111	89	65
Unionist Party	39	40	25							
Labour Party	4	4	21	9	18	8	4	3	9	6
Dominion Party								8	7	
Afrikaner Party										9
Independents and others	11		3	1	1	1	10	1	2	
Native representatives								3	3	3
TOTAL NUMBER OF SEATS	121	130	134	134	135	148	150	153	153	153

war, a position that both Botha and Smuts fully accepted. And they supported the country's active participation in the war when the British government called on South Africa to invade German South West Africa. The South African government's agreement to the British request was too much for some Afrikaners and it prompted a military rebellion against the government. The rebels were quickly defeated. Over 300 rebels and government troops died in the conflict. The invasion of German South West Africa followed and was completed by July 1915 with fewer casualties than in the country's brief civil war.

The impact of the divisions among Afrikaners, in part as a result of the war, was reflected in the results of the October 1915 general election. While the South African Party remained the largest party and retained power with the support of the Unionist Party, it no longer enjoyed the overwhelming support of the Afrikaner community. As Barber explains:

> The NP polled 78,000 against the SAP's 94,000. As the NP's voters were drawn almost exclusively from Afrikaners, whereas the SAP had English-speaking as well as Afrikaner support, the figures signified a substantial shift of allegiance. Probably as many Afrikaners voted for the NP as for the SAP.[13]

After the war, it became clear that the division among Afrikaners was not just a temporary product of the strain that participation in the war placed on the loyalty of Afrikaners to the British Empire. In the general election of February 1920, the National Party won the largest number of seats, but it was unable to displace the South African Party government.

Smuts and the British Empire

Jan Christiaan Smuts had become Prime Minister after the death of Botha in 1919. After the general election Smuts explored the possibility of reuniting Afrikanerdom in talks with the National Party, but differences over the issue of the country's relationship with the Empire prevented agreement. On this issue there was far greater accord between Smuts and the Unionist Party. It paved the way to the merger of the South African Party and the Unionist Party to meet the threat to the government posed by increasing support for the National Party, as well as for the South African Labour Party. The merger enabled Smuts to secure a clear overall majority in fresh elections held in February 1921. Smuts's commitment to the British Empire went far beyond the pragmatic acceptance of the reality of British power that motivated many of his Afrikaner contemporaries. He sought positive advantages in the relationship. But like Rhodes he also wished to pursue his own political agenda under the umbrella of the British Empire, relatively autonomously from the influence of the Westminster parliament.

At the time of the establishment of the Union, it had confidently been expected in both Britain and South Africa that the Union would be enlarged by the addition of Southern Rhodesia and the High Commission territories of Basutoland, the Bechuanaland Protectorate and Swaziland. Indeed, provision was made in a Schedule appended to the Act of Union for the transfer of the three High Commission territories and reference was also made to the possible incorporation of Southern Rhodesia. Botha and Smuts envisaged that South Africa would one day also include the two non-British colonies in the region, German South West Africa and the Portuguese territory of Mozambique, thereby creating a single dominion stretching from the Cape to the Zambezi, if not beyond. In the light of South Africa's transformation by the mineral revolution, such ambitions did not seem as in any way unrealistic. However, Smuts clearly understood that their realisation depended on an unequivocal commitment to the Empire.

The First World War presented Botha and Smuts with an early opportunity to displace German rule in South West Africa through conquest. The fact that at the end of the war South Africa was not permitted to incorporate the territory into the Union, thanks to President Wilson's insistence that there should be no annexation of enemy territories, was a disappointment to Smuts. However, South Africa was made the mandatory power of South West Africa as a C-class mandate, which meant that in practice the territory could be treated virtually as if it were part of the Union. As Hyam noted in his 1972 book on South Africa's territorial ambitions between 1908 and 1948:

The Mandate allowed the territory to be administered as an integral part of the Union, whose government had full powers of administration and legislation subject only to the observance of safeguards for the natives and the submission of annual reports to the Mandates Commission of the League of Nations. Smuts chafed under the inquisitorial supervision, and in practice treated the South-West as if it were annexed.[14]

The South African government looked on the acquisition as a welcome, new source of land for white settlement so that in Hyam's words, 'land-hungry South Africans were allocated huge farms virtually for the asking and then pampered'.[15] This process of South Africanisation (in practice, Afrikanerisation) of the territory underpinned the assumption that in due course its full legal incorporation into South Africa would follow.

When the Union of South Africa was established, the inclusion of Southern Rhodesia in the Union appeared to be only a matter of time. In particular, the representatives of the white settlers of Southern Rhodesia were favourably disposed to joining the Union in preference to the continuation of rule under the British South Africa Company. However, by the 1920s, when the settlers were given the choice by the British government of joining the Union or responsible government, they opted for the latter. In a referendum on 6 November 1922, the settlers voted by 8,774 votes (59.4 per cent) to 5,989 against Union. The result was a huge setback for Smuts's hopes of expansion. He wrote to the British Prime Minister, Arthur Bonar Law:

> The entry of Rhodesia is not only in her own interest and that of the Union but also in the interest of the British Empire. Rhodesia as a separate state struggling vainly with her impossible task is certain to become an embarrassment to the British government in the end.[16]

A variety of factors were instrumental in the settlers' rejection of Union. These included their reaction to the industrial strife that had afflicted the gold mines since Union, the manner in which the government had responded to industrial unrest, the Afrikaner rebellion against participation in the war and the rise of the National Party. In addition, the settlers feared that there would be an influx of poor whites into Southern Rhodesia and that there would be competition for African labour from South African mines and industry. Further, the alternative of creating a Central African Federation (realised in the 1950s) diminished enthusiasm for incorporation as a province in South Africa. It is striking that the settlers of Southern Rhodesia did not regard the residual veto that responsible government gave to the British government over 'native policy' as a reason to embrace the Union. It was a measure of how confident they were that the British government would not wield this power to interfere with Southern Rhodesia's own version of the policy of segregation. This confidence did not prove misplaced.

The efforts of Smuts and other South African leaders to secure the country's expansion ultimately all failed. Thus, the country's boundaries were the same in 1961, when South Africa became a republic, as they had been at the time of Union in 1910. Because of this failure, it is easy to underestimate the importance that hopes of expansion played in shaping the strategies of the country's leaders. This was especially true of Smuts. For Smuts, the external alliance with the British Empire, which he consistently supported in office through to his defeat in the 1948 general election, was of supreme political importance. It was of much greater significance to his career than were the various coalitions and domestic alliances he took part in as a South African politician. To his role as loyal advocate of the Empire, he owed his place on the world stage. The closest contemporary analogy is the standing of the British Prime Minister, Tony Blair, in the United States since 11 September 2001.

The Pact Government

In a memorable phrase Stanley Trapido characterised the support base of the South African Party of large landowners, industrialists and the mine-owners as 'the alliance of gold and maize'. In 1924 this alliance was defeated by another combination, that of the National Party and the segregationist South African Labour Party. Economic difficulties that had exacerbated industrial strife played an important role in Smuts's defeat at the polls. In particular, Smuts had used force to put down an armed rebellion among white mineworkers in 1922. The cause of the Rand Revolt was cost-cutting by the Chamber of Mines effected through enlarging the ratio of African to white workers. The threat this presented to the position of white workers led to the dispute. The violent nature of the subsequent strike prompted government intervention in the form of a proclamation of martial law and the use of troops against the strikers. The rebellion and its suppression resulted in a total of 230 deaths. A notorious feature of the strike was the slogan employed by the white mineworkers: 'Workers of the world fight and unite for a white South Africa.'[17]

It is tempting to argue that Smuts won the battle of 1922 but at the expense of losing the war through his defeat at the polls in 1924. However, Yudelman has shown at length that such a characterisation is simplistic if it is taken to imply that the defeat of the mineworkers was reversed by the election of the Pact government.[18] Given the importance of the mining industry to the economy, the Pact government could no more ignore the interests of the mining magnates than its predecessor. What the Pact government could and did do was to enact a series of measures designed to protect the position of white workers. The intention was that white workers should be paid a wage that would enable them to sustain a 'civilised' standard of living. This was defined as conforming to 'the standard generally recognised as tolerable from the usual European standpoint'.[19]

The most important of these measures was the Industrial Conciliation Act of 1924. It created Industrial Councils with the powers to lay down minimum wages in particular industries. Represented on the Councils were the government, employers and 'employees' defined so as to exclude Africans. Established in parallel to Industrial Councils was the Wage Board, set up under the 1925 Wage Act. Its purpose was to enable the government directly to set minimum wages for different grades in industries in which the 'employees', as defined in the Act, were not organised into a trade union. Like Industrial Councils, the Wage Board provided protection for white workers from undercutting or substitution by laying down the rate for the job, thus establishing a wage colour bar.

However, all the efforts of the Hertzog government to create jobs for whites and to protect white living standards were of limited effectiveness in stemming the growth of the 'poor white problem', as it was described. The origin of the problem lay in the closure of the land frontier in the last decades of the nineteenth century. With no new land to expand into, the extensive form of agriculture practised by many Afrikaners came under strain. Conditions were made worse by the sub-division of land under the Roman–Dutch law of partible inheritance, which divided up property among all of the deceased's offspring. Lacking viable holdings of land, many Afrikaners were turned into poverty-stricken *bywoners* (tenants) or forced out of agriculture altogether. Whereas fewer than 10,000 Afrikaners were urbanised in 1890, by 1926 391,000 or 41 per cent lived in towns or cities.[20]

United Party Rule

The Pact government was re-elected with an increased majority in 1929, though the number of seats held by the South African Labour Party was halved. However, the government soon ran into severe economic difficulties as a result of the impact of the worldwide depression on South Africa. To meet this emergency the National Party and the South African Party formed a coalition. The two parties won an overwhelming victory in the general election that followed in 1933. A year later they agreed to fusion, forming the United National South African Party, which soon became known as the United Party. The white consensus on the policy of segregation helped to facilitate agreement and one consequence of fusion was the enactment of further segregationist legislation.

In particular, the government's overwhelming majority in parliament made possible the removal of African voters from the common roll in the Cape. In compensation, provision was made for the election of three representatives of African voters, though the representatives themselves had to be white. The reserves were also extended in size to cover approximately 13 per cent of the country. Other measures included an amendment in 1937 to the Wage Act to enable the Wage Board to make determinations to set wages below a 'civilised' level. The thinking behind this change in policy was set out by the Wage Board in 1934. It declared that the introduction of machines that could be efficiently minded by unskilled employees (in practice, Africans) necessitated 'the raising of the level of wages of unskilled employees to a level at which the European employee can maintain his standard of living'.[21] At the same time, a report in 1935 of the Industrial Legislation Commission highlighted the limited effectiveness in practice of the attempts the government had hitherto made to protect white workers. It concluded:

> Though for many years efforts have been made to encourage the employment of Whites on unskilled work in place of Natives, no appreciable success has been achieved in any but Government

occupations where the loss in increased cost has been borne out of general revenue and from railway rates.[22]

Another factor facilitating agreement was the changing nature of the British Empire. The enhanced status of the dominions, including South Africa, within the Empire narrowed the differences between Hertzog and Smuts over the country's relationship with Britain. Nevertheless, this issue – to a larger extent than racial policy – remained a source of dissension, with the consequence that factions within both the National Party and the South African Party opposed fusion and ultimately provided the basis for the establishment of opposition political parties. Nationalists led by D.F. Malan formed the *gesuiwerde* (purified) National Party, while a grouping of English-speakers from Natal led by Colonel Stallard, a segregationist who had played an important role in the development of influx control, formed the Dominion Party.

The continuing importance of external relationships to the politics of South Africa was underlined by the further changes to the party system brought about by the onset of the Second World War. The Prime Minister, J.B.M. Hertzog, favoured neutrality. However, he was defeated by 80 votes to 67 in the House of Assembly and South Africa opted to participate in the war on Britain's side. Hertzog resigned and Smuts became Prime Minister once again. The parties realigned accordingly with the members of the Dominion Party joining the United Party while Hertzog and his supporters made common cause with the *gesuiwerdes*. Hertzog and Malan merged in a party called the *Herenigde Nasionale Party*, or reconstituted National Party, initially under Hertzog's leadership. However, Hertzog was soon at odds with the activists in the party and resigned, to be replaced by Malan. In 1941 some of Hertzog's followers constituted themselves as a separate party, the Afrikaner Party.

Afrikaner Mobilisation

Beyond the confines of parliamentary politics, more fundamental change was taking place in the country's white politics. Urbanisation and the concern over the poor white problem were creating the basis of a mass political movement among Afrikaners. By 1936 half of the Afrikaner population lived in towns and cities. The scale of the poor white problem was underlined by the five-volume report of the Carnegie Commission in 1932. It estimated the number of poor whites at 300,000 or 17 per cent of the white population. In response to these trends there was a mushrooming of extra-parliamentary organisations during the 1920s and 1930s. What they had in common was a strongly nationalist orientation and their commitment to enhancing the position of Afrikaners within South African society. The most important of these was the Afrikaner Broederbond, which was formed in 1918, originally under the name, Jong Suid-Afrika.

From small beginnings the Broederbond developed into a major force within the Afrikaner community. In 1929 the Broederbond organised a conference in Bloemfontein attended by the representative of a wide range of associations. That gave rise to the formation of the Federasie van Afrikaanse Kultuurvereniginge (FAK – Federation of Afrikaans Cultural Organisations) for the promotion of the Afrikaans language. By 1937 over 300 organisations were affiliated to the FAK. The high point of the social mobilisation of the Afrikaners came in 1938, with the centenary celebrations of the Great Trek. These centred on a five-month-long symbolic re-enactment of the Great Trek by nine ox-wagons. The arrival of the wagons at the site of the Voortrekker monument outside Pretoria was accompanied by a huge torchlight parade. As Sparks puts it:

> It was pure Nuremberg, and there was more to come at the foundation-stone ceremony two days later when 200,000 gathered on Monument-hill for the biggest, most elaborate, and most emotive folk rally in the history of the Afrikaner people.[23]

The Ossewa Brandwag (OB – Oxwagon Sentinels), founded in October 1938 to perpetuate the spirit of the celebrations, grew 'into a uniformed and armed organization along Nazi stormtrooper lines'.[24] Together these various organisations formed an interlocking network of people committed to Afrikaner nationalism in its most radical and uncompromising form, envisaging that South Africa would become an independent republic outside the British Empire.

Yet this is to tell the story of South Africa in the inter-war period from the perspective of a known outcome, the triumph of the Nationalists in 1948 and their subsequent domination of South African for nearly half a century. In the 1930s, thanks to fusion, the strength of the political trends among Afrikaners was not immediately apparent. Thus, in the general election of May 1938, the United Party government was re-elected with a massive majority. Admittedly, the scale of the United Party's victory in terms of seats disguised the large number of votes the *gesuiwerdes* secured, amounting to 31.1 per cent of the votes cast. Nevertheless, the dominance of the United Party both before and during the war made it possible for some contemporary observers of South Africa to arrive at the conclusion that the divisions within the white community were a thing of the past or rapidly becoming a thing of the past. After all, much that the National Party of Hertzog had sought had been achieved. Afrikaans had been recognised as one of the country's two official languages in 1925, South Africa had acquired its own flag in 1928 and South African sovereignty had been recognised through the Statute of Westminster in 1931. Such a background must have seemed more consistent with the waning of Afrikaner nationalism than its reinvigoration.

The Colour Question

The other side of the coin of the growth of social movements among the Afrikaners was black social and political mobilisation. The most important organisation in this context was a trade union, the Industrial and Commercial Workers Union (ICU), founded in Cape Town in 1919 by a clerk from Nyasaland, Clements Kadalie. It was initially based on dock workers but grew into a general union for black workers during the course of the 1920s. At its height it had 100,000 members. Strikes by black workers in the docks and mines, as well as the famous strike by African sanitation workers in 1918, underscored the development of a labour movement among the country's voteless communities. Histories written since South Africa's transition to democracy inevitably pay a great deal of attention to this record of militancy among black workers as precursors of sorts to the eventual achievement of majority rule. But even if it is accepted that future generations drew inspiration from their example, it is obviously easy to exaggerate their influence on politics at the time. Yet it would also be a mistake to imagine that whites were indifferent to the signs of black social and political mobilisation. The prominence of what was called the colour question in elections made white preoccupation with racial issues very evident. A notorious example was a poster used by the *gesuiwerdes* during the 1938 general elections. They high-lighted their campaign for the prohibition of mixed marriages with the question: 'How would you like your daughter to marry …?'. The United Party's response was to describe the poster as an insult to every white woman in South Africa.

South African politics in the period leading up to the 1948 general elections presents a conundrum. Radical Afrikaner nationalism grew in strength as the issues that had previously divided the white community diminished in importance and those of race increased in significance. Thus, the more central relations with the English and with Britain were to politics the more divided Afrikaners were, after the brief period of acquiescence in the Empire that followed the Anglo-Boer War. Paradoxically, as the issues of South Africa's status and the standing of Afrikaners within the society were resolved as a result of the loosening and the weakening of the British Empire, the more hostile the majority of Afrikaners became to imperialism. It is important in this context not to lose sight of how wider international developments affected the evolution of white politics in South Africa. For many radical Afrikaner nationalists, the challenge that the rise of Hitler presented to British power was welcome in the same way that radical Irish nationalists proclaimed England's difficulty to be Ireland's opportunity. For some, the embrace of Nazi Germany went beyond merely tactical calculation. They were enthralled by National Socialist ideology as a justification of racism that was not dependent on the existence of the British Empire and its graduated hierarchies.

South Africa's entry into the war polarised white politics. The immediate effect was to strengthen support for the Opposition in the House of the Assembly, with the departure of Hertzog and his supporters from the government benches. However, in the medium term, the challenge to Malan was greater than that to the country's new Prime Minister, Jan Christiaan Smuts. Enthusiasm among Afrikaners for the Nazis, which was reflected in the activities of the OB and a host of other organisations, threatened Malan's pursuit of power through parliamentary and constitutional means. The general elections of July 1943 provided the occasion for a showdown between Malan and the OB. While Smuts and the United Party won a landslide victory in what was dubbed the khaki election, the victory of the *Herenigde Nasionale Party* and Malan over other strands of Afrikaner nationalism was equally decisive. By refusing to cooperate with any of his rivals in 1943, Malan contributed to the scale of

Smuts's victory, but in the process established the *HNP*'s primacy over all other Afrikaner nationalist organisations.

Ironically, even Malan's breach with Hertzog over the issue of the rights of English-speakers in 1940 worked to the *HNP*'s advantage in 1948. Hertzog's followers in the Afrikaner Party had failed to win any seats in 1943. But thanks to its electoral alliance with the *HNP* the party won nine seats in 1948. Ironically, the party had become the means for the reintegration of the most radical Afrikaner nationalists back into the political mainstream. The Afrikaner Party opened its doors to members of the OB, whereas Malan had excluded anyone in the OB from membership of the *HNP* in the course of his battle for supremacy over extra-parliamentary and anti-parliamentary organisations. The process of their reintegration through the Afrikaner Party was not entirely smooth, however. Thus, the *HNP* vetoed a number of OB members whom the Afrikaner Party put forward for adoption as parliamentary candidates in the 1948 elections. One of those vetoed was a future Prime Minister of South Africa, B.J. Vorster.

It is possible that OB disaffection with this decision contributed to the narrow defeat of the *HNP* candidate in a nearby constituency. However, Verwoerd's defeat did not prevent the *HNP* and the Afrikaner Party from securing an overall majority in the House of Assembly. This was achieved despite the fact that the two parties between them secured far fewer votes than the United Party. In fact, the *HNP* and the Afrikaner Party put up candidates in only a little more than two-thirds of the seats. This extraordinary outcome was the combined product of the vagaries of the first-past-the-post electoral system and the provision that permitted rural constituencies to contain many fewer electors than urban ones. Thus, the United Party piled up huge majorities in English-speaking urban constituencies with a very poor return in terms of the ratio of seats to votes cast.

Apartheid and 1948

A matter of continuing controversy in the literature is how far the Nationalist platform of apartheid contributed to their victory in 1948. In a study published in 1979, Hermann Giliomee argued that there were 'serious problems' with the interpretation that the victory was clinched by the ideology of apartheid:

In the political campaign preceding this election, Nationalists often suggested that racial policies should not be allowed to become a political issue between the two parties. Some argued that the only hope South Africa had of solving its racial problem lay in taking the issue out of political contention. The electoral victory was in fact ensured by a decisive measure of Afrikaner unity. The appeal of the apartheid platform to classes such as the workers and the farmers was no doubt an important factor in attracting support for the National Party, but equally important were the party's demands for South African national independence, its promotion of Afrikaner business interests, and its championing of the Afrikaans culture. Or to put it differently, apart from 'putting the Kaffer in his place', 1948 also meant to the Afrikaners – particularly the professionals, educators and civil servants – 'getting *our* country back' or 'feeling at home once again in *our* country.'[25]

It is somewhat ironic that Giliomee should quote the notorious slogan: 'die Kaffer op sy plek' (in English 'the kaffir in his place') in this passage. In his most recent work he takes no less a person than Nelson Mandela to task for identifying the National Party's 1948 campaign with this slogan:

> Nelson Mandela maintains that the NP fought the election on the twin slogans of: 'The kaffir in his place' and 'The coolies out of the country'. But there never were any such slogans. The NP leadership had no desire to upset ministers and other apartheid theorists who believed in the capacity of apartheid to uplift people.[26]

Where the National Party differed from the United Party, according to Giliomee, was that it was united on its platform of keeping South Africa white.

From this perspective, the United Party's defeat was attributable in large part to the party's doubts over the continuing viability of segregation and to its internal divisions over the future direction of racial policy. However, apartheid meant more than simply putting a halt to the erosion of segregation under the United Party. In any event, segregation had been the product of a particular set of internal and external circumstances that no longer applied. The point is very well made by Paul Rich in his study of state power and black politics in South Africa in the first half of the twentieth century:

Until the war years many leading politicians such as Jan Smuts and Douglas Smit hoped that South African 'native policy' could serve as a model to be emulated elsewhere in Africa. There was an element of collective self-delusion about this, reflecting the degree to which debate about 'native policy' was conducted at an arcane level outside the pressure of popular opinion in the townships, locations and reserves. Smuts considered it essential to be able to demonstrate some liberal features to the state's 'trusteeship' policy as a means of maintaining external international approval for South Africa's domestic policies... During the inter-war period the shield of the Commonwealth helped to insulate the state's administrative apparatus from the changing international outlook on 'race relations'.[27]

During the 1930s radical Afrikaner nationalists had espoused not merely anti-imperialist opinions but also at times strongly anti-capitalist views. Economic nationalism was advocated alongside much greater intervention in the economy by the state in general. The economic situation facing South Africa after the war somewhat reduced the salience of these prescriptions, but a much more statist approach towards the economy remained part of the *HNP*'s approach. The argument that without rescuing the poor whites they might make common cause with black workers against capitalist rule had also lost much of its force, as wartime industrial expansion had largely solved the poor white problem. Nonetheless, the identification of the United Party with big business and private enterprise remained, while in its programme for the 1948 elections the *HNP* advocated nationalisation on a wide scale.

In his account of the 1948 elections Kenneth Heard emphasised the role that external factors played in the *HNP*'s victory, including the beginnings of the transformation of the British Empire into the Commonwealth, the independence of India, Pakistan, Burma and Ceylon, and the onset of the Cold War. Heard wrote:

These were some of the more obvious of the general currents that disturbed the minds of men, and that were in the end perhaps to be decisive in the overthrow of the United Party Government. For if there is one thing that is antipathetical to the disturbed it is the appearance of complacency in those in authority; and it was just this appearance that, rightly or wrongly, the Government tended to convey.[28]

Anti-Communism formed a significant theme in the *HNP*'s campaign. The defeat of Nazi Germany discredited a model that some of the more radical Afrikaner nationalists had been attracted to. However, the alignment of the world in terms of the Communist threat, as well as the eclipse of Britain as a world power, created a set of circumstances that also made possible the implementation of apartheid, the Afrikaners' 'radical survival plan'[29] in Giliomee's words. As we shall see in the next chapter, Giliomee's description of apartheid remains highly contentious for a variety of reasons. What seemed apparent at the time and remains largely accepted is that the outcome of the 1948 elections was a significant turning point in South Africa's history.

5

The Theory and Practice of Apartheid: Was There a Blueprint?

While there were (and still remain) sharp disagreements among analysts as to the role that the slogan of apartheid played in the *HNP*'s election victory in 1948, the Nationalists themselves had no doubt that they had been given a mandate to put apartheid into practice. Further, they acted on this assumption so that a number of apartheid's main legislative pillars were put into place during Malan's first term of office. This was in contrast to segregation, the legislation of key aspects of which was enacted over a period of decades. For example, more than thirty years passed between the recommendation of the Lagden Commission that the Cape's non-racial franchise should be abandoned and the removal of African voters from the common roll in the Cape.

Yet, in spite of the legislative framework enacted in the very first years of the post-war Nationalist government, the idea of apartheid as a blueprint has been strongly contested in the writings of Deborah Posel. Her arguments deserve careful consideration. Posel notes the prevalence of the grand design view of the development of apartheid by the 1960s and 1970s. First, she summarises some of the reasons why this view acquired so much verisimilitude:

Building on the foundations laid by previous segregationist regimes, the National Party (NP) government built Apartheid into a monstrously labyrinthine system which dominated every facet of

83

life in South Africa. From its election victory in 1948, the NP steadily consolidated its hold on the state, with a greater degree of ideological fervour than any previous ruling party. Long-standing state controls over the African labour market were restructured and greatly intensified. A national system of labour bureaux, introduced in the 1950s to monitor and control African employment, placed increasingly severe constraints on Africans' freedom of movement and occupational choice. The Population Registration Act (1950), Group Areas Act (1950), Bantu Education Act (1953), Reservation of Separate Amenities Act (1953), and others laid the groundwork for a more rigid and thoroughgoing system of racial domination than had existed to date.[1]

Secondly, National Party governments were not deterred from continuing to implement apartheid by concerted opposition to their policies:

> Buttressed by a large and powerful arsenal of security laws, the Nationalists also mounted an unprecedented assault on their political enemies. By the early 1960s organised black opposition had been smashed, and would take over a decade to recover. The 1960s then saw the launch of an ambitious and ruthless programme of social engineering, which stripped the majority of Africans of their South African citizenship, and forcibly removed over three and a half million from allegedly 'white' areas of the country to putative ethnic 'homelands'.[2]

She cites works by authors from a variety of political perspectives, including Willem de Klerk, Brian Bunting and Pierre van den Berghe who, she argues, explain this record by positing the existence of 'a single, systematic long-term blueprint'. Posel's criticism is not limited to those who posit the view that apartheid was implemented on the basis of a detailed blueprint. She also criticises writers who adopt a looser version of the grand design view, even those who acknowledge that only the broad parameters of policy were laid down in advance and that circumstances affected its detailed implementation. In particular, she takes Dan O'Meara to task for presenting in his book, *Volkskapitalisme*, 'a single, hegemonic "Apartheid-idea" as the ideological cement binding the Afrikaner nationalist class alliance together from the late 1940s'.[3]

Sauer Commission

An important source for the view that the National Party proceeded in office according to the plan the party had worked out in opposition was the report of the Sauer Commission. The National Party adopted apartheid as its official racial policy in 1945. In 1947 Malan appointed a commission under Paul Sauer to add flesh to the bare bones of the concept. It reported later that year and the report formed the basis of the party's manifesto for the 1948 election. Giliomee describes how the Sauer Commission went about its task:

> Accordingly, the commission sent out a circular, inviting opinions, to all elected representatives of the party, all chairmen and secretaries of the party's district councils, all 'well-disposed' Afrikaner lecturers at universities and to other 'knowledgeable experts and interested persons'.[4]

The Party recived approximately five hundred replies to the five thousand circulars it sent out. As Giliomee notes, the report called for the total separation of whites and Africans as the ultimate goal of policy, while recognising that the economy would require African labour for the foreseeable future. Posel argues that different factions supporting the National Party disagreed on such issues as the long-term need for African labour and that the report of the Sauer Commission 'reproduced rather than resolved these divergences, and therefore cannot have provided a single master plan for the building of Apartheid'.[5]

In spite of both the concessions to practical realities and the various strands of opinion represented, in its approach the report clearly differed sharply from the outlook articulated by the United Party government. This was encapsulated in the report of another commission. In 1946 Smuts appointed a former cabinet minister, Henry Fagan, to investigate the question of African urbanisation. Its report was published just before the 1948 general election. It rejected the feasibility of the theoretical option of total segregation or partition. It also rejected the theoretical option of racial equality in a common society, while acknowledging the irreversibility of wartime and post-war African urbanisation. O'Meara identifies the major differences between the two reports as being 'their view of the permanency of African urbanisation'.[6] He argues that there was widespread concern among all classes of Afrikaners over the issue of rapid African urbanisation. It was encapsulated in the Afrikaans term, *oorstromming*, which translates literally as inundation. However, the English word 'swamping', as used, for example, by Thatcher in the reference to immigration into Britain from the Indian sub-continent in the run-up to the 1979 British general elections, captures its political essence more accurately.

In *Forty Lost Years*, O'Meara accepts Posel's argument that there were differences among Afrikaner nationalists in their policy prescriptions and objectives:

> Yet if the policy content of apartheid remained vague, and if the various forces of Afrikaner nationalism had different interpretations of its meaning, the deep collective wish for apartheid reflected several of the fundamental principles underlying the emerging Christian-nationalist reworking of Afrikaner nationalism in the late 1930s and 1940s. Apartheid was presented as an ethical policy which would grant to other ethnic groups what Afrikaners demanded for themselves. It was the only way to avoid racial conflict in South Africa's *veelvolkigge* (multi-ethnic) situation, since it provided for the survival of Afrikaners (and other whites) while supposedly facilitating the development of other ethnic groups.[7]

O'Meara's language is perhaps anachronistic in its attribution of the language of ethnicity to South Africa in the late 1940s. However, the point remains that whatever differences there were among Afrikaner nationalists, the *HNP* and the Afrikaner Party presented a much clearer vision of the future direction of racial policy to the electorate than the United Party.

The contradictory character of the report of the Sauer Commission forms only the first of Posel's arguments in refutation of the notion that the Nationalist government from its election in 1948 implemented a pre-ordained blueprint. She argues, secondly, that forces outside Afrikanerdom influenced apartheid's implementation and these included the English-speaking business community and the black extra-parliamentary opposition. She contends, thirdly, that the development of apartheid 'underwent an important change of direction at the onset of the 1960s, which ushered in a discrete second phase of policy-making'.[8] Posel bases her argument on a detailed study of the government's policies on influx control. To comprehend the case she makes in greater depth, it is necessary to explain the history of influx control and its connection to the government's policies in other fields, as well as how it fitted into the overall scheme of apartheid.

Influx Control

Union-wide influx control was introduced by the Native (Urban Areas) Act of 1923, which placed restrictions on the rights of Africans to remain in urban areas. The principal reason for the introduction of the legislation was social rather than economic. That is to say, it was not introduced as a means of channelling labour into other sectors of the economy. Further, in practice, the Act was not very effective in limiting the growth of the African urban population, which doubled between 1921 and 1936. The measure's chief importance was that it laid the basis for far-reaching intervention in the labour market in the future. During the Second World War there was some relaxation of influx control as Africans flocked to the towns to match the demand for their labour in manufacturing and in defence projects. The war years were a period of unparalleled opportunity for African workers. While the increase in the white labour force was small, the numbers of Africans employed in manufacturing increased by 60 per cent. At the same time, the gap between white and African average earnings narrowed sharply, reflecting both the upgrading of African workers and a marked improvement in the wage rates of unskilled workers.[9] This was due in large part to the success that African trade unions had in pressing for the setting of higher minimum rates by the Wage Board. Alarmed by the growth and militancy of these unions, the government promulgated War Measure 145 in December 1942 which made it a criminal offence for African workers to strike.

After the war the United Party government attempted to restore the pre-war status quo by, for example, tightening up influx control. Thus, the 1945 Natives (Urban Areas) Act gave urban local authorities the power to prohibit the entry of any Africans into their jurisdictions. However, the growth of the urban African population continued at a rate of nearly 7 per cent per annum. An equivocal attitude towards the growth of a permanent African labour force in the towns was reinforced by the United Party's links with commerce and industry, which underlined the government's reluctance to abandon a laissez-faire policy towards the African labour market.

At the same time, considerable efforts were made to restore the privileges white workers had enjoyed in the pre-war period on an *ad hoc* basis through, for example, the enforcement of the rate for the job in the building industry. A state-aided scheme to encourage white immigration was introduced reducing the pressure on firms to upgrade African workers. The impact of these measures was significant and contributed to a marked widening of the wage gap between white and black in manufacturing between 1946 and 1948. This widening of the wage gap also reflected the cumulative impact of state expenditure on education and vocational training. Whereas twenty years earlier the newly urbanised Afrikaner labour force had few educational advantages over its African counterpart, by this time education was becoming an important factor in securing white workers a privileged access to white-collar occupations and thus facilitating a separation of the white labour market from the African.

Consequently, it is simplistic to view the defeat of the Smuts government in the 1948 election as a backlash against the failure of the United Party to protect white economic privileges. More significant was the manner in which the *HNP* and the Afrikaner Party played on the electorate's fears of the political and social implications of the growth of the urban African labour force. At the same time they cited the contrast between the surplus manpower in the urban areas that relatively high wages in manufacturing had attracted with the shortage of mining and farm labour as an economic imperative for a fundamental restructuring of the African labour market. A key element of the Nationalist programme of apartheid was that it linked proposals to deal with this imbalance with its plans to give a new lease of life to traditional 'native' policy. Central to the Nationalist government's policy of coordinating 'native' and labour policy were labour bureaux. They were set up under the Native Laws Amendment Act 1952. Regulations for their operation were promulgated by the Department of Native Affairs in the same year.

The purpose of labour bureaux can be summarised as follows. First, they provided a means of channelling African labour from the reserves to mining and farming, as well as, if required, to manufacturing industry, and even as between these different sectors of the economy. Secondly, labour bureaux were designed to perpetuate migratory labour. To this end, the government systematically restricted the terms under which an African could remain in an urban area. Under s. 10 (1)(a) Natives (Urban Areas) Act (1945), Africans were permitted to reside in an urban area if they had been born in the area and had permanently resided there. Under s. 10 (1)(b) Africans also had the right to be in the urban area if they had been employed continuously with one employer for not less than 10 years or had resided continuously and lawfully in the area for not less than 15 years.

Finally, under s. 10 (1)(c) residential rights were conferred on the wives, and children under 18, of those who qualified to be in the area under s. 10(1)(a) or s. 10(1)(b). Otherwise Africans required labour bureau permission to be in any urban area for longer than 72 hours. Complementary to the creation of labour bureaux was the bizarrely named Abolition of Passes and Co-ordination of Documents Act (1952). This required all Africans above the age of 16 to carry a reference book that gave detailed information on the individual and had to be produced to the police on demand. At the same time, under the Group Areas Act (1950), Africans were confined to segregated areas within the urban areas, while the Prevention of Illegal Squatting Act (1951) prohibited Africans from squatting just outside municipal boundaries.

Posel argues that when the Nationalists came to power, their aim was to slow down African urbanisation, with the intention that the labour demands of manufacturing industry would be met from within the urban areas. In other words they drew a distinction between those who had already settled in the urban areas and the rest of the African population. In so far as the policy was designed to halt the process of further African urbanisation, it implied that employers would be competing for limited supplies of labour in the urban areas. That would tend to drive the price up, increasing the differences between the living standards of urban Africans and the rest of the African population. Posel argues that this did not happen in practice as many of the labour bureaux in fact channelled labour where the employers wanted them, including into the urban areas. Further, some employers in practice illegally recruited migrant labour independently of the labour bureaux. This undermined the objective of the government's Urban Labour Preference Policy (ULPP).

The principle behind the ULPP was that further influx into the urban areas should not take place when labour resources were already sufficient within an area to meet the needs of employers. It was specifically intended to prevent employers from exercising a preference for migrant labour over permanently urbanised workers. In the case of the Western Cape, the ULPP had the additional racial purpose that employers should be obliged to utilise Coloureds in preference to Africans. This was buttressed by other measures to limit the African population of the Western Cape. Posel argues that the ULPP was 'weakened by a series of legal and administrative concessions' and concludes:

> Influx control unwittingly heightened the very tendency it was designed to overrule – namely the prevailing preference for so-called 'raw' migrant labour for unskilled work. Section 10 (1) of the Natives (Urban Areas) Act added to the vulnerability and insecurity of migrants in search of work, as compared with urbanised Africans whose residential rights afforded them more time, opportunity, and bargaining power in the choice of employment. The majority of industrial and commercial firms, with a predominantly unskilled African work-force, thus developed a vested interest in the influx control legislation, provided it was sufficiently flexibly applied as to render the ULPP a dead letter.[10]

Posel also demonstrates the extent to which opposition from business, fear of African unrest and anxiety not to put its re-election in jeopardy persuaded the government to modify its original legislative plans. In particular, Section 10 (1) was initially worded in a Bill put forward in 1949 so that only Africans who had been born in an urban area and had permanently resided there would have any right to live there. Anyone else – whether male or female – would require specific permission to be in a proclaimed area for longer than 72 hours. Posel notes: 'Probably the most explosive political issue was the state's declared intention to subject African women to all the notorious rigours of the pass system.'[11] Mass protests followed that temporarily persuaded the government to backtrack.

Change of Gear

The final element in Posel's argument is her explanation of the government's change of gear between 1959 and 1961 that paved the way for the ambitious social engineering of the 1960s. The lead in the change of approach was taken by the Department of Bantu Administration and Development, as the Department of Native Affairs was renamed in 1958. It proposed further state intervention to curtail the process of economic integration. In 1964 the law was amended to make qualification under s. 10 (1)(c) more difficult. The government proclaimed as its objective the removal of all Africans from the urban areas who were surplus to the cities' labour requirements. The government also introduced measures to encourage the location of industries on the borders of the reserves. New labour regulations promulgated in 1968 were designed to ensure that Africans could no longer qualify to stay permanently in an urban area by reason of long residence. They restricted the maximum length of service contracts to one year, at the end of which Africans were required to return to their 'homeland'. For the same reason, they could no longer qualify through continuous employment with one employer. Labour bureaux were established in the homelands to enforce the new rules.

To facilitate the training of such contract labour within the context of a policy to ensure that Africans remain 'temporary sojourners' in the 'white' areas, the government introduced the 'call-in' card system whereby 'the same worker may repeatedly return to the same employer...for a further contract with the minimum of red tape'.[12] Thus, the government hoped that the productivity of African labour could be raised within the context of a migratory labour system. It was a requirement of 'the ideal of separate development' that 'the government hold the numbers of Africans permanently resident in urban areas as low as possible'.[13] In practical terms, the restrictions on the mobility of African labour also enabled the government to curtail severely the bargaining power of Africans both economically and politically. Nevertheless, as in the 1950s, resistance to the government's policies did not prove entirely fruitless. In particular, it dissuaded the government from ending Section 10 rights altogether in line with the ideology that all Africans in the white areas were there as temporary sojourners. Nevertheless, the change in the government's outlook had a radical impact on the growth of the urban African population. The size of the urban African population increased from 2.4 million in 1951 to 3.5 million in 1960.[14] By contrast, 'during the 1960s there was no net inflow of Africans to the white cities' and 'it has been estimated that in the 1960s and 1970s, influx control kept between 1.5 and 3 million Africans out of the white urban areas'.[15]

To understand the change of direction in the government's policies on influx control, more explanation of the overall political context is necessary, since the change in this area of policy was related to a much broader change in the government's interpretation of apartheid. In the months that followed the Nationalists' election victory in 1948, there was a debate as to whether apartheid constituted a new approach to racial policy or simply represented a continuation and shoring up of the old policy of segregation. An interesting contribution to that debate was made by Hendrik Verwoerd in a speech in September 1948. At the time he was simply a member of the Senate as he had not been included in Malan's first Cabinet. He insisted that the policy was not new:

> The claim we have made is that we are propagating the traditional policy of Afrikanerdom, the traditional policy of South Africa and of all those who have made South Africa their home – that we want to apply that traditional policy to the full; that is our claim.[16]

Verwoerd devoted a considerable part of his speech on the issue of what was apartheid to ruling out the option of total territorial segregation as impracticable. However, he emphasised the value of treating it as an ideal that gave a sense of direction to policy. Another theme of the speech was his justification of the denial of political rights to Africans residing outside the reserves by analogy with the millions of Italian seasonal workers who worked in France without gaining political rights there. While the details changed over the years, the comparison of South Africa's migratory labour system with labour practices in Europe became one of Verwoerd's favourite lines of argument in justification of apartheid. Unlike the more widely used justification of the denial of African political rights in terms of white trusteeship, it did not depend upon or assume a colonial context.

Notwithstanding the reference to Italians in France, the most significant feature of Verwoerd's speech was its emphasis on continuity in racial policy and this included invoking the concept of trusteeship. It is striking that the man who later and quite justifiably came to be seen as the architect of apartheid in its most radical form should have taken such a conservative approach to the issue in 1948. It reflected the fact that notwithstanding the huge changes brought about by the Second World War, colonial rule was still a feature of the international political system. It therefore made sense for the South African government to continue to invoke the norms under which colonial rule was justified. This was so, despite the National Party's own opposition to British imperial influence in South Africa.

This is not to deny the importance of the change to the international political system as a result of the war. The point was well put by Colin Webb in a chapter on South African foreign policy in a book published in the early 1960s:

> [T]he decisive theatre of war...was not Europe, but the Far East. For it was there with the Japanese attack on South-east Asia, that the first of the death-blows was struck at that world of European political supremacy in which the South African system had had its appropriate place.[17]

However, colonial rule did not end overnight. Most of Africa remained under colonial rule through both the 1940s and the 1950s. Further, as long as colonial rule existed, the European powers that had colonies sought to legitimise their rule in a variety of ways. While the concept of white racial superiority based on a racist biology had fallen into discredit following the defeat of the Nazis, culturally based notions of civilisation and backwardness still underpinned continuing claims of trusteeship. While the British government championed the notions of multiracialism and of racial partnership in the 1950s as alternatives to apartheid, these notions like apartheid itself were based on the assumption of the existence of racial hierarchies and not equality. This was brutally underlined by the Prime Minister of the Federation of Rhodesia and Nyasaland who defined racial partnership as like the relationship between the rider and the horse.

In line with such thinking the South African government emphasised the difference between tribal and de-tribalised Africans. The purpose of influx control during the 1950s was to limit the growth in the numbers of de-tribalised Africans living in the urban areas. It was particularly concerned to limit the efflux from the reserves into the cities by ensuring the full utilisation of labour resources within the urban areas. In practice, economic circumstances did not facilitate such a segmentation of the labour market, not least because of the preferences of employers. The context of the change in gear described by Posel was the shift from a colonial to a post-colonial era. It involved the abandonment of the distinction between tribal and de-tribalised Africans and its replacement by the concept of ethnicity. The implication for the urban African population was stark. All Africans could be defined in terms of ethnicity. The logic therefore was that every African could be connected to one of the ethnic homelands. In principle, therefore, all Africans in the white areas could be regarded as temporary sojourners who were only entitled to exercise their political rights in their own ethnic homelands. Admittedly, in practice, even during the most radical phase of apartheid, which roughly coincided with Verwoerd's premiership between 1958 and 1966, the government did not succeed in the elimination of the Section 10 residential rights that a minority of the African population enjoyed.

Opposition

From the outset, the Nationalist government faced resistance to its policies and from the very start, the government took measures to suppress the opposition it faced. After the election, the Minister of Justice established a departmental committee to inquire into the question of Communist influence in South Africa. The outcome was the passage of the Suppression of Communism Act in 1950. The Act outlawed the Communist Party of South Africa. It also empowered the Minister to declare any similar organisations illegal, to list individuals and thus to restrict their political activities, and to prohibit gatherings the Minister considered were likely to further the ends of Communism. The Act contained an extraordinarily wide definition of Communism encompassing bringing about 'any political, industrial, social or economic change by the promotion of disturbances or disorder'.[18] Communists who had been elected to the House of Assembly as Native Representatives lost their seats or in subsequent cases were prevented from taking them up.

At the urging of its Youth League, the ANC adopted a Programme of Action at its conference in December 1949. This committed the ANC to the objectives of ending white domination and achieving self-determination, as well as to the use of mass protest, including civil disobedience. In 1952 the ANC and the South African Indian Congress (SAIC) launched the Defiance Campaign against what they deemed unjust laws. Volunteers deliberately courted arrest through the violation of minor apartheid regulations, such as ignoring the racial segregation of facilities at post offices and stations. By the time the Campaign fizzled out at the end of 1952, more than 8,000 people had been arrested. The government's response was to enact legislation that made the violation of minor regulations for the purpose of protest a serious criminal offence punishable by years of imprisonment and flogging. By and large the Defiance Campaign had been conducted peacefully, but rioting leading to 40 deaths accompanied the final stages of the protest. A lasting effect of the Defiance Campaign was the boost it gave to membership of the ANC. It also helped to lay to rest the legacy of a particularly serious episode of violence between blacks. In January 1949, 142 people had been killed in riots in Durban between Indians and Africans that followed the beating of an African youth near a crowded bus station.

In the light of the narrowness of their victory in the 1948 general election, a priority for Afrikaner nationalists was to strengthen their position ahead of the next general election. The *HNP* and the Afrikaner Party merged in 1951 to form the National Party. Soon after the 1948 general election, legislation of the previous government that provided for communal representation of the Indians including two white representatives in the House of Assembly and two in the Senate was scrapped. In 1951 the government abolished the Native Representative Council (NRC). These steps took place against the background of Indian dissatisfaction with the terms of the representation under Smuts's legislation and of African disillusionment over the functioning of the NRC. However, the most important initiative of the new government in relation to political representation was its attempt to remove Coloureds from the common roll in the Cape.

This attempt ran into legal difficulties. The Appellate Division of the Supreme Court ruled that the government needed to follow the special procedure laid down in the Act of Union for amending entrenched clauses of the constitution. The government's claim was that entrenchment had lapsed with the passage of the Statute of Westminster ending the Union's remaining subordination to Britain. Ahead of the 1953 general election, the government strengthened its position by creating six seats for South West Africa in the House of Assembly and four in the Senate. It correctly anticipated that these seats would be filled by National Party candidates. The government's attempt to disenfranchise Coloureds prompted strong protests which were led by an extra-parliamentary movement of ex-servicemen, the War Veterans' Torch Commando.

However, in spite of the protests the government increased its majority in the general election of April 1953. (The results of the elections between 1953 and 1966 are set out in Table 5.1.) Malan retired at the end of November 1954. He was succeeded as Prime Minister by the Transvaal leader of the National Party, J.G. Strijdom. Strijdom was a transitional figure. He died from heart disease in August 1958, after having led Afrikaner nationalism to a third election victory. His successor was the far more substantial figure of Hendrik Verwoerd. Strijdom justified apartheid in crudely white supremacist terms. He was identified with the slogan of *baasskap* (literally boss-dom, but best translated as white domination). During his premiership, the government finally succeeded in removing Coloureds from the common roll in the Cape. This was achieved through the device of enlarging the Senate and changing the terms of its composition so as to manufacture the two-thirds majority of both houses of parliament sitting together that was needed to amend entrenched clauses of the constitution. Coloureds were given separate representation consisting of four white members in the House of Assembly and one in the Senate. This separate representation was abolished through the Prohibition of Improper Interference Act 1968. The parliamentary representation of Africans created after the removal of Africans from the common roll in the Cape in 1936 had been ended under the Promotion of Bantu Self-Government Act 1959.

The other significant piece of legislation during Strijdom's premiership was the amendment of the Industrial Conciliation Act

Table 5.1   General election results in seats, 1953–66[19]

Party	1953	1958	1961	1966
National Party	94	103	105	126
United Party	57	53	49	39
Labour Party	5	–	–	–
Progressive Party	–	–	1	1
Independents and others	–	–	1	–
Native representatives	3	3	–	–
Coloured representatives	–	4	4	–
TOTAL NUMBER OF SEATS	159	163	160	166

in 1956. This created job reservation whereby the government could reserve specific categories of work for whites. Two other major developments occurred during Strijdom's premiership: the publication of the summary report of the Tomlinson Commission in 1955 and the adoption of the Freedom Charter by the ANC and its allies in the Congress Alliance in the same year. Frank Welsh describes the Congress of the People as 'the best achievement of racial unity for many years' and the Freedom Charter it adopted as 'the most authoritative statement of reformist aims'. However, he notes that although it advanced 'nothing more than demands for freedoms commonly accepted in any normal state', even these were 'enough to prevent its being accepted by any parliamentarians as a realistic programme'. In 1956 the government responded to this challenge by charging the leading figures in the Congress Alliance with high treason. Eventually they were all acquitted.

The Tomlinson Commission was appointed in 1950 to inquire into socio-economic conditions in the reserves. It delivered its massive, multi-volume report to the government in 1954, but the debate on its findings only took place in 1956 after the publication of a summary of the full report. The Commission's principal recommendation for the expenditure of £104 million to develop the reserves was rejected by Verwoerd on behalf of the government. Giliomee notes:

> In the years to come nationalist reformers bewailed Verwoerd's failure to heed the Tomlinson report and embark on the rapid development of the reserves. Some even thought that the political history of South Africa would have taken quite a different course had he done so.[20]

He rejects this view, while describing the tabling of the report in parliament 'the moment of truth for the apartheid theorists'.[21] Giliomee's implication is that for apartheid to have acquired any credibility as more than simply an attempt to maintain white privilege at the expense of the rest of the population required a positive response to the report, which was not forthcoming. At the same time, some of the ideological trappings of the report proved very influential, such as the central importance it attached to ethnic divisions among the African population. While rejecting the sacrifices the Commission's recommendations would have required of whites,

Verwoerd also used the Commission's demographic projections to press the case for stopping further African urbanisation.

Verwoerd

The years of Verwoerd's premiership were among the most eventful in South Africa's history. They included the Sharpeville massacre, the outlawing of the ANC, South Africa's becoming a Republic outside the Commonwealth, self-government for the Transkei and two general elections. They were also years of very significant external developments for South Africa, including independence for most of the states of Sub-Saharan Africa, the civil rights movement in the United States and Rhodesia's Unilateral Declaration of Independence (UDI). The combination of internal and external pressures they generated and Verwoerd's response to them shaped the course South African policy took during these years. The period after the crisis years of 1960 and 1961 is sometimes referred to as apartheid's golden age.[22] Though such language is scarcely appropriate, it may more reasonably be argued that this was when the policy of apartheid reached its apogee.

The first full year of Verwoerd's premiership (1959) was dominated by domestic developments. They included the formation of the Pan-African Congress (PAC), the founding of the Progressive Party and the passage of the Promotion of Bantu Self-Government Act. The PAC was formed by Africanists in the ANC who were opposed to the ANC's involvement in the multiracial Congress Alliance. They were particularly hostile to what they saw as the excessive influence of white Communists. The Progressive Party came into existence as a result of the defection of 11 MPs from the liberal wing of the United Party. Their reason for defecting was the failure, as they saw it, of the United Party as the official Opposition to oppose the policy of apartheid more strongly and more wholeheartedly. The Promotion of Bantu Self-Government Act was a major step towards the political and institutional transformation of the reserves into ethnic homelands that would eventually be offered independence in fulfilment of the policy of separate development.

The year 1959 was relatively uneventful in terms of South Africa's foreign relations. It is significant that although the government's adoption of the policy of apartheid had worsened South Africa's relations with the rest of the world, it remained open to argument as to whether the change of government in 1948 had actually occasioned any fundamental change in the country's international position. There had, after all, already been international criticism of South Africa's racial policies before the unexpected election of the Malan government. James Barber summed up the significance of 1948 as he saw it in his 1973 study of South African foreign policy between 1945 and 1970:

> While the different personalities of the Nationalist leaders played a part in shaping policy, their main concern, like that of the United Party government before them, was concentrated on the defence of white society. There was, therefore, much common ground in South Africa's foreign policy, whether it was being made by the United Party or by the Nationalists, by Smuts or by Louw. Because of this the exaggerated claim is sometimes made that there was no change when the National Party government first came to power. The argument is that Malan took little interest in foreign affairs, he made no dramatic gesture like leaving the Commonwealth, and he retained senior officials, like D.D.Forsyth, who had served Smuts, and so, it is said, there was no change in foreign policy. But while the changes may not have been spectacular, they could be detected, and detected early. They were changes that stemmed not only from the increasingly hostile international environment, but from the aims and ideals of the National Party which were being realized inside the Union.[23]

However, hostile external reaction to South Africa's internal policies did not preclude cooperation with South Africa in international affairs. That applied particularly to South Africa's main trading partners. A striking example of such cooperation was the election in 1959 of South Africa's representative as a Vice-President of the United Nations General Assembly as the candidate supported by the Commonwealth.[24]

Sharpeville

The real turning point in South Africa's relations with the rest of the world as a result of apartheid came about not in 1948 but in 1960.

The centrepiece of the crisis that brought about this change was the massacre at Sharpeville on 21 March 1960. Even without Sharpeville, 1960 would have presented a severe challenge to the South African government. A total of 15 African states achieved independence in 1960, more than doubling the number of independent states in the whole of Africa. The British Prime Minister, Harold Macmillan, visited South Africa in 1960 to spell out publicly significant change in British policy towards the continent. As Calvocoressi recorded in a book on the crisis in South Africa's relations with the rest of the world, this was:

> [t]o push British territories into independence instead of applying a half-hearted brake and so make a bid for the friendship of the African nationalisms which were becoming a force to be reckoned with in world affairs.[25]

On 3 February 1960, Macmillan delivered his 'wind of change' speech to the South African Parliament in Cape Town in which he underlined that Britain regarded African nationalism as an irresistible force. The speech had an immense impact:

> The South African Prime Minister was visibly dumbfounded and as Mr Macmillan's words spread beyond the Parliament Africans received them with a jubilation that was all the greater because it sprang from surprise.[26]

A factor in dampening (though not eliminating) criticism of Macmillan from rightwingers in Britain was the fact that ahead of the visit Verwoerd had given notice that the government intended to hold a referendum on the issue of turning South Africa into a republic.

For its part the ANC had announced that it would hold massive demonstrations against the pass laws on 31 March 1960. To pre-empt this protest, the PAC announced it would mount demonstrations to defy the pass laws on 21 March 1960. One of these demonstrations took place outside the police station in Sharpeville, a township outside Vereeniging in the Transvaal. Concerned that the station's perimeter fence would give way and perhaps panicking at the sheer size of the crowd, the police opened fire on the peaceful demonstration killing 69 protestors and injuring another 180. There was a very strong international reaction to the massacre, with the United Nations Security Council meeting in emergency session and passing a resolution strongly condemning apartheid. The crisis prompted a collapse in confidence in South Africa among foreign investors. J.E. Spence described the short-term economic consequences of Sharpeville in his seminal study of South African foreign policy in the early 1960s:

> The relation between domestic stability and external confidence emerged clearly in the months following the Sharpeville crisis of March 1960. In this period, capital left the country at the rate of 12 million Rand a month. By May 1961 gold and foreign exchange reserves had fallen from the January 1960 figure of R312 million to less than R153 million, and a severe balance of payments crisis was averted only by raising the bank rate and imposing import and foreign exchange controls.[27]

Inside South Africa the massacre prompted further protests over the pass laws. For a short period in the immediate aftermath of Sharpeville, the police suspended enforcement of the pass laws. At the same time, the government made clear its intention to regain control by introducing legislation to outlaw the PAC and the ANC. A state of emergency permitting detention without trial was declared at the end of March. Hundreds of political activists belonging to or sympathetic towards the two African nationalist movements were imprisoned under its provisions. On top of these developments and just a day after the ban on the PAC and the ANC came into force, Verwoerd survived an attempt on his life on 9 April. While Verwoerd was convalescing, it seemed possible that the government would change direction in response to the crisis, as a number of leading Nationalists made speeches in support of reform.

However, Verwoerd's response to the crisis was quite different from those of Cape Nationalists such as Paul Sauer. Like Thatcher and Blair, Verwoerd was not for turning or backtracking. In particular, he pressed ahead with the holding of a referendum on the republic. On 3 August Verwoerd announced that it would be held on 5 October 1960. On that day the white electorate was asked the simple question: 'Are you in favour of a republic for the union?' Questionably, the electorate for the referendum included not just the white voters of South Africa's four provinces, but also the white voters of South West Africa. In other ways, too, the government had done what it could to boost the prospects for the 'yes' vote. Soon after the 1958 elections, the minimum age for the franchise had been changed from 21 to 18. Coloured voters, who still elected MPs on a separate roll, were excluded from the poll. The outcome was a narrow 'yes' vote of 52 per cent in favour of the republic.

According to the 1960 census, whites made up 19.3 per cent of the population of South Africa. Afrikaners accounted for 58 per cent of that total and English-speakers 38 per cent. The balance was made up by those claiming to be fully bilingual or who spoke another home language. The narrow basis of support for the republic is evident. Even after 12 years of National Party rule, there remained a minority within the Afrikaner community opposed to this step, particularly in the Cape. Concern that the alienation of Cape Afrikaners would lead to defeat ensured that Verwoerd campaigned for South Africa to become a republic within the Commonwealth, to the disappointment of members of the party who wished to sever all ties with Britain. In the event, opposition to apartheid within the Commonwealth, particularly from newly independent African members, brought about the result that radical Afrikaner nationalists had wanted. When South Africa became a republic on 31 May 1961, it was outside the Commonwealth as Verwoerd had withdrawn South Africa's application for continuing membership in the light of the strength of opposition to it.

The achievement of the republic hugely strengthened Verwoerd's position within his own party. He used it to make clear that he did not intend to deviate by one iota from the vision of apartheid as separate freedoms that he had enunciated in 1959. In effect, Verwoerd had redefined apartheid in ethno-national terms for the coming of a post-colonial age and he intended to defend his creation. He became known as the man of granite (and satirised in cartoons as such) after he had spoken towards the end of 1960 of erecting walls of granite around his policies. He presented himself to the white electorate as a man of conviction who did not have 'the nagging doubt of ever wondering, whether, perhaps, I am wrong'.[28] Verwoerd ignored the advice he received on all sides to tackle the domestic turmoil by addressing the grievances of the urban African population. He opted instead for a security clampdown that entailed the passage of Draconian laws and a massive increase in expenditure on the military and the police.

Verwoerd sought endorsement of this approach by holding an early general election. It took place on 18 October 1961. A particular objective of the government was to eliminate the remaining liberal opposition to the government in the form of the Progressive Party. In this objective it almost succeeded (see Table 5.1). The National Party was returned to power with an increased majority, while Helen Suzman was the sole Progressive Party MP to secure re-election. The result reflected a hardening of white opinion in response to the unrest that had engulfed the country since Sharpeville and it was also a reaction to events in newly independent Africa, particularly the Congo. The main opposition to the government came from outside parliament. Following the failure of the ANC to sustain mass protests after being banned, the ANC and the South African Communist Party set up Umkhonto we Sizwe (Zulu for 'The Spear of the Nation'). MK, as it was dubbed, launched a campaign of sabotage on 16 December 1961. However, it did not deflect Verwoerd from the pursuit of his plan for the creation of separate states out of the reserves. A significant first step in this direction was the establishment of self-government for the Transkei in December 1963. It was presented as demonstrating how self-determination for the peoples of South Africa could be achieved under the aegis of apartheid. Thus, according to Munger, 'more than one Nationalist MP spoke privately of the Transkei as a smokescreen to deceive world opinion'.[29]

Verwoerd achieved an even greater triumph in the general election of 30 March 1966. A significant element in the National Party's landslide victory was the support the party secured for the first time among English-speaking voters in Natal. Disillusionment with Britain over decolonisation and the dispute with Ian Smith's regime in Rhodesia was a factor in their swing to the right. At the same time, the United Party hardly presented itself as a more liberal alternative to the government. It attacked Verwoerd for his intention to grant independence to the Bantustans, promising white leadership over the whole of South Africa. The National Party's response was that it would maintain white control in white South Africa. The United Party also criticised the government's 'policy of carefully balanced neutrality'[30] over Rhodesia and called for greater support to be given to the Smith regime.

Factors in Verwoerd's electoral triumph were a booming economy and the crushing of African nationalist opposition in all its forms. The outward appearance of political stability encouraged foreign investment, contributing to the high economic growth rates South Africa enjoyed through the 1960s once the impact of Sharpeville at the start of the decade had worn off. After the 1966 elections, Verwoerd's position appeared unassailable. The government was slightly ruffled by a visit to South Africa by Senator Robert Kennedy in June 1966. However, the outcome the following month of the case over South West Africa before the International Court of Justice was of much greater moment to the government. The court ruled by the casting vote of its presiding judge that the complainants, Ethiopia and Liberia, lacked legal standing to bring the case. It thereby removed a threat to the legal basis of South African rule in South West Africa that had hung over the government since the case had been initiated in 1960.

Then out of the blue on 6 September 1966 Verwoerd was assassinated by a deranged parliamentary messenger. At the time of his death, no figure had contributed more to the development of apartheid, both in theory and in practice, than Hendrik Verwoerd. The translation of any ideology into practice involves compromise and adaptation. In that sense, Posel is right to question the notion that apartheid's implementation from 1948 could ever have followed a preconceived plan. However, the perception of apartheid as grand design involving social engineering on a gigantic scale owed much to the coherence and consistency of Verwoerd's vision, as well as to his radicalism. The next chapter examines the development of his vision under more pragmatic stewardship.

6

South Africa in a Post-Colonial World: Modernising or Eroding Apartheid?

A week after Verwoerd's assassination on 6 September 1966, the National Party parliamentary caucus chose the Minister of Justice, Police and Prisons, Balthazar Johannes Vorster, as his successor. He was unopposed. Vorster owed his election as Prime Minister to the role he had played in crushing African nationalist opposition to the government. Having been interned during the Second World War for pro-Nazi sympathies as a member of the Ossewa Brandwag (OB), he had a controversial past that added to his reputation as a tough, authoritarian leader. In fact, he was by no means as formidable a figure as his predecessor. He was far more collegial in the way he ran his government. A great deal of leeway was left to individual ministers. While operating with the broad ideological framework established by Verwoerd, Vorster was also more flexible in his interpretation of policy. At the same time, the need for adjustments to existing practices became more pressing during Vorster's premiership as the world moved further into a post-colonial era. He was in power for just over twelve years. That left its mark on both the implementation and interpretation of apartheid, which is reflected in the literature on the politics of South Africa that appeared during his premiership.

After the Sharpeville massacre it became commonplace to predict that the implementation of apartheid would lead to a racial bloodbath and that South Africa would succumb to revolution, not in the distant future but, given the pace of change elsewhere in Africa, in a matter of years. The failure of these predictions to come to pass prompted an important study of the South African system by a German sociologist, Heribert Adam. His book was entitled, *Modernizing Racial Domination*. Adam's point of departure was reflected in the title of the opening chapter, 'South Africa's Stalled Revolution'. According to Adam, those forecasting revolution 'underestimated the effects of an increasingly streamlined and expanding system of sophisticated dominance'.[1] He argued: 'The Apartheid system has been viewed as simply the most outdated relic of a dying colonialism, yet possibly it is one of the most advanced and effective patterns of rational, oligarchic domination.'[2]

Adam highlighted a number of factors as contributing to the survival of South Africa's 'pragmatic race oligarchy'. He identified coercion as one element:

> The system of police informers in all potential opposition groups has been improved to such an extent that this surveillance alone guarantees an effective check on all opponents inside and outside the country. Wide powers, without interference of the courts, together with effective methods of interrogation, give the political police virtually unlimited authority.[3]

At the same time, he contended that the government's legalistic attitude towards coercion lent it a modicum of legitimacy. He argued: 'The insistence of white domination on properly legalized repression, to a certain extent clouds the content, and the power of the state seems impartial, merely abused by individual transgressions.'[4] In summary, Adam called South Africa a 'democratic police state'. However, a more apposite oxymoron would be that South Africa had become a constitutional police state through the passage of legislation permitting detention without trial for long periods.

Why White Rule Survived

However, Adam regarded two other factors as being more important to the explanation of the survival of the regime than coercion. They were the partial success of separate development as a programme and the effect of the economic boom in neutralising dissatisfaction.

In this context, Adam referred to Pierre van den Berghe's categor-
isation of three different spheres of apartheid, the micro, the meso
and the macro, to distinguish among the provision of separate public
facilities, residential segregation and the creation of ethnically
homogeneous homelands. Adam argued that the last of these, macro-
apartheid, differentiated the policy from segregation as well as from
the policies pursued by Ian Smith in Rhodesia or by the Portuguese
in Mozambique and Angola. While acknowledging the 'illusory
aspects' of separate development, he contended that psychologically
the Bantustans helped to compensate for the absence of real political
rights and also increased black political fragmentation. On the role
of the economic boom Adam noted: 'Even though half of Soweto's
500,000 Africans still live below the poverty line, the relative
improvement of their economic situation takes the sting out of their
deprivation.'[5]

Elsewhere Adam discussed the argument that 'an essential contradiction exists between an irrational race policy and the requirements of a rationally organized, expanding industrial society'.[6] He
concluded:

> In summary, it can be said that the analytical perspective which
> focuses on the essential compatibility between economic interests
> and white political power comes much closer to reality than the
> naïve belief in economic growth as the magic defeat of racial dis-
> crimination. It recognizes that the disputes between industrialists
> and the government's supporters are not about the abolition of
> white power but the distribution of its yields within a system of wage
> color bar and the suppression of labor organizations. However,
> while economic development may reinforce white supremacy in
> the short run, it also undermines it in the long run.[7]

Adam also considered why external pressures on the South African
government had not led to the demise of apartheid. On the first page
of 'South Africa's Stalled Revolution' he noted:

> In the context of sub-Saharan Africa, the economic and military
> power of the developed south occupies such a position of dom-
> inance as compared with the underdeveloped north, that South
> Africa has already succeeded in surrounding herself with a ring of
> more or less dependent satellite countries, in spite of the almost

universal ideological opposition against her internal political system.

Later in the book he considered the role of external pressures in greater depth. His point of departure was a highly influential sociological study of South Africa that had been published in the mid-1960s: Pierre van den Berghe's *South Africa: A Study in Conflict*. The message of the book was succinctly conveyed on the cover of the paperback edition of the book which first came out in 1967 and was reprinted in 1970. The cover proclaimed: ' "WHITE SUPREMACY," says the author of this up-to-date analysis of South African society and politics, "IS BUSILY DIGGING ITS OWN GRAVE." '[8] Van den Berghe concluded his study as follows:

> A South Africa divided against itself awaits the impending and inexorable catastrophe. The Whites claim a right to survival which hardly anybody denies them. But in claiming to assert that right, they have set themselves against the course of history, and have become an arrogant, oppressive albinocracy. Their pride and prejudice may well be their undoing. *Quos vult Jupiter pendere, dementat prius*.[9]

In the chapter on external pressures, van den Berghe predicted that the international isolation of South Africa would intensify and that South Africa's anti-Communist stance would count for little with the West, given the hostility of the Third World. He also forecast that South Africa's vulnerability to both infiltration and sanctions would increase with the spread of African majority rule to its borders. Further, he suggested that the High Commission territories would adopt a hostile attitude towards South Africa once they achieved independence and that the South West Africa case would increase the pressure on South Africa. As Adam noted, by 1970 events had confounded more or less all of van den Berghe's expectations. In the preface to the paperback edition of his book, van den Berghe conceded that his analysis of external pressures had been 'partially invalidated by events' and concluded the preface:

> The liberation of South Africa remains contingent on two main external factors. First, the territories north of the Limpopo must come under majority rule. Second, there must be effective outside

support for the South African underground and an escalation of sanctions.[10]

An assumption underpinning van den Berghe's analysis was that the West would be forced to take effective steps to bring about the demise of apartheid or otherwise it would alienate much of the Third World, but most especially the newly independent states of Sub-Saharan Africa. One of the major achievements of the first years of Vorster's premiership was his success in confounding this assumption. The point was underlined in a speech by the South African foreign minister, Hilgard Muller in 1968:

> As the West becomes aware of our fruitful co-operation with other African states, their attitude towards us improves. I believe that it will happen to an increasing degree because we must simply accept that our relations with the rest of the world is largely determined by our relations with the African states. In this connection we are giving the world considerable food for thought.[11]

The expectation had been that once the progress of decolonisation touched South Africa, it would spark off conflict. The decolonisation of Sub-Saharan Africa had taken place in stages. Territories in West Africa and West Central Africa, where there were no settler colonies, were the first to achieve independence. East Africa followed. Of the continental territories in this region, Kenya, which had been a settler colony, achieved independence last of all in December 1963. Next came the Northernmost territories of the Federation of Rhodesia and Nyasaland. Malawi became independent in July 1964, Zambia in October 1964. Neither actually bordered on South Africa. However, they were the first states under African majority rule to have close economic ties with South Africa. Further, Zambia did border a remote part of South African-ruled South West Africa.

South Africa's Neighbours

At this point, the progress of African nationalism southwards stalled. Portugal refused to grant independence to Angola or Mozambique. With the collapse of the Federation, the government of Southern Rhodesia resisted British demands for reform. It ultimately declared independence unilaterally on 15 November 1965 to free itself of British pressure. However, three land-locked British territories bordering South Africa did achieve independence under African majority rule in the 1960s. They were the three High Commission territories of Basutoland, Bechuanaland and Swaziland. The largest, Bechuanaland, was the first to achieve independence as Botswana on 30 September 1966. Basutoland, a territory wholly surrounded by South Africa, became independent as the Kingdom of Lesotho on 4 October 1966. Swaziland was the last of the three to achieve independence, which it did on 6 September 1968.

At the time of the setting up of the Union of South Africa in 1910, as touched on in Chapter 4, it had been envisaged that the High Commission territories would be transferred to South Africa. They were in a customs union with South Africa and employed the South African currency. South Africa contributed to the running of the transport services in all three and in two (Basutoland and Swaziland) ran the postal and telegraphic services. Precisely because Britain anticipated that they would indeed be transferred to South African rule, the character of their administration was different from that of other British colonies in Africa. In the event, transfer did not take place. Before the Second World War the main obstacle to their incorporation was not South African racial policy as such, but British unwillingness to effect the transfer without guarantees that their tribal lands would not be alienated for white settlement. South African assurances in this respect in the 1930s appeared to clear the way for their incorporation, but the negotiations were interrupted by the outbreak of the war. After the war hardening international attitudes towards South African racial policies constituted a larger obstacle, as did British concern that transfer should take place with the consent of the populations of the territories. Of that there was little prospect.

The attitude of the South African government also underwent significant change. At the time of Union, the government looked to the territories as offering new outlets for white settlement. By the 1950s the attraction of the territories was as African reserves that by their addition to the country would give credibility to the concept of separate development. In particular, the Tomlinson Commission envisaged the inclusion of the territories in its efforts to give the policy of apartheid credibility in the context of the international norms of the 1950s. Because of the sheer size of the Bechuanaland Protectorate, which was very nearly half the area of South Africa as a whole, including the territories made a very large difference to the saleability of apartheid. As Hyam explained:

> Although the Tomlinson Commission did not apparently make any detailed study of the High Commission Territories or assess their potentialities, it regarded them as 'artificially excluded' from the Union in 1910, and it claimed to follow the land legislators of 1913 and 1936 in relating them to the larger Bantu homelands, or 'geographical cultural-historical complexes', which bound together the Africans within the Union and in its vicinity. It stated that the High Commission Territories should be incorporated [*sic*] as soon as possible.

As Hyam demonstrated, the inclusion of the High Commission Territories made a very large difference to the Tomlinson Commission's presentation of the casc for separate development.

> Calculating that the future maximum extent of the Bantu Areas in the Union would be fixed at 13.7 per cent, this proportion would be completely altered if the High Commission Territories ('which are essentially Bantu Areas') were included. 'Greater South Africa' (the Commission's term) would then cover some 766,000 square miles (excluding the South-West), of which (allowing for European settlement in Swaziland), 45 per cent would belong to the Africans. Thus, on this basis, seven 'national homes' could be systematically expanded, with the least possible transgression of ethnic bonds, 'around historio-logical centres' or 'power stations', namely: Tswanaland, Vendaland, Pediland, Swaziland, Zululand, Xhosaland (i.e. the Transkei) and Sotholand. In each, the Africans themselves would exercise administrative functions to an ever-increasing extent. In this way, the problem of the existing scattered 110 African areas, together with the 154 'black spots', which formed no foundation for the growth of an independent community could be overcome.[12]

The Tomlinson Commission was by no means alone in factoring the High Commission territories into an overall solution of the conflict between the races in South Africa. Advocates of partition as an answer to the conflict typically included the territories in their schemes for resolving the problem on the basis of a 'fair' division of resources between white and black. Some advocated a South African version of the two-state solution, which assumed a consolidation of white and black areas of South Africa. Others posited the division of the land into a number of ethnic homelands. Proponents of apartheid imagined a future in which the High Commission territories would follow a similar political trajectory to that of the Transkei. Even without the addition of the High Commission territories, the concept of separate development attracted a measure of interest in the West after the grant of self-government to the Transkei. In this period there was almost as much scepticism among Western conservatives that South Africa might ever become a non-racial democracy as there is today about the prospects for political accommodation between Jews and Palestinians in the same polity.[13]

In 1961 Verwoerd acknowledged at last that there was no longer any likelihood that Britain would agree to the incorporation of the territories into South Africa. However, in September 1963, he raised the possibility in another form. He declared:

> If South Africa were to be, or to become, the guardian, the protector or the helper of these adjacent Territories, instead of the United Kingdom, we could lead them far better and much more quickly to independence and economic prosperity than Great Britain can do.[14]

Verwoerd went further, suggesting that there could be adjustments to the final boundaries of the territories so as to reflect ethnic divisions more accurately. He made an offer that South Africa 'would repurchase or exchange areas now wrongly occupied in order to include them in the white area or the black'.[15] The hostile international reaction to the speech, as well as the attitude in the territories towards apartheid South Africa, meant that Verwoerd's offer never received serious consideration from the British government. None of the territories' political leaders were attracted by the model Verwoerd presented of 'natural native democracy...as in the Transkei'.[16]

From the perspective of the advocates of separate development, the failure of South Africa to secure the incorporation of the High Commission territories before the rise of international hostility towards the country's racial policy represented a significant lost opportunity. However, the opposite case can as easily be argued. Giliomee considers the converse of what might have happened if South Africa had been able to develop the territories as Bantustans. This is that Britain might have taken over the governance of the Transkei in the late nineteenth century and Transkei's political development might have followed that of the High Commission territories. The former had been a serious possibility in the 1880s. Giliomee muses:

> It is tempting to speculate what would have happened if the Transkei had gone the way of the Basutoland, Bechuanaland and Swaziland, which had become British 'protectorates', and yet later High Commission territories. The Transkei would serve as the centerpiece of the ideology of segregation and apartheid. Had Britain also taken over the Transkei, the idea of a white South Africa existing side by side with some African 'reserves' would have lacked any credibility.[17]

Despite the rejection of the offer contained in his September 1963 speech, Verwoerd was credited with foreseeing 'what a windfall for Bantustan publicity the granting of independence to the former British Protectorates was going to become'.[18] However, he died before the independence of any of the High Commission territories. Just before his death, he had a meeting in Pretoria with the man who was shortly to become the Prime Minister of an independent Lesotho, Chief Leabua Jonathan. The main significance of the meeting was that it enabled Vorster to claim that he was following the path already set by Verwoerd when he sought to develop relations with the territories after their independence. After Vorster's accession to power, the South African foreign minister, Hilgard Muller, attended the independence celebrations of both Botswana and Lesotho. Vorster met Jonathan in January 1967. These developments were taken to herald a new departure in South Africa's relations with Africa and South Africa's efforts to cultivate such ties were dubbed the outward-looking policy.

The emergence of conservative leaders in majority-ruled Africa ready to come to terms with the reality of South African power on the continent and to take advantage of it was apparent even before Vorster came to power. For example, the conservative and strongly anti-Communist Moise Tshombe became Prime Minister of the

Congo in July 1964. He recruited white mercenaries in South Africa to assist the government to suppress a rebellion in the East of the Congo. He had previously had friendly relations with South Africa when he had headed the secession of Katanga from the Congo in the early 1960s. However, the Tshombe government did not last. It was overthrown in a military *coup d'état* in November 1965. In fact, it was one of a series of military coups that occurred across Sub-Saharan Africa in late 1965 and early 1966. They underlined the fragility of constitutional government in Africa after decolonisation. Among those overthrown was the radical nationalist leader, Kwame Nkrumah of Ghana. As the leading advocate of Pan-Africanism, Nkrumah had practically embodied the notion that the West could not expect to maintain cordial relations with both independent Africa and apartheid South Africa.

When Malawi and Zambia became independent in 1964, their leaders recognised that their countries' economic ties with South Africa necessitated the adoption of a non-confrontational approach to their relations with the Republic. In fact, prior to independence the Zambian leader, Kenneth Kaunda, had gone so far as to offer to exchange diplomatic representatives with South Africa. However, Verwoerd turned down Kaunda's offer. Verwoerd remained wedded to the use of roving ambassadors in relations with African states and, in any event, gave a higher priority to the development of economic over political relations. A complicating factor in the development of South Africa's relations with both Zambia and Malawi was Rhodesia's unilateral declaration of independence (UDI) on 15 November 1965. In its wake Zambia embarked on a policy of reducing its economic links with the white South. However, in the short term, Zambia's trade with South Africa actually increased as the country gave higher priority to cutting its ties with Rhodesia.

By contrast, UDI prompted Malawi's leader, Hastings Banda, to seek closer relations with South Africa. The first indication of this policy was Malawi's despatch of a top-level trade mission to South Africa in March 1967. It was led by three cabinet ministers. The success of the mission and the favourable reaction of the white elect-orate both to the trade mission and to Vorster's earlier meeting with Jonathan paved the way to a major breakthrough for the outward-looking policy. In December 1967 Banda announced that South Africa and Malawi had agreed to exchange diplomatic representa-tives. The agreement had significant implications for the policy of apartheid since, very obviously, Malawi's envoy could not be treated in the same manner as South Africa's own African population was under apartheid. Vorster developed the concept of multinationalism to justify racial integration that occurred as a consequence of South Africa's foreign relations. The argument he advanced was that South Africa could not impose its own domestic racial norms on other countries and had to accept this in its international dealings. (This issue is explored further in Chapter 10.)

Dialogue with Africa

The political importance of the relationship to the two governments was underscored by an exchange of visits. Vorster paid a visit to Malawi in May 1970, while Banda toured South Africa in August 1971. Banda's triumphal tour included the staging of a state banquet loyally described by the Afrikaans press as '*veelvolkig*', i.e. 'multinational' and not multiracial. At a more modest level South Africa also established relations with the Malagasy Republic in the late 1960s. The success of the outward-looking policy forced African states that had sought to bring about South Africa's isolation to reconsider their approach. In April 1969 a meeting of East and Central African states held in the Zambian capital issued a joint declaration dubbed the Lusaka Manifesto after the conference venue. Without compromising on the issue of the liberation of South Africa from apartheid, it held out the prospect of negotiations as the preferable route to change. The declaration was endorsed by the Organisation of African Unity (OAU) and by the United Nations General Assembly.

But differences remained among the African states in their inter-pretation of the declaration. In particular, the more conservative African leaders regarded the declaration as implicitly a recognition that the OAU strategy of achieving change through support for liberation movements in countries still under white minority or colo-nial rule had failed. In an attempt to exploit the differences among African states Vorster made an offer in September 1970 to enter into negotiations on a non-aggression pact with any African state that responded to his invitation. This initiative was fruitless. However, on 4 November 1970, a major breach occurred in the solidarity of African states over the issue of apartheid when the veteran President of the Ivory Coast, Felix Houphouet-Boigny, called for a dialogue with South Africa. His call was reported to have the support of a number of other Francophone African states.[19] In December the Ghanaian Prime Minister, Kofi Busia, indicated his support for dialogue as well. However, he made it clear that the objective of dialogue had to be the elimination of apartheid. Further, he argued in line with the Lusaka Manifesto that negotiations did not rule out continuing to support the use of other means, including force, to achieve this end.

Yet it soon became apparent that the states advocating a dialogue with South Africa in the manner proposed by Houphouet-Boigny remained in the minority. At a meeting in June 1971 of OAU foreign ministers, the Ivory Coast initiative was opposed by 27 of the OAU's 41 members. The OAU's rejection did not put an end to the advocacy of dialogue. For example, very briefly, Idi Amin of Uganda espoused the cause, but it remained clear that the push for dialogue had lost momentum. By the end of 1972 the South African government's hopes of a major breakthrough had faded. In the end, the concrete results of dialogue were slight. Whereas the African states advocating dialogue hoped that it would give rise to reform of apartheid, the South African government approached dialogue from a very different perspective. By showing that it could enter into constructive relations with African states, it hoped to demonstrate that apartheid was compatible with a post-colonial world and there was no need for change. In this context, the controversy in Africa over dialogue did much to transform Western attitudes towards South Africa. In particular, it helped to dispel the notion that conflict between apartheid South Africa and states under African majority rule was inevitable. This had consequences for the policies of Western states towards South Africa.

The American Pay-off

The change was most evident in American attitudes towards South Africa. In fact, well before Houphouet-Boigny's initiative, the American government had already decided upon a change of policy towards Southern Africa. Shortly after his inauguration in January 1969, President Richard Nixon ordered a review of American policy towards Southern Africa. He asked the National Security Council's Interdepartmental Group for Africa to produce an assessment of the area's future prospects and to suggest 'the full range of basic strategies and policy options open to the United States'.[20] The study was completed in August 1969 and subsequently leaked to the press. The NSC Group put forward five policy options. The most important were Options Two and Three. Option Two proposed:

> Broader association with both black and white states in an effort to encourage moderation in the white states, to enlist cooperation of the black states in reducing tensions and the likelihood of increasing cross-border violence, and to encourage improved relations among states in area.[21]

Option Three was:

> Limited association with the white states and closer association with the blacks in an effort to retain some economic, scientific and strategic interests in the white states while maintaining a posture on the racial issue which blacks will accept, though opposing violent solutions to the problems of the region.[22]

The study described Option Three as 'a codification and extension of present policy'.[23] (Option One envisaged closer association with the white regimes. Option Four put the emphasis on further dissociation, while Option Five entailed general disengagement from the problems of the area.)

Option Two was the one adopted by the Nixon Administration. This represented a considerable gain for the South African government. While the success of South Africa's outward-looking policy played a part in influencing the Nixon Administration in this direction, more important was the stalling of African nationalism in Southern Africa. The NSC Group took the view that the white redoubt round South Africa consisting of the Portuguese colonies of Angola and Mozambique. Rhodesia and South African-ruled South West Africa would endure. Its report stated:

> There is no likelihood in the foreseeable future that liberation movements could overthrow or seriously threaten the existing white governments. Rebel activity may expand and contract from time to time, but there will be no definite victory or defeat resulting from guerrilla activities. In Angola and Mozambique, where

insurgency is most active, the rebels cannot win militarily – but neither can the Portuguese. In the longer run, the most likely prospect is a continuation of present trends – a rise in activity, but no conclusive results.[24]

As far as Rhodesia was concerned, the NSC study was of the view that 'despite the effects of sanctions, the white regime can hold out indefinitely with South African help'.[25] On South West Africa, the study stated:

> South Africa will continue to occupy and administer the territory while the African and Asian nations press for stronger measures to force South Africa out. The South African police and military will be able to successfully counter any insurgent or dissident activity for the foreseeable future.[26]

However, clearly influenced by the instability that had beset majority-ruled states in the mid-1960s, the study was far less sanguine about the political prospects of the newly independent states in the region. It argued that 'Zambia shows latent instability for tribal reasons, and may face internal crises'.[27] The comment reflected the superficiality of the NSC Group's analysis. In particular, it did not take into account the most striking feature of Zambian society, the extent of its urbanisation. The study also predicted that the Soviet Union would continue to accord Africa a low priority and that the extent of its involvement in the affairs of the continent would be limited. While this prediction, like its forecast of political instability in Zambia, proved false, there was a much stronger basis for it. It was in line with the expectations of academic experts such as James Mayall, who argued that 'the very incoherence of African state structures and the volatility of African politics were likely to undermine any sustained attempt at political influence'.[28]

In general, the climate of opinion in the West was favourable to the conduct of South Africa's outward-looking policy in the first half of Vorster's premiership. Nixon's election as President of the United States was followed by the election of a Conservative Party government in Britain in June 1970. The Heath government resumed arms sales to South Africa. At the same time, it sought to disengage from Africa through seeking a settlement of the Rhodesian problem. The early 1970s were a time of détente between the super Powers, an era of negotiations that gave credibility to the pursuit of foreign policy objectives through diplomatic means. However, the main reason for increasing confidence among Western conservatives in the survival of apartheid South Africa was the white buffer around the Republic.

Ironically, the South African government and its advisers were less complacent than were Western conservatives in their view of the durability of this white buffer. Further, the fact that the South African government had managed to establish workable relationships with a number of majority-ruled states meant that its fear of the consequences of majority-ruled states on the country's borders had diminished. Thus, in his 1968 book, *The Third Africa*, which envisaged South Africa's dominating Southern Africa in the manner in which the United States dominated Latin America, Eschel Rhoodie argued:

> Whether a black, mixed, or white government is in power would really be immaterial, for in the *long run* close co-operation with its southern neighbour (and Mozambique) is the only certain formula for sustained economic growth and political stability in Rhodesia.[29]

The headway made by South African foreign policy in the late 1960s and early 1970s reduced the pressure on the government to introduce domestic reforms. Thus, Vorster made only relatively minor adjustments to apartheid as it had evolved under Verwoerd and these adjustments arose for the most part out of South Africa's relations with other countries in the context of the norms of a post-colonial world. Indeed, it may fairly be argued that Vorster's success in reducing the country's isolation helped to make the continued implementation of apartheid according to Verwoerd's blueprint possible.

The Extreme Right

Nonetheless, Vorster encountered opposition to his policies from rightwingers who accused him of deviating from the path of his predecessor, a charge which Vorster vigorously and by and large justifiably denied. However, there was one area of policy in which Vorster's approach clearly did differ from that of Verwoerd. A year before his death Verwoerd had made a speech at Loskop Dam setting out his attitude towards apartheid in sport. It was delivered just as a highly successful tour of New Zealand by the Springboks (South Africa's rugby team) was drawing to a close. It shattered illusions that the South African government would accommodate the demand in New Zealand that a fully representative All Blacks rugby team should be allowed to tour South Africa in 1967. The gist of the speech was that he expected others to abide by South African customs while in South Africa, just as South African teams on tour necessarily abided by the customs of the countries they were visiting. The implication was that South Africa would not admit racially mixed sporting teams for the sake of maintaining relations with other countries in this field. This was confirmed by the terms of the invitation issued to the All Blacks in February 1966. As a consequence the All Blacks cancelled their planned tour of South Africa.

Vorster unveiled his government's new sports policy in April 1967 in a lengthy speech in the House of Assembly. It represented significant change from previous policy though Vorster took considerable pains to disguise the fact. He reaffirmed existing policy against mixed sport in domestic competitions. However, he argued that at the international level, different considerations applied. The distinction formed the basis for his declaration that South Africa would not prescribe the racial composition of teams visiting South Africa that came from the country's traditional sporting partners. The implication was that South Africa would not raise objections to the inclusion of Maori players if the All Blacks rugby team were to tour South Africa. Vorster also made clear that in the context of the Olympic Games, he accepted the rule that only one team could represent South Africa. The implication of this was that South Africa would send a racially mixed team to Mexico if it were permitted to take part in the Olympic Games in 1968. While Vorster's policy had only limited success in overcoming the trend towards the isolation of South Africa in international sporting competition, it became the focus of extreme rightwing opposition to the government. Vorster's opponents claimed that the policy would lead to social integration, including the opportunity for the Maori players to dance with Afrikaner girls.

The extreme right's appeal to racial prejudice on this issue was connected to a larger divide in attitudes among Afrikaner nationalists that emerged during Vorster's premiership. Shortly after Vorster's accession to power, Willem de Klerk, brother of the future President,

F.W. de Klerk, coined the terms *verligte* (enlightened) and *verkrampte* (constricted or narrow-minded) to encapsulate the conflict between modernisers and traditionalists within the National Party. This was in a speech in Warmbad in October 1966.[30] The principal representative of the *verkramptes* in the Cabinet was Albert Hertzog, whom Vorster first demoted and then dismissed in 1968. However, the internal contention over Vorster's policies continued. The party leadership sought a showdown with the *verkramptes* at the Transvaal Congress of the National Party in September 1969. The delegates were invited to support the government's policies on four of the contentious issues. The four issues were: the outward-looking policy, including the special treatment accorded to black diplomats; the promotion of white unity between Afrikaners and English-speakers; the government's immigration policy; and its sports policy, including the invitation to the All Blacks to tour South Africa without any racial restrictions on their choice of players.

It was made clear that anyone who continued to oppose government policy after the votes had been taken would be faced with expulsion from the National Party. The government was supported unanimously on three of the four issues. A handful of delegates took a stand against the government's sports policy. Hertzog championed the cause of the dissidents in a speech that sharply attacked Vorster for departing from the stance on sports policy taken by Verwoerd. The expulsion from the National Party of Hertzog and the other dissidents followed. They launched a new extreme rightwing political party, the Herstigte Nasionale Party (the reconstituted National Party – HNP) in October 1969. The party's religiously fundamentalist character was reflected in its membership policy. While being restricted to whites as required by this time by South African law, the party also barred Catholics, Jews and atheists from membership. Even before the launch of the HNP, Vorster had announced his intention to hold a general election in 1970, a year ahead of schedule. The election took place on 22 April 1970.

The bizarre character of the campaign was underlined by an exchange between the Prime Minister and a questioner at a public meeting in Springs. It graphically illustrated the government's sensitivity to charges of corruption. Vorster's response to being asked about loans made to National Party politicians by the Land Bank was to tell his interrogator that the police would pay him a visit the next day. After this duly happened the questioner told the waiting press that he would not be intimidated and that he still considered Vorster to be a dangerous liberal.[31] The election achieved the government's main aim of crushing the extreme right (see Table 6.1). The HNP's share of the vote in the 77 seats it contested was 7.2 per cent and it won no seats. However, this outcome did not end National Party divisions between *verligtes* and *verkramptes* over the direction of government policy as many of the leading *verkramptes* had opted to stay inside the party. Further, the government paid a price for its victory over the HNP. For the first time since the 1948 general election, the ruling party lost ground. The United Party increased its representation in the House of Assembly. While the Progressive Party did not add to its single seat in the House of Assembly, there was a substantial increase in its vote. However, the significance of the Opposition's gains should not be exaggerated. They scarcely affected the National Party's overall position of dominance.

Indeed, the main challenge to the government after the 1970 election came from outside parliament. But the election did have consequences for party politics in the white community. The increased support for the Progressive Party caused tensions between the conservative and liberal wings of the United Party. The condition of the Opposition was one of the reasons why Vorster opted again to go to the country a year before the parliament had run its full term. The general election took place on 24 April 1974. A weakened United Party lost ground to both the National Party and to the Progressive Party. The latter won a total of seven seats. The HNP once again failed to win any seats (see Table 6.1).

Table 6.1   General election results, 1970 and 1974[32]

Party	1970		1974	
	Seats	*% of vote*	*Seats*	*% of vote*
National Party	118	54.9	123	56.2
United Party	47	37.5	41	32.0
Progressive Party	1	3.5	7	6.4
Herstigte Nasionale Party	0	3.6	0	3.9
Others	0	0.6	0	1.5
Total	166		171	

African Nationalist Resurgence

However, of far greater moment than the electoral contests of 1970 and 1974 was a resurgence of African nationalism across the region of Southern Africa that took place between the two elections. It took different forms in different countries. There were two dimensions to the recovery of African nationalism in South Africa. One was ideological; the other industrial. Black Consciousness emerged as a strand of thinking among black (i.e. African, Coloured and Indian) activists in the late 1960s. Their slogan, 'Black man, you are on your own', accorded well with the government's desire to encourage separatism and its hostility towards the concept of a non-racial society. It also chimed in well with the government's hatred of white liberals, particularly the students at English-medium universities who had provided the main opposition to apartheid during the nadir of African nationalism in the 1960s. These factors persuaded the government to tolerate and even to encourage the Black Consciousness movement. This included permitting the distribution of Black Power publications from the United States from which many of the activists drew their inspiration. Unwittingly the government provided its African nationalist opponents with the space to reorganise. By the mid-1970s it regretted the fact and the Black Consciousness movement was repressed with much the same ferocity as the government had crushed the ANC and the PAC.

One of the central aims of the Black Consciousness movement and its leading theorist, Steve Biko, was to encourage a philosophy of self-help and self-assertion among South Africa's subordinate communities. How far the influence of the Black Consciousness movement actually extended beyond intellectuals and students remains a matter of debate. Nevertheless, the movement did coincide with growing self-confidence among black workers that was reflected in increasing militancy. In the first three months of 1973 there were 160 strikes involving over 61,000 black workers.[33] They were followed by a revival in the fortunes of African trade unions. The greater bargaining power of black workers reflected changes in the nature of the South African economy, particularly an increase in the employment of semi-skilled workers from the subordinate communities. The economic boom in the 1960s, which had been partially fuelled by the availability of cheap, unskilled labour, had generated a demand for more skilled workers that the white labour market had been unable to meet. The skills shortage resulted in the training of black workers that made employers reluctant to involve the police in breaking strikes, since police involvement brought with it the likelihood that any African strikers would be endorsed out of (i.e., expelled from) the urban area.

The end of African nationalist quiescence in Rhodesia occurred at a point when it appeared that the Smith regime had achieved total victory. The Conservative Party government elected in June 1970 was committed to making one last attempt to reach a negotiated settlement, but not to the indefinite maintenance of economic sanctions. It was a weak bargaining position, which was weakened still further by a vote of the United States Senate authorising the import of Rhodesian chrome contrary to the mandatory sanctions of the United Nations. It was therefore not surprising that the settlement Britain reached with Rhodesia in November 1971 made very substantial concessions to the Smith regime. However, before the settlement could take effect, it had to meet the test that the British government had previously laid down of being acceptable to the people of Rhodesia as a whole. A Commission under Lord Pearce was appointed to consult opinion. When the commissioners arrived in Rhodesia in January 1972 they were greeted with a chorus of 'noes'. Not merely did the strength of African opinion against the deal torpedo the settlement, it also made it impossible in the circumstances of such a clear demonstration of the illegitimacy of the Smith regime to lift sanctions. Further, the mobilisation of African opinion behind the 'no' campaign paved the way to more violent defiance of white rule reflected in the beginnings of sustained guerrilla warfare against the regime.

In the case of South West Africa, the nationalist upsurge took the form of a strike by Ovambo workers against the contract labour system. This was in December 1971 and followed the declaration by the International Court of Justice in an advisory opinion that South Africa's occupation of South West Africa was illegal. The strike was a prelude to further disturbances in Ovamboland, the most populous part of the territory. Three different African nationalist movements launched guerrilla warfare against Portuguese rule in Angola in the first half of the 1960s, while Frelimo (the Front for the Liberation of Mozambique) launched its campaign for the freedom of Mozambique in September 1964. To begin with, the guerrilla campaigns tended to be confined to relatively remote areas of the two colonies, but there was an increase in both the level of the violence and its scope in the early 1970s. The seriousness of the conflicts was underlined by the failure of major offensives by the Portuguese army to quell the rebellions.

While the upsurge of African nationalist militancy tended to undercut South Africa's outward-looking policy and to strengthen the position of African states espousing a strategy of liberation, it did not fundamentally alter Western expectations of South Africa's continuing political stability or of further growth in the South African economy. That justifies Barber and Barratt's characterisation of the decade between 1965 and 1974 as 'the years of confidence'.[34] Even in the economic realm, it is only with the benefit of hindsight that it can be argued that the close of the period actually marked the start of South Africa's economic decline after the boom of the 1960s. Not surprisingly in these circumstances, the government did not change course but proceeded apace with the implementation of Verwoerd's grand design. This entailed preparing the political development of the homelands in the direction of self-government and independence.

To this end, the Vorster government – often considered pragmatic in contrast to its predecessor – enacted two ideologically significant pieces of legislation, the Bantu Homelands Citizenship Act of 1970 and the Bantu Homelands Constitution Act of 1971. The former turned the entire African population into citizens of one or other of the homelands, regardless as to whether they had ever lived in the homeland in question. The latter empowered the government to confer self-government on the territorial authorities it had created. The two Acts raised the spectre that with the complete realisation of separate development, South Africa would literally have no African citizens. Even the partial implementation of the policy would mean that the right of millions of Africans to reside in South Africa's major urban centres would disappear. As Terreblanche puts it:

> As several Bantustans became self-governing, and after a while also supposedly 'independent', migrants from these areas who were illegally in 'white' urban areas were now regarded as 'foreigners'. As a result they could be deported, and these deportations were no longer subject to legal appeal. In this way even the limited legal

rights granted to African migrants under the pass laws were removed.[35]

At the time of the general election in 1974, little appeared to stand in the way of the further implementation of apartheid on these lines, despite increased instability on the country's borders.

7

From Vorster to Botha: New Departure or Militarised Cul de Sac?

On 25 April 1974, the day after South African whites voted in a general election, the outcome of which strengthened the Vorster government's hold on power, there was a leftwing military *coup d'état* in Portugal. It overthrew the country's long-standing dictatorship. The *coup* was a reflection of the strains placed on Portuguese society by the continuing wars in the country's African colonies. It had profound implications for the whole of Southern Africa. The abrupt change in Portugal meant that the transition to majority rule in the country's colonies would follow a revolutionary rather than an evolutionary path. In fact, the overthrow of Portugal's dictatorship reinforced the trends towards radicalism in the other countries in Southern Africa. Whereas the sources of the radicalism of the early 1970s had been primarily internal in each case, after the *coup* the interaction between events in the different countries became marked. There was a widening and intensification of the guerrilla war in Rhodesia as a result of Frelimo's coming to power in Mozambique. Demonstrations by supporters of Black Consciousness in 1974 in favour of Frelimo underlined the impact of the changes flowing from the Portuguese *coup* on black opinion in South Africa. But far more significant was the role that events in Angola, particularly the defeat of South African military intervention in the country's civil war, played in encouraging the Soweto uprising that began in June 1976.

The Soweto uprising marked a turning point in South Africa's political development on a par with the Sharpeville massacre. Nationwide unrest followed the brutal suppression of protests by schoolchildren protesting at government policy to impose Afrikaans as a medium of instruction in secondary schools in the Transvaal. One consequence of the uprising was to revive questions as to the durability of apartheid South Africa. A notable contribution to that debate was made by an Oxford academic, R.W. Johnson. His book, which was published in 1977, was entitled *How Long Will South Africa Survive?* The jacket explained the context in which the question had arisen:

> In 1976, as Portugal's African colonies fell to guerrilla fighters, South Africa's black townships exploded in demonstrations and rioting. Without its Northern buffers and torn by internal strife, it seemed that the last years of the Republic of South Africa had arrived.

But it immediately disabused the reader that the book's author was predicting the imminent collapse of the regime:

> This view is far too simple, as R.W. Johnson shows in this vivid and dramatic book. In spite of humanitarian posturing and resolution mongering in the United Nations, South Africa is too important to the West and has too many bargaining counters – gold, uranium, platinum and industrial investments – to be allowed to go the way of the Congo, Mozambique or Angola.[1]

Johnson's Prognosis

While the title of R.W. Johnson's book by no means had the same resonance as Andrei Amalrik's *Will the Soviet Union Survive until 1984?*, it had a considerable impact on the analysis of South African politics and was widely acclaimed. Some of the assumptions that underpinned the book seem contestable from the perspective of post-apartheid South Africa. Thus, it equated South Africa and its white establishment with apartheid, with the implication that majority rule would mean South Africa's becoming a very different country. In doing so, it basically excluded the possibility that South Africa might change through a process of evolution rather than revolution. In the context of the period it was an understandable assumption. Thus, while Vorster had introduced elements of greater flexibility into the implementation of apartheid, there was no indication that he had any intention of departing from the fundamentals of the blueprint that had been developed by Verwoerd. Against the possibility of an evolutionary outcome, Johnson argued:

> There is no precedent in history anywhere of an ethnic minority of over 4 million people voluntarily dismantling the dominance they enjoy over more than 20 million ethnically different others. Anything other than white supremacy *is*, in this sense, unthinkable.[2]

Further, in the case of the transition to majority rule of the other white regimes in Africa (including the outcome he expected in Rhodesia), 'none of them' he contended 'have [*sic*] managed this process peacefully'.[3]

While Johnson considered some of the proposals for reform that were being put forward by *verligtes*, he believed that white opinion was more likely to embrace the *verkramptes* and he presented the issue of the regime's survival in stark either/or terms:

> White South Africa now stands under heavy and increasing pressure. The entire structure of social and political power in South Africa is under stress, utterly taut. Cracks within it have clearly developed. These *may* be contained. If not, if they grow, if the whole structure is brought down, then the consequences are almost incalculable. To ponder the fall of South Africa's White Establishment is to think about the unthinkable. There are, simply, few larger questions one can ask than whether – or how long – White South Africa can survive.[4]

An innovative aspect of his analysis was his insistence that South Africa's future would be critically affected by the international environment. He underlined this point as follows:

> In most of the enormous literature on South Africa there is a strong tendency, in which left-wing radicals and Afrikaner Nationalists are at one, to depict South Africa's development as if it were dictated solely by the internal dynamics of her own history. This assumption is false at least for the whole period since white settlement in South Africa began in 1652.[5]

Further, in analysing the role of the international environment, Johnson by no means confined his analysis to the impact of events in the region. In particular, he ranged over the indirect effect on South Africa of such events as the Yom Kippur war in the Middle East, examining not just the political significance for the Republic of such developments but also their economic implications.

Johnson was acutely conscious of the numerous predictions of the imminent demise of the apartheid regime that had been made in the wake of the Sharpeville massacre. In fact, Chapter 1 of the book was entitled, 'The Sharpeville Crisis and the Defeat of Revolution'.[6] He was fully aware of the danger that history might repeat itself, given the regime's 'formidable resilience and strength'.[7] Indeed, on an analogy with the course of the Russian revolution, he argued that 'South Africa may well experience more "1905s" without a "1917" ever arriving'.[8] He was cautious in his assessment of the prospects and did not exclude the possibility that the government could weather the immediate storm.

> To put it bluntly: if the Pretoria regime adopts a sufficiently ruthless and brutal policy at home it may be able to repress black rebellion well into the twenty-first century; if it is willing to be sufficiently tough and flexible over Rhodesia and Namibia (allowing truly representative regimes to emerge there) *and* it is wise enough to keep its troops at home, its future would seem secure enough well into the 1990s.[9]

Nevertheless, the implication of his analysis was clearly that the regime faced a qualitatively more difficult situation than it did in the early 1960s, because of the combination of internal and external threats it faced. Johnson considered some of the structural factors that were undermining apartheid, including both demographic change and economic development.

However, central to the case that Johnson made that there were circumstances in which apartheid South Africa might not survive was a new version of an argument that Pierre van den Berghe had put forward in the mid-1960s. This was that change in South Africa would be in the West's own interests and that Western policy would increasingly reflect that reality.[10] Johnson treated as a precursor of Western policy towards apartheid the switch effected by Kissinger in American policy towards the Smith regime in 1976, in which

Kissinger had enlisted South Africa's aid in an attempt to end the Rhodesian conflict by forcing Smith to accept African majority rule. Kissinger's diplomacy ultimately failed because of President Ford's defeat in the American Presidential election of November 1976. Nevertheless, the fact that a right-of-centre Administration in the United States calculated that its best interests would be served by promoting rather than resisting change in Southern Africa was an indication of what might happen in future. In particular, if it appeared that stability could only be restored through ending white supremacy in South Africa, then it was evident that the demise of white rule would become the objective of Western policy-makers.

Added credibility had been given to this argument by Soviet intervention in Africa in the wake of Portugal's revolutionary *coup*. The Vorster government made a carefully calculated response to the change of regime in Lisbon. It immediately recognised the new government. In fact, South Africa was the first country in the world to do so. The Vorster government hoped to demonstrate to the West its capacity both to accommodate and to manage change in the region. On the basis that the economic dependence of Rhodesia and Mozambique would dictate how any government that emerged in the two countries would behave, it did not try to prevent the radical changes in prospect from occurring. In particular, it gave tacit approval to Portugal's decision to transfer power in Mozambique to Frelimo. It also enlisted the aid of the British and Zambian governments to promote a negotiated transition in Rhodesia in an initiative dubbed détente. The Vorster government adopted a more cautious approach to change in South West Africa or Namibia, as it was now widely known. The existing policy was one of separate development, which as in South Africa involved the setting up of ethnic homelands. Thus, in 1973 self-government was accorded to Ovamboland, a homeland for nearly half the population of the territory. However, the initiation of negotiations among the representatives of the different ethnic groups of the territory in September 1975 put paid to the notion that Namibia would ever be split into fully independent ethnic homelands.

Vorster's Strategy

The overall strategy of the Vorster government can be summarised as follows. It hoped to replace the unstable white-ruled buffer on

South Africa's borders with governments with sufficient internal legitimacy to generate international legitimacy, so that sanctions and other forms of pressure on these states would be removed. In the absence of a viable alternative this might entail accepting that a long-standing liberation movement, such as Frelimo, would come to power. In line with the thinking that Eschel Rhoodie had outlined in *The Third Africa*, it expected economic self-interest to determine their relations with South Africa. Further, by demonstrating that South Africa was able to play a constructive role in stabilising the region and thereby limiting opportunities for the growth of Soviet influence, the South African government aimed to secure a place for the Republic in America's global strategy in accordance with the Nixon doctrine. This placed emphasis on the role of regional powers as the linchpin of American foreign policy. The objective of foreign policy was not merely to reduce external pressures on South Africa, but also to make possible the continuing implementation of apartheid.

However, the approach taken by the government was open to criticism. In particular, the policy could be presented as one of sacrificing white minorities elsewhere in Africa in order to secure the position of whites in South Africa itself. Even more dangerous for the government was the implication that the changes it required of whites in other settler societies might set a precedent for the Republic's own transformation. These dangers were reflected in the manner in which the government conducted its strategy and presented its position. They also account for the existence of disagreements within the government on the approach to adopt in particular cases. For example, the government's acquiescence in Portugal's transfer of power to Frelimo in Mozambique, which it characterised as a policy of non-intervention, occasioned disagreement within the government.[11] However, Vorster's approach prevailed with the government thwarting attempts to organise opposition to Frelimo from South African territory. At the same time, the government took action to suppress black demonstrations in support of Frelimo.

Reasons for Breakdown

The strategy ran into difficulties for three main reasons. The first was that the government failed in its efforts to bring about a swift, negotiated end to the Rhodesian conflict. While the government was able to force the Smith regime to enter into negotiations on the future of Rhodesia, Smith proved adept at frustrating agreement. Under the rubric of a Southern African détente, the Zambian and South African governments worked in unison to bring Rhodesia's warring African nationalist factions together so as to lay the basis for a negotiated settlement. However, the Smith regime successfully directed its efforts at keeping them divided and even Kissinger's involvement in 1976 failed to deliver a settlement. In this context, the widening of the guerrilla war actually enhanced the regime's bargaining power in the short term, because of the pressure it put on those African nationalist factions without significant guerrilla support to reach an accommodation with the whites. The culmination of Smith's efforts was the signing of an internal settlement in March 1978. While the implementation of the settlement would spell the end of undiluted white rule, its achievement helped to lend credibility to the regime's portrayal of the guerrilla war as primarily entailing a battle between East and West rather than a racial conflict. The result was that much of conservative opinion in Britain and the United States urged support for the internal settlement.

The second was South Africa's disastrous intervention in Angola in late 1975 and early 1976. Unlike other countries in the region, Angola was not economically dependent on South Africa. At the same time, the country was strategically important to South Africa because of its long border with South West Africa. Consequently, the South African government had a considerable stake in what sort of government emerged in Angola and what its attitude would be to the Republic. African nationalist divisions in Angola gave the South African government the opportunity to influence the outcome of the power struggle among the different contending parties. In addition, as the South African government later revealed, there was covert support for South African intervention from the Ford Administration, which was hampered in its own efforts to support particular Angolan factions by Congressional opposition to American involvement in the conflict.[12] The two governments' calculation was that South African military intervention would result in the quick defeat of the MPLA (Popular Movement for the Liberation of Angola). This did not happen because of large-scale Cuban support for the MPLA, as well as assistance from the Soviet Union. Ironically, the very fact of South Africa's own military intervention helped to legitimise Soviet intervention among African states.

The third reason why the strategy ran into difficulties was the election of Jimmy Carter as President of the United States in November 1976. At the outset, the Carter Administration took the view that it was in America's interests to give its backing to mainstream African opinion in the non-aligned bloc as the best way to secure a reduction in foreign military intervention in the continent's conflicts. An implication of this approach was that America would also align itself with the non-aligned bloc's commitment to the liberation of Southern Africa from minority and colonial rule. This included the liquidation of apartheid. Consequently, the South African government no longer had an interest in working with the United States for a settlement in Rhodesia. Indeed, a primary objective of South African policy was to secure a reversal in the Carter Administration's stance. That also meant seeking to demonstrate the viability of alternatives to supporting radical African nationalism. The government found the means to further both objectives by supporting internal settlements in Namibia and Zimbabwe-Rhodesia. However, this represented a far-reaching change in South Africa's approach to African affairs so it was not surprising that it came about in the context of a change in South Africa's political leadership.

Elections

After the 1974 general election the Vorster government pressed ahead with the implementation of separate development. Full independence was extended to the Transkei in October 1976 and to Bophuthatswana in December 1977. Bophuthatswana consisted of several land-locked pieces of territory and had no history as a political entity prior to apartheid. Consequently, it was even less credible than the Transkei as an independent state. In any event, neither achieved any measure of international recognition and both homelands were treated by the outside world as if they remained integral parts of the Republic of South Africa. The unwillingness of the international community to treat Transkei and Bophuthatswana as legitimate entities comparable to other former colonies added to the catalogue of difficulties the government faced. The boom years were over. The economy had been hit hard by the quadrupling of oil prices and the reaction of international investors to the Soweto uprising made matters worse.

Characteristically the government responded to a widespread sense that the country was in crisis by adopting repressive measures to reassert its control. In September 1977 the Black Consciousness leader, Steve Biko, died in police custody. The following month the government banned a very wide range of organisations it associated with the Black Consciousness movement. Hostile international reaction to these developments was not confined to the media. The existence of liberal and left-of-centre governments opened the way for the United Nations Security Council to adopt a mandatory ban on the sale of arms to South Africa. This was in November 1977. While the ban had the perverse effect of facilitating the development of a major arms industry in South Africa, it raised the spectre that at some future date the international community might impose mandatory economic sanctions on South Africa.

In September Vorster had announced that there would be a general election at the end of November, eighteen months ahead of schedule. The election had three main objectives. First, it was intended to demonstrate the strength of support for the government within the white community to the outside world, so as to encourage opposition in the West to the strong stand against apartheid that had been taken by President Carter. Secondly, it was timed to take advantage of the disarray of the opposition parties. The United Party had begun to disintegrate shortly after the 1974 general election. Defections in 1974–5 had lead to the transformation of the Progressive Party into the Progressive Reform Party. With further additions it had been transformed into the Progressive Federal Party (PFP) in September 1977. The United Party dissolved into two more conservative parties, the New Republic Party and the South African Party. At the time of the dissolution of the House of Assembly, the New Republic Party was the largest of the opposition parties, though with only 23 seats. Thirdly, the election provided the government with an opportunity to gauge reaction to the plans for constitutional reform being discussed within the National Party.

The outcome of the general election was a massive victory for the National Party. It won over 80 per cent of the seats in the House of Assembly, the highest proportion of seats ever won by a single party (see Table 7.1). The PFP came a very distant second, replacing the New Republic Party as the Official Opposition. However, the scale of its electoral landslide did little to reinvigorate the government. Thus, Dan O'Meara maintains:

Table 7.1   General election results, 1977 and 1981[13]

Party	Seats in 1977	Seats in 1981
National Party	134	131
Progressive Federal Party	17	26
New Republic Party	10	8
South African Party*	3	-
Herstigte Nasionale Party	0	0
Total	**164**	**165**

Note: * The party merged with the National Party and did not contest the 1981 election.

By the end of 1977, virtually all commentators were agreed that on the burning issues of economic, social and political policy, behind the overt face of hardline control and repression, the government was virtually rudderless.[14]

Less than a year after the election, Vorster retired as Prime Minister, officially on grounds of ill-health. However, a major precipitating factor in his fall from power had been a scandal over the misappropriation of funds in connection with the government's efforts to buy influence abroad. What was known as the info scandal or Muldergate not only put an end to Vorster's long premiership, but also helped to shape the battle for the succession. In particular, it broke the Transvaal's hold on the leadership, enabling the leader of the party in the Cape, P.W. Botha, to secure election as party leader and hence Vorster's successor as Prime Minister.

Fresh Face

Botha's leadership of the party was to last nearly as long as that of Vorster. He became leader in September 1978 and resigned from the leadership on grounds of ill-health in February 1989. However, he clung on to the post of State President, which had become an executive and not just a ceremonial position until August 1989. By this point, as in the case of his predecessor, his continuing in power had come to be seen as an obstacle to political progress. Initially, however, Botha's rise to power did appear to lift the government out of the *impasse* of the mid-1970s. Thus, Barber and Barratt head their chapter on the succession as 'The Advent of P.W. Botha and the Return of Confidence'.[15] The reformulation of racial policy under Botha, the rightwing tide in the West and the credibility of the internal settlements that emerged in Namibia and Zimbabwe-Rhodesia changed opinions on the prospects for the survival of white rule in South Africa. In particular, the election of Thatcher in Britain and of Reagan in the United States removed any likelihood of further measures being taken against the Republic through the United Nations Security Council. The changes in South Africa's external environment influenced views on the durability of the South African system in the literature of the time.

An example was the publication in 1981 of a book by two conservative American-based Africanists, Gann and Duignan, entitled *Why South Africa Will Survive*.[16] Botha's emphasis on military strength was clearly reflected in their analysis:

> In military terms, South Africa is well equipped. It is a match for any conventional opponent except a superpower. South Africa is equally prepared to deal with guerrilla incursions. It is true that Portugal, after a ten-year conflict, was forced to shed its colonial empire after the military revolted. It is equally true that Rhodesia, after 14 years of UDI, was forced to negotiate for a black majority government. But South Africa's position is different in both a qualitative and a quantitative sense.[17]

Gann and Duignan acknowledged that 'South Africa, like Israel, will certainly face long-drawn-out partisan operations'.[18] However, they contended that South Africa, like Israel, would be able to contain their impact and that as 'the military and industrial giant of the African continent', the South African economy 'should therefore be capable of coping with the military expenditure that the country must now shoulder'.[19]

However, the analysis put forward by Gann and Duignan was by no means widely accepted and the authors themselves acknowledged that their views ran counter to 'the orthodoxy of the lectern and the pulpit'.[20] In fact, rather more influential than their book was another study of the Republic that was published in 1981. Its title with a quite different resonance was *South Africa: Time Running Out*.[21] It contained the findings of a study commission into American policy towards Southern Africa. The commission chaired by the President of the Ford Foundation, Franklin A.Thomas, and funded by the Rockefeller Foundation, had been formed in 1979. Conscious that 'over the decades, South Africa has confounded students of its affairs',[22] the authors of the study attached no timetable to the alternative scenarios of the country's future they presented, which were based on whether reformist trends prevailed over regressive ones or vice versa. Their reformist scenario envisaged the eventual installation of a multiracial government but not majority rule:

> Any analysis of South Africa must begin with a fundamental reality: Both blacks and whites hold certain positions to be nonnegotiable. For blacks, an acceptable solution must give them a share in genuine political power. For whites, that solution cannot be based on a winner-take-all form of majority rule. This is the core of the problem. Short of an outcome involving sustained and large-scale violence, any solution to the South African problem must incorporate these two positions. Whether such a solution can be achieved with a minimum of violence is an open question.[23]

It is worth emphasising that a number of the elements of policy associated with the Botha era had already been mooted or set in train in the last years of Vorster's premiership. Thus, the main outlines of what Giliomee and Schlemmer later dubbed 'reform apartheid', including proposals for the political co-option of the Coloured and Indian communities, were apparent well before Vorster stepped down. The concept of the 'total strategy' was laid out in a Defence *White Paper* in 1977. The appointment of two Commissions of Inquiry into labour issues, the Wiehahn Commission and the Riekert Commission, also took place in 1977. Conversely, some aspects of policy associated with the Vorster era continued under Botha. Two further homelands achieved independence, Venda in 1979 and Ciskei in December 1981. Botha also pursued the notion of a Southern African common market, an idea that went back to Verwoerd.

Destabilisation

Nonetheless, the broad thrust of Botha's approach to policy was quite different from that taken by Vorster. Whereas Vorster had sought to secure acceptance in the West for apartheid by demonstrating that the South African system could accommodate to decolonisation on its borders, Botha adopted a much more belligerent policy towards South Africa's neighbours. Botha sought to influence Western opinion towards South Africa directly through domestic reform. He posed as an ally of the West who shared its aim of reducing Soviet influence in Africa. He sought to further this objective through the destabilisation of Soviet-backed governments and by aiding guerrilla movements that were trying to overthrow Marxist regimes. This agenda had considerable appeal to conservative and rightwing forces in the West.

However, Western liberals were appalled by the human costs of the policy of destabilisation. A series of books appeared through the 1980s that detailed the misery caused by South Africa's export of violence, which displaced the struggle over the country's racial policy onto neighbouring states. They included the following titles: *South Africa at War, Apartheid's Second Front, Beggar your Neighbours* and *Apartheid Terrorism*.[24] Further books on, or dealing with, the same theme appeared in the 1990s including *Exporting Apartheid, Apartheid's Last Stand* and *Apartheid's Contras*.[25] The earliest of these studies was Leonard's *South Africa at War*. It contained an analysis of the intellectual origins of the total strategy in the writings of a French general, André Beaufré. However, the most significant contribution of Leonard's book was its assessment of the Reagan Administration's policy towards South Africa. His analysis was buttressed by leaked documents from the State Department enunciating the Administration's intention to establish a close working relationship with South Africa based on strategic calculations. This was the policy of 'constructive engagement'[26] developed by the Assistant Secretary of State for African Affairs, Chester Crocker.

In a memorandum in May 1981 Crocker set out a number of talking points for a meeting that was to take place between the Secretary of State and the South African foreign minister. They included:

- We want to open a new chapter in relations with South Africa.
- We feel the new relationship should be based upon our shared hopes for the future prosperity, security and stability of Southern Africa and our shared perception of the role of the Soviet Union and its surrogates in thwarting those goals.

- We can foresee co-operating with you in a number of ways in our efforts to re-establish regional stability.
- US-South African co-operation is indispensable for the success of those efforts. Failure to co-operate will encourage further Soviet gains and jeopardize the interests of both our countries.
- We will not allow others to dictate what our relationship with South Africa will be as evidenced by our recent veto of sanctions. But just as we recognize your permanent stake in the future of Southern Africa, so you must recognize our permanent interest in Africa as a whole.[27]

Even for its time and allowing for Crocker's desire to curry favour with his South African visitors, his lack of a realistic appreciation of the sources of political instability in the region is striking. What the new relationship meant in practice was that during the early 1980s there was virtually an American *carte blanche* for the South African government to lay its neighbours to waste.

The results were succinctly summarised by Joseph Hanlon on the opening page of his 1986 book, *Beggar Your Neighbours*:

Since 1980, in the eight majority ruled states of the region, South Africa has:

- invaded three capitals (Lesotho, Botswana, Mozambique) and four other countries (Angola, Swaziland, Zimbabwe, and Zambia);
- tried to assassinate two prime ministers (Lesotho and Zimbabwe);
- backed dissident groups that have brought chaos to two countries (Angola and Mozambique) and less serious disorder in two others (Lesotho and Zimbabwe);
- disrupted the oil supplies of six countries (Angola, Botswana, Lesotho, Malawi, Mozambique, and Zimbabwe); and
- attacked the railways providing the normal import and export routes of seven countries (Angola, Botswana, Malawi, Mozambique, Swaziland, Zambia, Zimbabwe).[28]

Hanlon argued that the deaths of more than 100,000 people and the displacement of a million people could be attributed to South Africa's policy. Further he contended: 'Over the five-year period 1980 to 1984 South Africa cost the region $10,000 million – more than all the foreign aid these states received in the same period.'[29]

Constitutional Reform

The other side of the coin of the external policy of destabilisation was internal reform. This had two principal dimensions, constitutional change and the significant modification of the country's labour laws and policies. Both had a long genesis and grew out of initiatives taken during Vorster's premiership. In March 1973 a commission had been established to examine the position of the Coloured community. The report of the Theron Commission in June 1976 recommended that 'provision should be made for satisfactory forms of direct Coloured representation and decision-making at the various levels of authority and of government'.[30] The response of the government was to set up a cabinet committee to come up with proposals for the incorporation of the Coloured and Indian communities into the political system. Its proposals were presented to the parliamentary caucus of the National Party in August 1977 and reported in the press. The nub of the proposals was the establishment of a tricameral parliament with separate chambers representing whites, Coloureds and Indians. The committee also recommended the creation of an executive presidency and a council that would contain representatives of the three chambers and deal with matters of mutual concern.

In broad outline there was little or no difference between these proposals and the constitutional reforms ultimately enacted in the Republic of South Africa Constitution Act of 1983. However, the emphasis the Botha government placed on power-sharing in its attempts to win international legitimacy for its reforms provoked fierce controversy within the National Party. This led to defections from the parliamentary party and the formation of a new rightwing party, the Conservative Party in 1982. A general election had taken place in April 1981. The main change was a modest increase in the representation of the PFP at the expense of other parties (see Table 7.1). The HNP once again failed to win a single seat. However, the party's share of vote had more than quadrupled, indicating the electoral potential of parties of the extreme right if the government pressed ahead with reform. The 1983 Act set up a tricameral parliament with each chamber serviced by its own ministerial council and having jurisdiction over its respective community's 'own affairs'. Provision was made for disputes among the chambers in relation to 'general affairs' to be referred to the President's Council.

This body represented the chambers on the racially proportional basis of 4 : 2 : 1.

The new constitution provided for the election of the State President, who was to be both head of state and head of the government. The State President was to be elected by an electoral college consisting of 50 members of the white House of Assembly, 25 members of the Coloured House of Representatives and 13 members of the Indian House of Delegates. However, of vital importance was the fact that the members of the electoral college would be elected by simple majority so enabling the majority party in each chamber to monopolise representation. In short, the constitution meant not merely that whites would be the majority in both the President's Council and the electoral college, but that the National Party would have a majority in both as long as it secured a majority of the seats in the House of Assembly. Rightwing opposition to the constitution focused on what were in reality weak elements of power-sharing with the Coloured and Indian communities. Liberal opposition focused by contrast on the exclusion of Africans from the system. Despite the opposition, the proposals were endorsed by a large majority of white voters in a referendum in November 1983.

Opposition

Elections to the Coloured House of Representatives and the Indian House of Delegates took place in August 1984 and the new constitution formally came into effect in September 1984. The elections were a major test of the new constitution's legitimacy both internally and externally, which it spectacularly failed thanks to boycotts of the elections organised by the United Democratic Front (UDF). The UDF forged out of a wide-ranging alliance of community-based organisations had been founded in August 1983. In order to give the new system credibility, the government had been obliged to permit a larger measure of free political expression among the subordinate communities. In the same way, Ian Smith had been obliged to allow greater scope for the expression of different viewpoints during the test of the acceptability of the 1971 proposals for a Rhodesian settlement. The results were similar: the subordinate communities took advantage of their newly found freedom to reject any entrenchment of white supremacy.

Worse for the Botha government followed. The elevation of the status of the Coloured and Indian communities under the new constitution intensified the impact of the continuing denial of political rights to the African population outside the homeland system. It was resented particularly strongly by the urban African population whose grievances the government had begun to address in the wake of the Soweto uprising. However, the creation of elected local authorities had done little to assuage their resentment. Indeed, the resentment had turned to anger when the local authorities, which had been elected on minuscule turn-outs, introduced large increases in rent and service charges. The consequence was serious unrest in the townships that coincided with the introduction of the new constitution. The government's use of the army to quell unrest contributed to a sharp deterioration in South Africa's relations with the rest of the world, but particularly with the major Western powers. Ironically just a few months before his inauguration as State President, Botha had been well received by a number of governments during a very successful tour of Europe that appeared at the time to herald a substantial easing of the Republic's isolation.

Labour Reform

The other dimension of reform took the form of changes to the country's labour laws and to the system of influx control. In 1979 the Wiehahn Commission issued the first of a series of reports recommending changes to the country's labour laws, while the Riekert Commission reported separately on legislation relating to the utilisation of manpower. The reports were broadly reflective of the shift in the attitudes of the white establishment in the wake of the Soweto uprising and represented a further break with the assumptions that had underpinned Verwoerd's conception of apartheid. As O'Meara puts it:

> Verwoerdian apartheid had cast all blacks into the same ethnic boat and suppressed the mechanism of social differentiation and mobility 'normal' to capitalist society. Under pressure from the Urban Foundation and other business groups, the Botha government now relaxed *some* of the restrictions on the black middle class, allowing it a measure of social mobility.[31]

At the time, the *Survey of Race Relations in South Africa 1979* characterised the change as follows:

> A marked feature of the Government's policy this year was its concern to promote the creation of stable urban African communities. The concern no doubt resulted in part from the 1976 riots, and of an awareness of the possible social and political instability to which growing unemployment in urban areas could lead.
>
> This feature of its policy is evidenced ... in its acceptance in the main of the Riekert Commission's recommendations which were designed to accord a better deal to urban Africans ... The Riekert Commission's view was that the development of a stable urban African community was dependent on giving urban Africans preference over migrant workers in regard to existing facilities.[32]

In general, the position of 'Section 10' Africans who qualified to stay in the urban areas without labour bureau permission was strengthened by the report. This included 'Section 10' Africans who had become foreigners as a consequence of the independence of the Transkei and Bophuthatswana. However, the threat to their children's position was not removed.

The main recommendation of the first of the reports of the Wiehahn Commission was that African trade unions should be accorded legal recognition. In response to its recommendations the government amended the Industrial Conciliation Act, ending the notorious exclusion of Africans from the definition of an 'employee' under the Act, though the change initially did not apply to migrant workers. The Wiehahn Commission also recommended – and the government accepted – that job reservation should be phased out. The principle that underpinned the government's approach to reform in these areas was that 'unnecessary' racial discrimination which damaged South Africa's reputation in the West should be removed. Further reports of the Wiehahn Commission were published in 1980 and 1981. The Commission recommended aligning the law with international labour conventions. It also recommended the ending of one of the longest-standing forms of discrimination in the mining industry, the denial of blasting certificates to African workers, which prevented them from undertaking skilled work. However, the objections of the white trade union persuaded the government not to act on this recommendation at this juncture.

Capitalism and Apartheid

The state of the economy in the late 1970s and early 1980s provided further impetus to the process of reform. The South African economy was adversely affected by the oil crises of the 1970s and the limitations of an economy reliant on the export of primary products and in which the growth of manufacturing had come about through import substitution were exposed. The booming economy of the 1960s had given way to a situation in which the annual percentage rate of economic growth was generally failing to match the annual percentage rate in the growth of the country's population. The country's relative economic stagnation led to increasing dissatisfaction with apartheid, particularly in the wake of the Soweto uprising. This was despite greater flexibility in the implementation of the policy under Vorster. In 1985 a major study of South Africa's political economy, *Capitalism and Apartheid*, was published. A paperback edition of the book with the addition of an epilogue on the crisis of the mid-1980s came out in 1986.[33]

Merle Lipton systematically analysed the interests of agricultural capital, mining capital, manufacturing capital and white labour and demonstrated how the changing interests of capital in particular were providing a driving force behind reform of the system. She outlined the changes to apartheid that had occurred after 1970 in a chapter entitled 'The Partial Erosion of Apartheid, 1970–1984'.[34] From the perspective of the changes that were to occur over the next decade, in part as a consequence of the erosion of apartheid she described, her assessment appears cautious. She concluded:

> While the reforms have made significant inroads into apartheid, and created hopes and possibilities that seemed inconceivable fifteen years ago, SA remains a racially-ordered society, especially in those areas perceived as affecting white security – population distribution, mobility, political rights.[35]

Lipton argued that apartheid had been rooted in the political dominance of white agriculture and white labour until the mid-1960s but that thereafter there had been growing conflict within the Afrikaner alliance, with Botha's election as Prime Minister in 1978 marking a further shift towards capital.

The argument that apartheid and capitalism were in conflict was not new. Indeed, it had been advanced by a number of economists in the 1950s and the failure of their predictions in the 1960s had helped to inspire what had initially been a revisionist thesis, that capitalism had thrived on the cheap labour that apartheid had provided. A third position was that capitalists adapted to political circumstances and made the best of what was laid down by government. What Lipton demonstrated was that only certain sectors of the economy benefited from the cheap, unskilled labour of migrant workers. Further, she showed that even in such sectors as agriculture and mining, changes were occurring as a result of, for example, mechanisation that were increasing the interest of employers in securing both a more settled and a more skilled labour force.

The weakening of the South African government's position had begun as a result of changes in the region of Southern Africa that had been magnified by a leftwing military coup in Portugal. That had stirred revolt within South Africa as a result of which substantial reform of the system of apartheid was undertaken within the overall framework of maintaining white supremacy. However, reform did not stabilise the situation. On the contrary, the changes the government introduced had the effect of strengthening the opponents of white minority rule, as became clear during the crisis of the mid-1980s. That crisis is addressed next, as well as how external events beyond the African continent impinged on the country so as to provide a new leader of the National Party with what he hoped would provide a path out of the *impasse* the government had found itself in.

8

The Pursuit of a Negotiated Settlement: Choice or Necessity?

The crisis of white rule in South Africa in the mid-1980s was multi-dimensional. It began with the boycott in August 1984 of the elections to their chambers in the tricameral parliament by Coloured and Indian voters. This dealt a near-fatal blow to the country's new constitution even before it had formally come into force. This was followed by a revolt in the townships in the Vaal Triangle in September 1984. The South African Institute of Race Relations (SAIRR) estimated that 175 people were killed in unrest-related incidents in 1984, 149 of them between 3 September, when the revolt in the Vaal Triangle had begun, and the end of the year.[1] The use of troops to quell the unrest politicised the trade unions, leading to a major stay-away from work on 5 and 6 November, 'the largest political stay-away on record'.[2] There was also a strong international reaction to the violence in the townships. In particular, the November stay-away, which coincided with President Reagan's re-election for another four-year term, prompted a wave of protests against apartheid in the United States. Demonstrations coordinated by Transafrica focused on the South African embassy in Washington attracting extensive media coverage.

The violence in the townships and the international protests against the South African government continued in 1985. On the 25th anniversary of the Sharpeville massacre, the security forces shot dead 20 people going to a funeral in Uitenhage in the Eastern Cape.

Funerals had become the occasion for protest and confusion over the prohibition of the holding of the funeral on the anniversary of Sharpeville was a factor in the confrontation between mourners and the police. In the course of the year as a whole, 859 people died in political violence according to the SAIRR, just over half of whom were killed by actions of the security forces.[3] On 20 July the government declared a state of emergency in 36 magisterial districts. The violence and repression continued to fuel international protests against white rule. The pressures on Reagan were such that he introduced limited sanctions against South Africa in an attempt to pre-empt Congress from adopting far more stringent measures. To the alarm of both the South African government and conservative governments in the West espousing the policy of constructive engagement with South Africa, the disorder completely overshadowed further efforts by Botha to reform the system. In particular, the repeal of the legislation that made sexual relations across the colour line a criminal offence, the removal of the prohibition on mixed marriages, and the ending of the bar on mixed political parties had little impact on international opinion. However, the issue of mixed marriages was sufficiently potent to secure the HNP its first parliamentary seat in a by-election.

Wrong Message

An attempt was made by the South African government and its Western allies to highlight the government's reform programme by arranging for unprecedented, international live television coverage of the address Botha was due to give to the Natal Congress of the National Party on 15 August 1985. This was a relatively early example of the use of a technique for the manipulation of public opinion that has become commonplace in many Western societies. On this occasion, however, the choreography went spectacularly wrong. In particular, advance publicity for a speech billed as representing a crossing of the Rubicon in South Africa's affairs put Botha's back up. According to F.W. de Klerk:

> The speculation infuriated President Botha, who called us together and told us he was not going to use the suggestions for the speech in the form and formulation in which they had been submitted to him. He rewrote the speech himself and, in so doing,

completely failed to capture the spirit of fundamental reform which had characterized the recommendations that had been submitted to him.[4]

Botha's strong expressions of resentment at the external pressure being placed on the government dominated coverage of the speech. By contrast, his briefly stated acknowledgement that the remaining homelands could not be forced to accept independence and that a large segment of the African population would therefore have to be accommodated politically within South Africa as South African citizens made little impact. It can be argued that its significance was underplayed as it represented the final, irreversible abandonment of Verwoerd's grand design. However, since the outside world had long ceased to set any store by this blueprint and such a step had in any event been foreshadowed in previous speeches from the government, reaction was muted. With good reason, De Klerk calls the speech 'probably the greatest communication disaster in South African history'.[5]

Far from restoring confidence in the South African government, the speech undermined it with almost immediate financial consequences, as the SAIRR's annual survey recorded:

> The sharp decline of confidence in South Africa led to a dramatic decline in the foreign-exchange value of the rand. On 28 August it plunged to 34 American cents – the lowest point ever reached – leading to a summary suspension of trading on the Johannesburg Stock Exchange (JSE) for three days from 28 August as a prelude to the introduction of restrictions on outward capital movements. The last time the JSE had been summarily closed was in the early 1960s after the Sharpeville political crisis.[6]

Events in 1986 followed a similar pattern. The government lifted its partial state of emergency in March. However, tensions grew following the collapse of the Commonwealth Eminent Persons Group mission to South Africa after South African military attacks on Botswana, Zambia and Zimbabwe in May and ahead of a planned stay-away the government imposed a nationwide state of emergency in June. According to the SAIRR, 1,298 people died in political violence during the course of 1986.[7] With an increase in conflict between rival political organisations, particularly in African townships, the proportion killed by the security forces fell to approximately a third of the total. Once again the violence and the government's measures to quell it dominated international reaction to events in South Africa, overshadowing further reforms, including the abolition of influx control. Overriding President Reagan's veto, the American Congress passed public law 99–440, the Comprehensive Anti-Apartheid Act, in October 1986.

The Act imposed a very wide range of sanctions, including the cutting of direct air links, on South Africa, but it also provided for the suspension of these sanctions in the event of specified progress towards the establishment of a non-racial democracy through the ending of racial discrimination. It listed six measures it encouraged the South African government to undertake:

(1) repeal the present state of emergency and respect the principle of equal justice under the law for citizens of all races;
(2) release Nelson Mandela, Govan Mbeki, Walter Sisulu, black trade union leaders, and all political prisoners;
(3) permit the free exercise by South Africans of all races of the right to form political parties, express political opinions, and otherwise participate in the political process;
(4) establish a timetable for the elimination of apartheid laws;
(5) negotiate with representatives of all racial groups in South Africa the future political system in South Africa; and
(6) end military and paramilitary activities aimed at neighboring states.[8]

In the light of American policy earlier in the decade, the last of these was somewhat ironic. It reflected not merely differences in attitude between members of Congress and the Reagan Administration, but also the change that had taken place in Soviet–American relations since Mikhail Gorbachev had become General Secretary and effective leader of the Soviet Union in March 1985.

New Books

The dramatic developments of the mid-1980s prompted a raft of new books on South Africa. Unsurprisingly, the word 'crisis' featured in the title of many of them. Among books published in 1986 and 1987 were *Apartheid in Crisis, South Africa in Crisis, The Crisis in South Africa* and *Endgame in South Africa?*[9] O'Meara argues that the existence of a crisis does not *per se* spell the demise of an existing political order, noting that 'in the real world crises can and do persist for long periods without producing change'. And, in fact, the crisis in South Africa in the mid-1980s did not prompt analysts to predict a rapid or easy transition to a new dispensation. Robin Cohen expressed the conviction that white minority rule could not survive and that there would be black majority rule, 'though after a period of prolonged and continuing political unrest and instability'.[10] However, he was less certain that this would signify apartheid's total demise.

> The achievement of state power does not, however, dislodge imbedded social structures, or alter the economic 'facts of life'. In tropical Africa, decolonisation signalled the formal end of empire; it did not prefigure substantive independence. Likewise, in South Africa, the achievement of black majority rule will not signify the end of apartheid, but its legal and formal abolition.[11]

Other analysts were less willing to make a firm prediction of the end to white minority rule. The fact that the regime had survived the previous crises associated with the Sharpeville massacre and the Soweto uprising induced a measure of caution. Mark Uhlig referred to this history in his introduction to *Apartheid in Crisis*:

> It is tempting to predict, on the basis of this record, that current and future crises will follow the same pattern – that white rule is resilient enough to withstand still further shocks and emerge stronger as a result. Yet such a view underestimates the important changes that have occurred beneath the surface of racial relationships in South Africa. It ignores the facts that the black opponents of the regime have also learned from the past and grown stronger, and that every successful effort to frustrate black political demands has fueled a new round of anger and confrontation.[12]

But Uhlig went on to argue, 'There can be no doubt that the obstacles to any change in South Africa's political structure remain formidable and have in many ways been strengthened over time.'[13]

Similarly, Jesmond Blumenfeld summarised the message of *South Africa in Crisis* as follows:

The chapters in this volume make it plain, however, that to conclude – as many people both within South Africa and outside it did
conclude, especially at the height of the crisis in 1985–86 – that
black rule is 'around the corner', is to misunderstand the nature of
South African society and of the forces operative within it.[14]

Blumenfeld used the term *'impasse'* to characterise the situation in
South Africa. This is also the term employed by John Brewer in
concluding an edited collection with the title, *Can South Africa
Survive?*, which was published in 1989. But, like Cohen, he was clear
on the general direction in which South Africa was headed:

> This is not to say that in the short term South Africa will become
> more unstable than at present – stalemates can persevere for a
> long time. But the current impasse reflects a shift in the balance
> of forces in favour of black South Africans, and the scales will
> continue to tip, if crescively [i.e. gradually], in their direction.[15]

In a book published in 1990, but the product of a conference in
September 1989, Bernard Crick described the problems of South
Africa, Northern Ireland and Israel-Palestine as 'insoluble'. He did
so primarily on the grounds that 'no internal solution likely to guar-
antee peace can possibly satisfy the announced principles of the
main disputants'.[16]

By the late 1980s there was at least in the South African case little
dispute among analysts as to which were the main disputants. By this
time, the ANC was widely seen as having established its indispensability
to the creation of a legitimate and stable order in South Africa. At the
same time, nobody expected the collapse of the National Party government or regarded the state as vulnerable to overthrow in military
terms. Logic pointed in the circumstances for the necessity of there
being negotiations between the government and the ANC. However,
the obvious difficulty was the gulf in their minimum requirements of any
settlement. Mandela provided a lucid statement of their differences
at the end of a memorandum he sent to P.W. Botha in March 1989:

> Two political issues will have to be addressed: firstly, the demand
> for majority rule in a unitary state; secondly, the concern of white
> South Africa over this demand, as well as the insistence of whites
> on structural guarantees that majority rule will not mean domin-
> ation of the white minority by blacks. The most crucial tasks which

will face the government and the ANC will be to reconcile these two positions.[17]

But the government's initial response to the events of 1985–86 had not been to seek to initiate negotiations with the ANC. Rather it sought to rally white support for its resistance to external pressures, but within the context of a continuing commitment to domestic reform. Botha dissolved the House of Assembly to provide a test of white opinion. He was not obliged to do so. In terms of the new constitution, the life of the House of Assembly had been extended, with the next general election of all three chambers being due to take place in 1989. More specifically:

> the State President justified the calling of an election by stating that he wanted a mandate from the white electorate to proceed with negotiations with blacks – in order to incorporate the latter in the political dispensation in one way or another.[18]

However, the agenda of reform tended to play a less prominent role in the campaign than did the issue of security. In particular, the government portrayed the PFP as ready to treat with the ANC, which the National Party depicted as both a Communist and a terrorist organisation.[19] The tactic was successful and the PFP suffered a sharp reverse in both votes and seats (see Table 8.1). However, the

Table 8.1   General election results, 1987 and 1989[20]

Party	1987		1989	
	No. of seats	*% of vote*	*No. of seats*	*% of vote*
National Party	123	52.5	94*	48.0
Conservative Party	22	26.4	39	31.2
Progressive Federal Party	19	14.0	–	–
Democratic Party	–	–	33	20.4
New Republic Party	1	2.0	–	–
Herstigte Nasionale Party	0	3.1	0	0.2
Independent	1	1.3	–	–
Total	166		166	

Note: * Including one seat originally tied.

gains the National Party secured among English-speaking voters were offset by its losses among Afrikaners to two extreme rightwing parties, the Conservative Party and the HNP. Between them the two parties won just under 30 per cent of the total vote. The Conservative Party was much the more successful of the two, winning 26.4 per cent of the vote and 22 seats to the *HNP*'s 3.1 per cent and no seats. In the process the Conservative Party overtook the PFP in seats and became the official Opposition in the House of Assembly.

Impasse

After the election the government continued to excoriate critics who advocated and indeed practised dialogue with the ANC, such as the Afrikaner intellectuals who travelled to Dakar in Senegal to meet with leading figures in the ANC in exile. The state of emergency was renewed in June 1987, while in February 1988 the government placed a ban on the political activities of the UDF, COSATU (Congress of South African Trade Unions) and 16 other organisations. By this time power was concentrated in the State Security Council, which oversaw the National Security Management System and Joint Management Centres the government had set up. However, apart from repression, the Botha government had run out of ideas to find a way out of the country's political *impasse*. Just as Vorster's electoral triumph in 1977 had failed to reinvigorate his government, so the landslide in seats won by Botha in 1987 did little to solve South Africa's political problems. In particular, the government was unable to secure significant support for its concept of a national council among African political leaders inside the country. This constituted the government's interim solution to the issue of African representation, but without the willingness of credible political figures to participate, the idea made little headway.

O'Meara provides a graphic picture of the Botha government's immobility in this period:

P.W. Botha and his generals appeared to wield absolute power after the 1986 Emergency. Nobody in the NP or government seemed prepared to risk Botha's ire by questioning this strategy, let alone fight for alternatives. Clearly ageing, and probably ill,

Botha became, if possible, even more imperious, but also ever more dependent on his generals. Having thrown his weight behind the securocrats, he appeared to close his mind to alternative advice. His usually petty, often brutal and always demeaning treatment of those in his caucus and Cabinet who did not immediately bend to his wishes, and his open disdain for those outside his new magic circle made him a deeply loathed, but feared figure.[21]

It was clear that the Total Strategy had run its course, but also that a change in approach was unlikely under the existing leadership.

As in the case of Botha's predecessor, Vorster, illness was the trigger for a change in the leadership of the National Party. On 18 January 1989 P.W. Botha had a stroke and on 18 February he resigned as leader of the National Party. But he did not resign as State President. His intention seems to have been to await the outcome of the vote in the National Party caucus for his successor as party leader so as to allow for a smooth transition of power. Another possible motive of his pointed if temporary separation of the two offices was to retain an influence over the ultimate outcome of the succession.[22] When the caucus failed to elect the reformist candidate he favoured and chose instead the Transvaal party leader, F.W. de Klerk, Botha refused to step down as State President. It is worth noting that at the time De Klerk was considered the most conservative of the candidates who had contested the leadership. What followed was a prolonged power struggle between Botha and De Klerk. The fact that the security establishment backed Botha during this power struggle did not endear the securocrats to De Klerk when he finally became State President.

De Klerk Takes Over

P.W. Botha's political isolation in his own cabinet led to his resignation on 14 August 1989. F.W. de Klerk became Acting State President the following day. As scheduled there was a general election for the tricameral parliament in 1989. In the voting for the white House of Assembly on 6 September, the National Party lost ground both to the liberal Democratic Party, which had replaced the PFP, and to the extreme rightwing Conservative Party (see Table 8.1). However, it still emerged with an overall majority and the nature of the campaign was quite different from that in 1987, with De Klerk stressing that the combined vote for the National Party and the Democratic Party gave the government a strong mandate for reform. F.W. de Klerk was sworn in as State President for a new term on 20 September.

One of his first acts was to dismantle the National Security Management System of his predecessor. In addition, eight long-term political prisoners, including Mandela's closest lieutenant in gaol, Walter Sisulu, were released on 15 October 1989. However, these steps were dwarfed by the measures De Klerk announced on 2 February 1990 when he opened a new session of the tricameral parliament. These included the unbanning of the ANC, the Pan-Africanist Congress (PAC), South African Communist Party (SACP) and a number of other prohibited organisations, and the announcement that the world's most famous political prisoner, Nelson Mandela, would shortly be released. This marked a far-reaching liberalisation of the South African political system with momentous consequences for the future of the country, even if they went far beyond what De Klerk anticipated when he launched his initiative.

Before examining the various explanations that have been put forward to account for this watershed in South Africa's history, the extent of continuity between the Botha and De Klerk eras is worth underlining. As in the change from Vorster to Botha, some of the actions most closely associated with De Klerk actually had their origins during Botha's tenure of office. In particular, Botha authorised officials to talk to ANC leaders in 1986. And in July 1989 before he left office, President Botha had a meeting with Nelson Mandela, which was publicly acknowledged at the time. Further, an important ANC figure, Govan Mbeki, was released from prison unconditionally in November 1987, with the clear implication that this action presaged the release of Mandela himself at some future date. Another example is that South Africa's acceptance of majority rule in Namibia under the aegis of the international community had its roots in accords the South African government agreed to in December 1988. At the same time, the government of De Klerk persisted with a key strategy from the Botha era of seeking to weaken the ANC in any way it could.

Explanations of Liberalisation

The accounts of the principal figures in the transition provide a useful starting point for considering explanations of De Klerk's initiative. In his autobiography F.W. de Klerk argues that he began to lay the foundations for the announcements he made on 2 February 1990 when he gave permission for protest marches that had hitherto been prohibited under the state of emergency. He also attaches importance to the release of Sisulu and others in October 1989. But he confirms too the huge importance to both his own thinking and that of his party colleagues of the coming down of the Berlin Wall. He writes as follows:

> The first few months of my presidency coincided with the disintegration of Communism in Eastern Europe which reached its historic climax with the fall of the Berlin Wall in November 1989. Within the scope of a few months, one of the our main strategic concerns for decades – the Soviet Union's role in southern Africa and its strong influence on the ANC and the SACP – had all but disappeared. A window had suddenly opened which created an opportunity for a much more adventurous approach than had previously been conceivable.[23]

The cabinet took stock of the situation in a *bosberaad* (literally a bush council, i.e. a meeting held in relative isolation, usually at a game reserve or similar location) on 3–5 December 1989. De Klerk does not disclose in detail what was decided at the *bosberaad*, but he makes it clear that the whole cabinet accepted the principle of power-sharing and the involvement of the ANC in the process.

Mandela's account of 2 February 1990 underlines the significance of De Klerk's initiative, describing it as 'a breathtaking moment for in one sweeping action he had virtually normalized the situation in South Africa'. He adds 'Our world had changed overnight'.[24] He stresses more generally the significance of De Klerk's accession to the State Presidency. Mandela met De Klerk on 13 December 1989 and his impression from that meeting was that he was 'a man we could do business with', echoing Thatcher's description of Gorbachev. Earlier Mandela had been impressed by De Klerk's release of Sisulu and seven other political prisoners in October 1989, concluding that the terms of their release implied that the ban on the ANC 'had effectively expired'.[25] Of course, the view that both De Klerk and

Mandela take of 2 February 1990 in their autobiographies has to be seen against the backdrop of the influence of subsequent events.

Nevertheless, their accounts are largely consonant with those that were published at the time. Thus, in his famous speech of 2 February 1990, De Klerk made frequent references to the events in Eastern Europe. A prominent section of the speech devoted to foreign affairs focused on the implications for South Africa of the changes and he returned to the issue to justify the lifting of the ban on the ANC and the SACP. De Klerk referred to the advice he had been given on the consequences of liberalisation of the political system. He highlighted four points, the first of which was: 'The events in the Soviet Union and Eastern Europe, to which I have referred already, weaken the capacity of organisations which were previously supported strongly from those quarters.'[26]

It may be objected that politicians frequently make opportunistic references to current events in justifying their actions and that if, for example, there had been a *coup* against Gaddafi in Libya at this time, De Klerk would have made much of the links between Libya and the ANC. However, Willem de Klerk's biography of his brother, published in 1991, suggests that the influence of the events in Eastern Europe was real and significant. Willem de Klerk noted that as late as October 1989 he was subjected, along with others, to public criticism for his readiness to engage in talks with members of the ANC in exile. He also had his arm twisted in private.[27] Of course, it would be to overstate the case grossly to suggest that the coming down of the Berlin Wall was the sole factor that impelled De Klerk's liberalisation of the system at this point.

Most analysts at the time quite reasonably argued that it was the product of a range of factors. Thus, in an assessment published in 1991, Frederik van Zyl Slabbert listed the factors weighing on the government under the heading of internal and external pressures. He further sub-divided these into planned and unplanned pressures, a distinction based on whether they involved an identifiable agent's seeking to bring about or prevent transition. His list of internal factors included significant structural factors such as population growth, urbanisation and the demands of the economy, in addition to the role of political actors. Sanctions form the most significant of the planned external pressures listed by Slabbert. His list of unplanned external pressures included the changing relationship between the United States and the Soviet Union, the decline of South Africa as a gold producer, the decline of Africa as an area of geo-political influence and the collapse of Communism in Eastern Europe.[28]

What set the coming down of the Berlin Wall apart from most of the other factors that analysts identified was its positive nature from the perspective of the National Party government. In short, it was seen as presenting an opportunity rather than as a threat. There was an assumption more or less across the political spectrum that its effect was to strengthen the position of the National Party and weaken that of the ANC. Some examples will illustrate the point. Lawrence Schlemmer, in a contribution to a book published in 1991, explained the beginnings of negotiations by comparing the situation the government faced in 1990 with that in 1986. Schlemmer acknowledged that the National Party government exaggerated the external Communist threat in the 1970s and 1980s, but argued that nevertheless the changes in Eastern Europe and their implications for Southern Africa as a region allowed 'the security establishment to recalculate the strategic balance in South Africa'. He characterised the situation in 1986 as follows:

- The ANC/SACP still endorsed Soviet imperialism.
- The Soviet Union, albeit with increasing uncertainty and a crumbling economic base, still pursued strategies aimed at securing at least strategic influence in various international tension zones, including southern Africa.
- The Cubans were ensconced in Angola, and Soviet advisers were building the military technology of Angolan and Cuban forces.
- The ANC/Umkhonto we Sizwe (MK) had functioning base camps in Angola, Soviet military support, and a persisting belief in the inevitable success of the armed struggle.
- Mozambique, while cautious, was still trying to ward off destabilising South African pressure to force it to become neutral and semi-cooperative, like Zimbabwe.
- The effects of new US and international sanctions on South Africa could not yet be calculated.
- South Africa was locked in a war in Namibia in which the ANC was a semi-active opponent.
- Unrest in South Africa had serious revolutionary dimensions which included the possibility of 'ungovernable' townships becoming liberated areas.
- The only relevant models of 'transition' in the region were distinctly unappetizing. Half of the white Rhodesians had fled

Zimbabwe, which was starving itself of foreign capital. Lesotho was under military rule. Mozambique and Angola were implementing scientific socialism, re-education camps, and had crude East European equipment which could not be repaired and silted-up, non-functioning harbours. The relative successes of Botswana and Swaziland were too quiet to be noticed.

• The NP voter constituency was still overwhelmingly in favour of political, residential, and educational segregation, maintained in perpetuity.[29]

Schlemmer contrasted this scenario to what he called the 'vastly different' scenario prevailing in 1990 when De Klerk liberalised the South African political system. He highlights the following:

• The Namibian settlement process led to the ANC losing its base camps in Angola. The ANC also faced virtually no prospect of re-establishing them elsewhere in southern Africa. The 'armed liberation' of South Africa became an absurdly remote ideal. The ANC was left with no real option but to seek negotiations in good faith.
• The hugely changed international stance of the Soviet Union, the US-Soviet disarmament talks, the disintegrating Soviet economy and the transformations in Eastern Europe eliminated the threat of Soviet influence operating to the detriment of white establishment interests in southern Africa.
• The Namibian settlement itself had won for the South African government a large measure of respect in international forums. At least a degree of moral support from abroad could be expected for internal negotiations.
• The US, the Soviet Union, and major Western powers had displayed an even-handed approach in the Namibian settlement.
• Economic factors, the weakening role of the Soviet Union, and the awesome damage attributed to South African destabilization had led to Mozambique unambiguously accepting that it would have to co-operate with the South African government.[30]

Schlemmer sums up: 'A comparison of these two boundary effect scenarios makes it abundantly clear that the strategic balance had shifted in favour of the South African government.' He continues: 'Stripped of its Soviet superpower leverage, the ANC could be reassessed as an internal political factor only' and 'in early 1990 government could view the possible outcomes of compromise with the ANC far more positively than at any time since it came to power'.[31]

Schlemmer's optimism (from his perspective) was matched by the pessimism of leftwing analysts. Kathryn Manzo argued that the demise of Communism in Eastern Europe had specific consequences for South Africa that arose from the reassertion of American hegemony and the absence of any apparent alternative to capitalist democracy. These consequences were in addition to the impact on the ANC of the drying up of military support as a result of the fall of Soviet Communism. She argued:

> Pressure on the ANC for a negotiated settlement has been reinforced by the revolutions in Eastern Europe, from whence a good deal of support came. East Germany, once the major military supplier of Umkhonto (the armed wing of the ANC), ceased supplying aid even before the reunification of East and West Germany; since then all military aid has come to a halt.[32]

She concluded that the Eastern European revolutions had significantly weakened the ANC's position.

> The ANC will almost certainly figure largely at the negotiating table, but unless it can harness the enormous stock of support that it still enjoys at the grassroots level, it will be forced to enter negotiations from an unenviable position – that of a junior and weak partner to the National party.[33]

Manzo's view that the ANC had been adversely affected by global trends was widely held on the left in the early 1990s. The SACP intellectual, Jeremy Cronin, took a similar view, concluding an article published in 1992 with reference to the revolutions in Eastern Europe that 'the world balance of forces that encouraged and sustained mass propelled negotiated transition there, is more or less an entirely unfavourable balance for us here'.[34]

Impact of Eastern Europe

While the outcome of the transition ran counter to these assumptions, analysts examining the transition after Mandela's inauguration as the first President of a democratic South Africa have nonetheless continued to ascribe a role to the coming down of the Berlin Wall. However, understandably, they have also emphasised factors more favourable to the ANC's emergence as a dominant force in the country's politics. For example, in his 1994 Chatham House discussion paper, *Forging the New South Africa*, James Barber argued that the collapse of Communism in Eastern Europe was one of three factors that determined the timing of De Klerk's initiative of 2 February. The others he identified were the problem of disorder in the townships and continuing economic stagnation.[35] A further example is provided by Hermann Giliomee's account of South Africa's democratisation in the 1995 volume of *Political Science Quarterly*, the journal of the New York-based Academy of Political Science. He argues that the decision to open negotiations with the ANC represented a fundamental shift in the government's policy that was the product of debate among the Afrikaner elite, in which three forces received special consideration. They were 'a weakening demographic base, a dramatically different external environment, and economic stagnation'.[36] It is worth mentioning that Giliomee dates the fundamental shift in government policy as taking place at the end of 1989. The conjuncture with the changes in Eastern Europe is not accidental.

Giliomee discusses a variety of factors under the heading of 'A Changing Ideological and External Environment', but he put greatest emphasis on the weakening of the Soviet Union. He argues that the success of the Namibian settlement played a part in the process, though here it is perhaps worth interjecting that the victory of the South West African People's Organisation (SWAPO) and, perhaps even more significantly, the failure of the Democratic Turnhalle Alliance (DTA) to exploit the fact that SWAPO had fallen short of a two-thirds majority, to insist on power-sharing, had upset some in government and in the security forces.[37] To be fair to Giliomee he does not present the Namibian settlement as an unambiguous triumph for the South African government, but merely argues that it 'made all sides appear winners'. He continues:

> Yet De Klerk would not have moved toward negotiations with the ANC as long as it was strongly backed by the Soviet Union. As late as September 1989, De Klerk sent word to his brother to stop talking to the ANC. In his view, this movement could never have a role in negotiations… In the last months of 1989, the external environment

improved dramatically from the government's point of view. For the first time it considered negotiations a viable option. The crucial development was the severe internal troubles experienced by the Soviet Union. Moscow told the ANC that it was up to the South Africans themselves to reach a political accommodation. At the same time Pretoria believed that without Soviet backing it had a much better chance to contain a legalized ANC.[38]

Furthermore, Giliomee argues that the changed international environment was a decisive factor in the ANC's abandonment of its revolutionary struggle:

> For the ANC the late 1980s also represented a watershed. It had long favoured the nationalization of large sectors of the economy, but it was now confronted with mounting evidence of the malperformance of economies under centralized control in Eastern Europe and Africa. With the South African economy already in trouble, the leadership saw the need for negotiating functional political and economic structures that could deliver on the greatly raised expectations of its followers. Even more important in its decision to begin negotiations were two major setbacks it received in the form of the New York Accords of 1988 and the collapse of the Soviet Union.[39]

Like Schlemmer, Giliomee paints a picture of ANC weakness as the context for De Klerk's initiative. However, while this analysis provides an answer to the question why De Klerk embarked on the transition, or, to put it another way, why he liberalised the South African political system on 2 February 1990, it poses a rather large problem. If the ANC entered negotiations from such a position of weakness, how then did it achieve such a position of dominance at the end of the negotiating process?

Solving the Conundrum?

One author who provides an answer to this conundrum is Allister Sparks. Admittedly, Sparks does not treat the coming down of the Berlin Wall as a decisive moment in South Africa's transition. He dates the influence on South Africa of events in Eastern Europe back to Gorbachev's accession to power in 1985 and his subsequent reforms. He contends that the decline of the Soviet empire helped De Klerk 'to justify to his people what would otherwise have appeared to them a suicidal course of action.[40] At the same time, Sparks argues that De Klerk did not anticipate the consequences that would flow from his speech on 2 February 1990:

> Just as Gorbachev could not have known that his restructuring of the Soviet system would lead to the loss of his East European empire, the collapse of Communism, and the dismemberment of the Soviet Union itself, so, too, De Klerk did not expect his reforms to lead to black-majority rule and the end of Afrikaner nationalism before the end of the decade.[41]

To put the point at its simplest, the case made by Sparks is that De Klerk miscalculated. In fact, the clear implication of Sparks's analysis is that if De Klerk had foreseen the outcome, he would have chosen a different course.

Some analysts did not accord a leading role in the initiation of the transition to either the coming down of the Berlin Wall or the end of the Cold War more widely. Thus, when this author published a piece on the transition and the end of the Cold War in 1996, a response by John Daniel discounted the impact of the end of the Cold War as such.[42] He put the emphasis on the toughening of American policy towards South Africa under President George Bush (Sr). Specifically, Daniel claimed on the basis of reports in *Africa Confidential* that Bush threatened to approve further economic sanctions against South Africa if De Klerk did not liberalise the political system. But even in Daniel's account there was a link to events in the Soviet Union and Eastern Europe since he argues that the toughening of American policy on South Africa followed Gorbachev's giving the United States *carte blanche* to shape events in Southern Africa.

In fact, Daniel's approach suggests an answer to the question that the analysis by Sparks begs. That is, why did De Klerk's assumption that the ANC would be weakened by the end of the Cold War turn out to be an illusion? Part of the answer lies in the role that anti-Communism played in justifying the stance taken by Western governments towards South Africa. Without a geo-political case for allying with white minority rule in South Africa, Western governments came under irresistible pressure from domestic opinion not merely to distance themselves from the South African government but to impose sanctions. Through the 1980s conservative opinion had placed a great deal of emphasis on the Communist threat to justify support for white minority rule in South Africa. The ANC's alliance with the SACP in creating Umkhonto we Sizwe (MK) in the early 1960s and the ANC in exile's links with the Soviet Union provided a factual basis for these arguments. But conservatives undoubtedly overstated the case. The broadly nationalist orientation of the ANC remained largely unaffected by such tactical alliances. Further, the existence of such alliances arose at least in part because of the unwillingness of most Western societies to support the liberation of Southern Africa by means that included the use of violence. This reflected a measure of sympathy for the white predicament in Southern Africa that was strongest on the right of the political spectrum but by no means confined to it.

The paradoxical manner in which the end of the Cold War impacted on the balance of forces in South Africa during the transition provides one element in the surprising emergence of the ANC as the dominant force in the country at the end of the transition. However, it was only one element in a much more complex process and it is to the larger question of South Africa's transition to majority rule that the next chapter is addressed. It is worth underlining at this point that very few analysts of the country's politics in the early 1990s anticipated such an outcome. What is more, even at the time of Nelson Mandela's inauguration as President on 10 May 1994, there was a tendency among analysts to fail to recognise just how large a change had taken place. However, by the time of South Africa's second democratic election in 1999, the magnitude of the shift in political power had become crystal clear.

9

The Unexpected Transition to Majority Rule: Analysing a Miracle?

At the time of Nelson Mandela's inauguration as President on 10 May 1994 after South Africa's first democratic elections it was common to represent the country's transition as a compromise between the forces of African and Afrikaner nationalism. Such a picture was powerfully reinforced by the fact that the last leader of the country under white minority rule, F.W. de Klerk, was inaugurated on the same day as one of his two Deputy Presidents. An extreme example is provided by Arend Lijphart's explanation of the reasons for his optimism that South Africa's first democratic system would work:

> The first reason is that the newly founded democracy is clearly a consociational democracy. Second, it is not only a power-sharing system, but close to the optimal power-sharing system that could have been devised. Third, the background conditions for its satisfactory operation have become considerably more favourable than they were in the 1980s. Fourth, the outcome of the April 1994 elections augurs very well for South Africa's democratic future.[1]

Lijphart then proceeds to elaborate on these points. His arguments are examined further below. But in the first instance, the sharp contrast between Lijphart's view of the transition and that presented by Giliomee in his 2003 book, *The Afrikaners*, deserves to be underlined.

Giliomee berates De Klerk precisely for his failure to secure for South Africa the system described by Lijphart. He explains that the National Party's acceptance of the ANC proposal for a government of national unity for a period of five years after the first democratic elections amounted to conceding the principle of simple majority rule as a basic element in any deal. He acknowledges that 'simple majority rule took much of the needle out of the white-black political conflict',[2] but he contends it held out risks in a number of policy areas. He continues:

> More importantly, simple majority rule was not what De Klerk had set out to achieve and not what the NP [National Party] had promised the electorate. In the election of 1989 and the referendum of 1992 the NP undertook to ensure that the majority party did not get all the say in the government. In one of its principal press advertisements before the first democratic elections in April 1994 the NP stated boldly: 'We have kept all our promises. We have got a Government of National Unity, which means that the political parties will share power.' But the new constitution certainly did not mean that.[3]

As Giliomee explains, what the interim constitution laid down was that parties winning more than eighty seats in the four-hundred member National Assembly would be able to nominate one of two executive deputy presidents. It also decreed that any party winning at least twenty seats would be entitled to cabinet posts in proportion to its share of the vote. But crucial was the fact that participation in government of minor parties did not restrict the right of the majority in the cabinet to determine the country's policies.

This chapter examines the contention in the literature over the nature of the transition. On this issue at least the author is in agreement with Giliomee's view that the transition was to African majority rule and not to the consociational democracy touted by Lijphart and others (see p. 235). However, a different view is taken of the failure of South Africa to follow this path advocated by consociational theorists. It is argued that a settlement that fell short of majority rule would have lacked legitimacy, given the scale of the country's social and economic inequalities.[4] It is evident that few writers at the start of South Africa's transition anticipated the outcome of majority rule. Consequently, another task of the chapter will be to explain how majority rule came about and why whites accepted an outcome that they had always been expected to resist to the point of civil war. Indeed, the assumption that the African population would accept nothing less than majority rule and that whites would resist such an eventuality to the death had long underpinned predictions that the fall of apartheid would be accompanied by a racial bloodbath.

How the Deal was Done

The issues of the nature of the transition and of how it was achieved tend to be linked in the literature. Most accounts of the transition present it as essentially a deal between the National Party government and the ANC. They emphasise the role that talks between the two played in the process, whether these talks took place in a formal or informal setting, whether they were secret or openly acknowledged. A selling point of a number of accounts of the transition is their privileged access to what went on in some of the more significant of the exchanges between the government and the ANC behind the scenes prior to or during the formal negotiations. Examples are: *Tomorrow is Another Country: The Inside Story of South Africa's Negotiated Revolution; The Politics of Transition: A Hidden History of South Africa's Negotiated Settlement; The Fall of Apartheid: The Inside Story from Smuts to Mbeki*; and *Anatomy of a Miracle: The End of Apartheid and the Birth of the New South Africa.*[5] Of the four, only the last fails to make play in the title or subtitle of its special access to information on secret contacts between the government and the ANC, though the text devotes considerable space to secret meetings that occurred during the 1980s.

In his account, Sparks traces the origins of attempts of the government to initiate negotiations through Nelson Mandela and he demonstrates how chance encounters facilitated the beginning of a dialogue between the government and the world's most famous prisoner. Sparks explains how after Winnie Mandela had been banished to the small town of Brandfort, the town's only lawyer, Piet de Waal, had been obliged to take her on as a client. Out of that relationship a friendship had developed between Winnie Mandela and the lawyer's wife, Adele de Waal. As it happened, the then Minister of Justice, Police and Prisons, Koebie Coetzee, was an old friend and tennis partner of Piet de Waal from university days. As Sparks tells the story, it was the De Waals who persuaded Coetzee to initiate talks between the government and Nelson Mandela, resulting in four years of secret talks between them which began in 1985. Sparks also relates how a strong relationship developed between the government's chief negotiator and his ANC counterpart. This was a result of an accident at a holiday lodge in 1991 that obliged Roelf Meyer to trust Cyril Ramaphosa to remove a fish-hook that had become deeply embedded in one of Meyer's fingers.

In a somewhat similar vein, Patti Waldmeir's book contains anecdotes of encounters between members of the ANC in exile and intermediaries and officials of the South African government engaged in what might be called talks about talks or pre-negotiations. These also began in the mid-1980s. The most important of the meetings described by Waldmeir were the encounters between ANC officials headed by Thabo Mbeki and members of the Afrikaner elite at Mells Park House, a stately home made available for the purpose by the mining company, Consolidated Gold Fields. These took place between November 1987 and May 2000. Robert Harvey's book provides a more detailed account of both the origins and the content of the Mells Park House meetings based on the access he was given to the written record of the talks kept by Michael Young, the public affairs director of Consolidated Gold Fields. Harvey puts the meetings in the context of what he describes as the extraordinary story both of the rise of apartheid and of its collapse when it appeared that the society was heading for mutual self-destruction. He concludes:

> This 'miracle' was not achieved out of the blue, although it appeared so at the time, but through the heroic and drawn-out struggle of South Africa's blacks, aided by a few liberal whites, the patience and intelligence of the more enlightened members of the Afrikaner community, and the prolonged dialogue between blacks and whites that began at Mells Park and ended with the constitutional agreement between Cyril Ramaphosa and Roelf Meyer in 1993.[6]

Spitz's book is somewhat different in character in that it is primarily about the nuts and bolts of the settlement reached in the interim constitution. The 'hidden' dimension of the story it tells lies in its access to material during the various stages of drafting of the interim constitution and to the detailed discussions that took place in technical committees of the Multi-Party Negotiating Process (MPNP).

In fact, a considerable number of books, the central focus of which is the constitution, have been published. They include: *Democratization in South Africa: The Elusive Social Contract; The Small Miracle: South Africa's Negotiated Settlement; South Africa: Designing New Political Institutions*; and *South Africa: The Battle over the Constitution*.[7] A common feature of these four books, as well as of Spitz's book, is the emphasis they place on the interim constitution as a compromise between ANC leaders and the National Party government, a compromise between elites. Timothy Sisk puts it this way:

> As the old order suffered its demise, the realization set in among the major actors that the benefits of a potential positive-sum outcome to the conflict – the creation of a jointly determined set of institutions to govern a future, common, and democratic society – were greater than the costs of continued confrontation in an environment ungoverned by common rules. Once this realization was made among a core set of elites, convergence on exactly what kinds of rules should replace authoritarianism evolved as a result of the strategic interaction among the political parties that committed themselves to a negotiated settlement.[8]

Steven Friedman explains the context of the deal in the book he co-edited with Doreen Atkinson. He summarises the findings of the book's various contributors as follows:

> The evidence the team has gathered suggests that the two largest parties' shared sense that they would have to achieve a quick settlement if the country was not to be laid waste did indeed produce a remarkable political achievement. As the parties sought to gain a settlement which would avert national disaster on their terms alone, they came to accept many compromises, and principles, which seemed unattainable, not long before.[9]

To be fair, Friedman has the wit not to make these his final words and he goes on to acknowledge that the settlement 'left many battles to be fought'.[10]

In the introduction to their edited book, Faure and Lane make emphatic assertions about South Africa's new dispensation, though they do qualify their initial statement:

If constitutionalism is the first major feature of the new regime in South Africa, then consociationalism is the second. The key players from the large social groups, in Arend Lijphart's (1977) interpretation, share executive power. Whether the consociational mechanism, recommended for the RSA by Lijphart himself (1985), will prove a lasting conflict-resolving mechanism is too early to tell. Ethnic mobilization of the different *zuilen* or camps, although strong, is far from complete, as both Mandela and de Klerk try catch-all strategies, whereas Buthelezi mainly attempts to catch the Zulu vote. All three players are of considerable age; it will be interesting to see how the second generation of leaders will position themselves in relation to consociationalism, or making concurrent majorities in the late 1990s.[11]

Even more misleadingly, the back cover of the book connects the drawing up of the final constitution to the authors' tendentious characterisation of the interim constitution:

Key political players in the RSA have drawn up a new constitution, and are engaged in the design and implementation of new institutions. Consociationalism – different social groups sharing executive powers – has been the key to success.[12]

The editors make brief reference to the adoption of the final constitution by the Constituent Assembly in May 1996 in a very brief postscript to their introduction. In this context, they note the National Party's decision to leave the Government of National Unity. However, they make no comment on the abandonment of power-sharing as a principle of the final constitution. It may perhaps be argued in their defence that the final constitution had not received certification as yet and it was therefore too early to tell what might happen. However, it is a very weak argument. The temporary nature of the provisions in the interim constitution for the inclusion of the main political parties in the government of the country, though without a veto on decisions of the majority party, had clearly been foreshadowed in the outcome of the negotiations that had taken place in 1993.

Siri Gloppen's book, in the author's own words, 'juxtaposes the basically majoritarian justice model with the consensus-orientated consociational model in a manner indicating a dichotomy between them'.[13] However, Gloppen argues that if theoretically contradictory, in practical politics a mix, indeed, any mix, is possible. In a somewhat similar vein, Spitz argues that the MPNP was a resounding success. He concludes:

> The talks produced a compromise settlement, dominated by the ANC and the NP/government, which reconciled the democratic and majoritarian concerns of the former with the latter's insistence on power-sharing and constitutional checks and balances. In satisfying the key interests of the two parties, the Interim Constitution attained the level of support – the controversial benchmark of sufficient consensus – needed for its adoption.[14]

There is a brief postscript on the final constitution. It attempts to justify the book's preoccupation with the MPNP. It notes:

> On 3 February 1997, less than three years after the Interim Constitution came into effect, it was replaced by the final Constitution. Notwithstanding its short life span, the Interim Constitution has left South Africa with a substantial legacy, most obvious in the provisions of the final Constitution. While the final Constitution was shaped by the political strength of the ANC in the Constitutional [*sic*] Assembly, it would be fair to describe it as a version of the Interim Constitution modified in the light of the changed political conditions obtained in the Constitutional [*sic*] Assembly.[15]

The picture these books paint of the transition is of a series of negotiations at the heart of which were talks on the provisions of the interim constitution. Their outcome was determined by a rational, deliberative process in which the parties sought to arrive at workable compromises and in which they drew on global best practice as a model. In so far as the actual negotiations of the terms of the interim constitution were confined to the last year of the transition, it was – so these authors would argue – because the right conditions for the conduct of such negotiations had to be created. In particular, the threat that violence posed to the process had to be overcome. From this perspective, the major landmarks in the process were a series of agreements between the government and the ANC, but sometimes extending to other parties, that ultimately paved the way to the MPNP at Kempton Park in 1993. These agreements included the Groote

Schuur Accord of May 1990, the Pretoria Minute of August 1990, the National Peace Accord of September 1991, and most importantly of all, the Record of Understanding of September 1992 following the failure of the Convention for a Democratic South Africa (CODESA) in 1991–2.

Looking beyond the Interim Constitution

The focus on the interim constitution as the very core of the transition tends to produce a rose-tinted view of the process. It detracts from the role that other factors played in determining the outcome of the transition, including the success of the ANC's strategy for securing mass support, the impact of political violence on the balance of political forces and the result of the 1994 election. This is not to deny the importance of the interim constitution. It provided a bridge to a new era and ensured constitutional continuity between old order and the new, an achievement of immense significance. However, the terms of the interim constitution do not explain why the ANC emerged in a position of such dominance in 1994. Indeed, they are positively misleading in so far as they encourage a view of the outcome of the transition as a compromise between the government's wish for a dispensation based on group rights and the ANC's insistence on majority rule. Such a view does not take into account the fact that part of the reason for the negotiation of the interim constitution was to provide the government with a face-saving formula for its retreat from its previous insistence on the entrenchment of power-sharing in the new order. The concession of a diluted form of power-sharing in which parties other than the ANC would have places in cabinet, but without any veto on its decisions, was made by the ANC on the basis that it would be temporary and not part of the final constitution.

In fairness to Sisk, Friedman, Faure and Lane, as well as Lijphart, who was quoted at the start of this chapter, it may be argued that the full extent of the ANC's domination of the polity was not apparent at the time they wrote. (However, even before the 1994 election the trend towards ANC dominance was apparent to most political analysts in South Africa, including government ministers keen by mid-1993 to get to elections before the position of the National Party deteriorated further.) In his contribution to Reynolds's book on the 1994 election,

Lijphart expands on his claim that South Africa after the election was 'clearly a consociational democracy'.[16] He argues that the country's interim constitution embodied all four basic principles of consociationalism: government by grand coalition; group autonomy; proportionality; and minority veto. To the objection that the constitution was only an interim one, he stressed that there was a 'general expectation' that the final constitution would 'bear a strong resemblance to the interim constitution'.[17]

The favourable view Lijphart takes of the limited and temporary elements of consociationalism in South Africa's interim constitution is in marked contrast to his condemnation of the tricameral constitution of 1983 as the embodiment of 'sham consociationalism'.[18] However, it is hardly surprising that the theorists of consociationalism should wish the concept to be associated with the miracle of South Africa's transition to democracy rather than with the era of reform apartheid. Admittedly, the ANC did not have a completely free hand in drawing up the final constitution. It was obliged to respect 34 constitutional principles that had been agreed in the MPNP. However, these did not include the principle of power-sharing. Further, the principles applied only to the drafting of the final constitution and not to any subsequent amendment of it. The fact that the ANC did not have a two-thirds majority in the Constituent Assembly also meant that the party had to consider the views of the other parties. However, the option of a referendum in the event of deadlock limited the willingness of the other parties to block the ANC's wishes.

Even before the 1999 election and the expiry of the interim constitution's provisions on power-sharing, the dominant position of the ANC within the political system was evident. A book edited by Giliomee and Simkins appeared in 1999 comparing South Africa to other cases of dominant party regimes, including Mexico, Taiwan and Malaysia. In their conclusion the editors firmly assert that South Africa's 'present system is neither corporatist nor consociational'.[19] Their reference to corporatism is an allusion to the view that the involvement of business in forums established by the government to discuss macro-economic policy and industrial relations has provided a measure of compensation for the absence of the entrenchment of power-sharing. For example, Adam, Slabbert and Moodley contend:

> Corporatism in the decisive economic realm guarantees the consensual type of democracy that simple majoritarianism lacks in the

political sphere. Moreover, given the volatile and fragile state of South African society and its new political institutions, corporatism constitutes an effective and necessary substitute for interest mediation that would be difficult to achieve with electoral politics alone.[20]

Giliomee and Simkins accept that business has accommodated to ANC dominance, but reject the notion that the relationship amounts to an alliance.

Economic Perspectives

The positing of such an alliance forms the basis of a number of books on the transition. However, it is only in *Comrades in Business* that a relatively favourable view is taken of the relationship. The notion that the ANC accepted the emasculation of its economic radicalism as the price of political power underpins the others. Examples are *South Africa: Limits to Change – The Political Economy of the Transition; Elite Transition: From Apartheid to Neoliberalism in South Africa*; and *The ANC and the Liberation Struggle: A Critical Political Biography*.[21] To these can be added the section on the transition in *A History of Inequality in South Africa, 1652–2002*.[22] What gives this approach a measure of credibility is that it provides a basis for explaining how South Africa managed the transition from apartheid to majority rule without a racial bloodbath. Its obvious weakness is its lack of incontrovertible evidence for the forging of an explicit deal between capitalists and the ANC beyond the gradual conversion of ANC leaders to an acknowledgement of the economic constraints on South Africa in the post-Cold War world. In fact, it is arguable that the ANC leadership's recognition of such constraints provided a surer basis for white confidence in the economic consequences of the transition than any deal could have done.

Marais sketches the basis of the relationship between capital and the ANC in a democratic South Africa as follows:

The fundamental importance of 1994, therefore, was not just the end of apartheid, but the dissolution of the dominant alliance of social, economic and political forces in South Africa. The ANC's ascent to political power did not immediately fill the resultant vacuum. Rather, it recast and intensified a struggle to reshape state and capital relations, to determine which alliance of social forces would come to constitute a new ruling bloc and to establish the decisive terms of that alliance.[23]

Patrick Bond sets out to explain why 'to the chagrin of many in the Democratic Movement, macroeconomic management during the 1989–93 late apartheid depression became a model for *post*-apartheid policy'.[24] He argues that 'two closely associated influences – turbulent financial markets and "globalisation" – were extremely important in all of this'.[25] Bond further attributes the ANC's adoption of a neoliberal macroeconomic strategy to an 'analytical failure of nerve' and 'a political retreat, paved with consensus formation in cosy seminars sponsored by business-oriented think-tanks, of which Anglo American, Old Mutual/Nedcor and Sanlam stand out'.[26]

McKinley contends that the ANC lacked the will to seek the radical transformation of South African society, arguing that the ANC wrongly adopted a perspective that left it 'with no other option than to see socioeconomic change as secondary to the parallel struggle for political change'. In the process he claims it privileged 'the economic status quo – capitalism'.[27] Terreblanche is bluntest in asserting the existence of an informal deal between the corporate sector and the ANC that was achieved in parallel with the political negotiations at Kempton Park. He refers in this context to a statement of economic policies by the Transitional Executive Council, which held sway in the final months of the transition. The statement was agreed with the International Monetary Fund as the basis of a loan to help the country with its balance of payments through the election. He goes on:

> The joint TEC-IMF statement shows clearly that ANC leaders must have changed their strategic and ideological thinking in important ways from mid-1992 onwards. Those in favour of making concessions in order to keep the formal constitutional negotiations on track were winning the battle within the democratic alliance, and have maintained their ascendancy ever since.

Terreblanche claims that in their eagerness to achieve a constitutional settlement as quickly as possible, ANC leaders were 'prepared to yield to the severe pressure from the corporate sector to accept its neo-liberal and export-oriented approach'. The consequence according to Terreblanche was that the country's social crisis caused by the abject poverty of the majority would remain unresolved, addressed only indirectly and in the long run 'via the high economic growth rate and "trickle-down" effect promised by the "super-salesmen" of the corporate sector'.[28]

A very different view to these primarily Marxist perspectives is presented by Giliomee and Simkins. After noting that socio-economic conditions for the consolidation of liberal democracy in South Africa are unfavourable, they summarise their understanding of South Africa's transition as follows:

> In these unpropitious conditions there are two pacts to consider in order to understand the political process in South Africa during the first half of the 1990s. The first pact was between the white and black elites, based on a white and a black dominant party respectively, to make possible the founding of a democracy. After the elections this was replaced by a second pact, that between an African elite and the poor African masses. It has two projects: to establish an African middle class mainly through the occupancy of senior positions in the civil service and state contracts to African suppliers, and to entrench a black labour aristocracy. The pre-April 1994 pact and the post-April 1994 pact are quite different and it was not possible to predict purely on the basis of the first pact what type of democracy was to be expected. What was predictable was that big business would quickly switch from the erstwhile dominant party to meet the needs of the new one. It has sponsored the enrichment of a small African elite, accepted labour legislation that only the bigger companies can afford and has not spoken up against affirmative action.[29]

The authors' recognition that the election of April 1994 created a new political reality is of fundamental importance. However, their implicit criticism of big business is open to the objection that both the government and business have been doing too little, not too much, to promote greater socio-economic equality. Indeed, the one element of the radical critique of South Africa's transition that has a measure of credibility is its denunciation of the scale of inequality in post-apartheid South Africa. This is an important issue that will be addressed in greater depth in the conclusion. It will not be pursued further here since the issue of inequality as such does little to explain why the ANC emerged in such a dominant position after the South Africa's transition to democracy. To understand this, we need to turn to other factors.

Political Violence

In the rest of this chapter the impact of political violence and of the 1994 election itself will be examined. In Chapter 10, the role that the transnational anti-apartheid movement and international opinion more widely played in the demise of apartheid will be analysed. The period from Mandela's release from prison to his inauguration as the first President of a democratic South Africa was an extraordinarily violent period as the monthly figures for political fatalities attest (see Table 9.1). According to the SAIRR figures, in the period from the beginning of February 1990 to the end of May 1994, there were a total of 14,807 deaths. This is best treated as a rough estimate for the transition as a whole of 15,000 deaths, making the transition the most violent period in the country's history. Admittedly, this total

Table 9.1   Monthly totals of political fatalities in South Africa, 1985 to 1996*[30]

	Jan	Feb	Mar	Apr	May	Jun	Jul	Aug	Sep	Oct	Nov	Dec	Total
1985	4	35	76	46	66	45	96	163	69	86	101	92	879
1986	105	112	179	145	221	212	122	76	40	16	37	33	1298
1987	40	22	40	40	33	36	39	35	73	93	89	121	661
1988	211	107	62	48	58	76	94	112	108	90	85	98	1149
1989	126	95	89	99	89	38	96	104	135	116	129	287	1403
1990	210	283	458	283	208	150	247	698	417	162	316	267	3699
1991	187	129	351	270	318	150	164	184	282	218	283	170	2706
1992	139	238	348	300	230	324	278	361	339	332	299	159	3347
1993	135	129	143	212	339	309	547	451	425	398	370	317	3775
1994	239	259	537	436	207	119	136	106	109	106	94	128	2476
1995	131	87	79	138	100	82	92	61	69	49	54	102	1044
1996	39	47	59	67	45	53	64	63	81	57	47	61	683

Total number of fatalities in 12 years of political violence = 23,120

Note: * In the months September to December 1984, there were 149 fatalities.

was dwarfed by the numbers killed in neighbouring countries during the 1980s as the direct or indirect consequence of the country's policy of destabilisation. In fact, it can truly be stated that South Africa's neighbours bore the brunt of the violent struggle to end apartheid, as they became the battleground in the South African government's war against the forces of African nationalism. Within South Africa, most of the violence was concentrated in two regions, the Pretoria–Witwatersrand–Vereeniging (PWV) metropolitan area and the province of Natal. According to the Human Rights Committee, these two regions accounted for over 90 per cent of the deaths as a result of political violence in 1992 and 1993. Most of the violence took place in townships, rural settlements or squatter camps and the overwhelming majority of the victims of violence were African. Very little violence took place in the suburbs.

Lethal political violence took four main forms during South Africa's transition: aggressive action by the security forces; conflict between the Inkatha Freedom Party (IFP) and the ANC; racial attacks by the Azanian People's Liberation Army (APLA), the armed wing of the Pan-Africanist Congress (PAC); and spoiler violence by the extreme right. However, reliable statistics on who or what organisations were responsible for what number of deaths are hard to come by, as there is little agreement on the attribution of responsibility among the agencies monitoring the violence. A selection of 25 prominent episodes provides a broad indication of the pattern of the violence (see Table 9.2). What can be stated with some certainty is that a large majority of the deaths occurred in the context of the conflict between the IFP and the ANC. APLA and the extreme right caused relatively few deaths, though the episodes in which they were involved had a very considerable impact. Overt violence by the security forces caused a considerable number of deaths. Examples include the Sebokeng, Daveytown and Bisho massacres. What is much harder to estimate, as well as a source of much greater contention is the extent of security force involvement in covert violence.

There are widely differing interpretations of the violence in the literature on the transition, though it is worth noting that there are fewer studies of the violence of the transition than of the constitutional negotiations. Examples of books on the subject are *Beloved Country: South Africa's Silent Wars* and *The Natal Story: 16 Years of Conflict* (extending well beyond the transition in its scope).[31] Three overarching theories of the violence can be identified. The first is

Table 9.2   A selection of twenty-five prominent episodes of
political violence[32]

Year	Date	Episode/Location	Region	Perpetrator/Context
1990	4 March	Gqozo coup in Ciskei	Eastern Cape	Security forces
	26 March	Sebokeng massacre	PWV	Security forces
	End March	Seven Day War	Natal	ANC–IFP conflict
	22 July	Outbreak of violence on the Reef	PWV	ANC–IFP conflict
	22 November	Duli attempted coup in Transkei	Eastern Cape	Security forces
1991	10 February	Kwashange massacre	Natal	ANC–IFP conflict
	14 March	Daveyton massacre	PWV	Security forces
	12 May	Swanievale massacre	PWV	ANC–IFP conflict
	9 August	Ventersdorp confrontation	Transvaal	Security forces
	3–4 December	Bruntville massacre	Natal	ANC–IFP conflict
1992	March	Battle for Alexandra	PWV	ANC–IFP conflict
	17 June	Boipatong massacre	PWV	ANC–IFP conflict
	7 September	Bisho massacre	Eastern Cape	Security forces
	28 November	King Williamstown golf-club attack	Eastern Cape	APLA
1993	Early March	Table Mountain killings	Natal	ANC–IFP conflict
	10 April	Assassination of Chris Hani	PWV	Extreme right
	1 May	Highgate Hotel attack	Eastern Cape	APLA
	25 June	Invasion of the World Trade Centre	PWV	Extreme right
	25 July	St James's Church massacre	Cape Town	APLA
	25 August	Murder of Amy Biehl	Cape Town	APLA
	8 October	Raid on APLA 'base', Umtata	Eastern Cape	Security forces

	31 December	Heidelberg Tavern attack	Cape Town	APLA
1994	10–11 March	Battle of Bop	Bophuthatswana	Extreme right
	28 March	Shell House killings	PWV	ANC–IFP conflict
	24–25 April	Pre-election bombings	PWV	Extreme right

that a 'third force' from within the state acted throughout the transition to weaken and to destabilise the ANC. The second is that violence was a product of the strength of racial and ethnic antagonisms within the country. The third is that violence was a legacy of the structures of inequality put in place by apartheid. To these theories, two further broad views of the violence are often counterposed. They are that the violence was primarily a product of very specific local circumstances and finally, that the violence was a product of the political competition among the parties contending for power in a post-apartheid South Africa.

The first of these explanations is difficult to reconcile with the fact that the ANC emerged in a position of dominance after the transition. Admittedly, the motivation for violence and its consequences may differ. Nevertheless, if it appeared that a particular strategy was proving counterproductive, one would expect it to be abandoned and not persisted with over a period of four years. The fact that much of the violence took place within both the same racial and ethnic group constitutes a powerful objection to the second explanation. The concentration of the violence in PWV and Natal would seem to rule out the explanation that attributes prime responsibility to structures created by apartheid. It also poses a considerable problem for the explanation of the violence in terms of much more narrowly based local factors. By a process of elimination, that suggests that political competition between the ANC and the IFP provides the most credible explanation of the violence.

However, the evidence of state involvement in the violence in the first years of the transition is too strong to be dismissed. In particular, it is evident – and hardly surprising – that the security forces failed to operate impartially as between the conservative IFP and the revolutionary ANC. It is also clear that Inkatha received material assistance on a large scale from the state in the late 1980s and early 1990s. Stephen Ellis has argued that support for Inkatha amounted to a strategy to weaken the ANC based on the experience of the covert campaign South African security forces mounted against the South West African People's Organisation (SWAPO) in the run-up to Namibia's pre-independence elections in 1989.[33] The success of that campaign in preventing the SWAPO from winning a two-thirds majority led to its adoption as a model for South Africa, where the ambition of the government at its most extensive was to secure the actual defeat of the ANC at the polls.

Yet by mid-1992 it is widely recognised that the continuing political violence was damaging and not helping the National Party. In particular, both the incapacity of the government to prevent the violence and, worse still, the widespread impression that it was colluding in the violence led to a haemorrhaging of support among Africans for the National Party. As late as February 1992, an opinion poll suggested that the National Party might secure 9 per cent of the African vote, a figure that rose to 14 per cent for 'a party with De Klerk as leader'.[34] In the election of 1994 its actual support among African voters was estimated at between 3 and 4 per cent.[35] The violence was also damaging the government's relations with Western governments who took their cue from reports in the media and by monitoring agencies that highlighted allegations of collusion. De Klerk's frantic efforts to secure the prosecution and conviction of the IFP-supporting hostel-dwellers who carried out the Boipatong massacre in June 1992 showed his appreciation of how his position was being undermined by the violence. However, as Table 9.1 shows, the violence continued. This was despite De Klerk's efforts to root out senior members of the security forces suspected of involvement in the 'third force'. With the Record of Understanding between the government and the ANC in September 1992, in which the government ditched its previously close relationship with the IFP in favour of cooperation with the ANC, any remaining rationale for the government's previous strategy had disappeared.

In so far as Buthelezi persisted with a campaign directed at opposing ANC hegemony, he did so independently of the government and in purely tactical alliances with other conservative and extreme rightwing political forces. Violence between the ANC and the IFP continued even after the 1994 election, though increasingly it was limited to the IFP's stronghold of KwaZulu-Natal. The turning point in relations between the parties occurred with local elections in the province of KwaZulu-Natal in 1996. Those elections demonstrated that the IFP for all its support in the rural areas did not enjoy sufficient support in the urban areas of the province to be able to press its case for turning South Africa into a loose confederation, let alone for secession. Thereafter the IFP had to settle for co-option as a junior partner of the ANC in government. Co-option also ensured that the ANC's interest in pressing to establish the IFP's culpability for much of the violence of the transition diminished.

Buthelezi was the only one of the homeland leaders to have organised political support in the form of a mass-based political party. In this context, Mandela's policy of reconciliation paid huge political dividends. Just as the real significance of the policy of reconciliation pursued by Botha and Smuts after the Anglo-Boer War was that it addressed divisions among Afrikaners, so too Mandela's policy of reconciliation was most successful in overcoming potential divisions among Africans. At the beginning of the transition, the ANC tended to be viewed by sceptical political commentators as a party rooted in the urban African population but with shallow support elsewhere. However, in the 1994 election, with the exception of KwaZulu-Natal it was the people of the homelands, including those employed by homeland political structures, who voted most overwhelmingly for the ANC.

Prelude to Democracy

The dramatic events of the 12 months before the election set the scene for the ANC's triumph. After a period of drift in the early months of 1993, the assassination of the SACP leader, Chris Hani, on Easter Saturday, 10 April, provided a powerful spur to the negotiations between the government and the ANC. There were fears that anger at the assassination in the townships, where Hani was an immensely popular figure, would engulf the country in violence. They were dissipated by Mandela's appeal for calm. The indispensable role played by Mandela in the crisis greatly strengthened the ANC's bargaining position in the negotiations. It paved the way to the setting of 27 April 1994 as the date for the country's first democratic, general election on 3 June. That furthered strengthened the ANC's position. As Adam, Slabbert and Moodley explain, 'once the Nationalists had agreed to Slovo's proposal of an election date *before* having settled most contentious issues, they had handed the initiative to their opponents and had to go along with their proposals'.[36]

The attempt of the extreme right to prevent the formal setting of the date for the general election in the MPNP by invading the World Trade Centre in Kempton Park where the talks were taking place was to no avail. By the end of 1993 a Transitional Executive Council (TEC) had been set up to oversee the holding of the election under the terms of the freshly agreed interim constitution. The settlement arrived at by the ANC and the National Party left a number of matters to be determined by the incoming government. Most importantly, the interim constitution was intended merely to provide a bridge to a new era. It was not the final constitution. However, its design gave the impression of much greater permanence. That was very helpful to the National Party in the election. Helpful to both parties was the assurance the settlement provided against retribution, whatever the outcome of the election. In October 1993 a coalition of forces centred on the IFP had formed the Freedom Alliance to oppose the pact between the ANC and the National Party. Overcoming the opposition of the Freedom Alliance became the TEC's main priority in the early months of 1994.

Chief Lucas Mangope, President of the independent homeland of Bophuthatswana, announced early in March 1994 that the homeland would not be seeking incorporation into South Africa and hence would not be participating in the election. His announcement prompted a strike by civil servants who were fearful that unless the homeland opted for incorporation they would no longer be paid and their pensions would be in jeopardy. A counterproductive and bloody intervention by the neo-Nazi Afrikaner Weerstands Beweging (AWB – Afrikaner resistance movement) in support of Mangope brought about the speedy collapse of his government and Bophuthatswana's incorporation in South Africa on 12 March. In the wake of these events, one of the leaders of the extreme right, Constand Viljoen, decided to register the Freedom Front for the election so that his supporters could participate in the April general election. The collapse of the Gqozo government in the Ciskei followed. That left the IFP as the main obstacle to a fully inclusive election. After a day of violence in the centre of Johannesburg on 28 March, which caused a rift between Buthelezi and the King of the Zulus, Goodwill Zwelithini, Buthelezi finally opted to take part in the election, just a week before polling.

Despite bombings by the extreme right, the elections themselves passed off in a remarkably peaceful and good-humoured atmosphere. The conduct of the elections was far from perfect and there were undoubtedly irregularities. When the Independent Electoral Commission announced the final results of the elections on 6 May, the manner in which the interests of the major parties were satisfied by the outcome prompted suggestions that the result was a negotiated one (see Table 9.3). However, for all the weaknesses of the electoral process, there is little reason for supposing that the outcome did not broadly reflect opinion among the electorate. In particular, although intimidation restricted the capacity of the parties to campaign on the ground in every part of the country, awareness was high that the ballot was secret, an important criterion for a free and fair election.

The Electoral Outcome

The scale of the ANC's victory was the most significant aspect of the outcome. The party had fallen short of achieving a two-thirds majority that would have enabled it to write the final constitution without reference to the opinions of other parties. However, it was in a position to get its way on its core concerns as it was clear that if it came to a referendum on a draft constitution, the view of the ANC would be likely to prevail. In these circumstances, the National Party did not seek to resist a final constitution based on the principle of majority rule, but sought concessions elsewhere. In any event, the party had discovered that power-sharing in the Government of National Unity did not provide it with a veto over the decisions of the majority. Following the approval of the draft of the final constitution in the Constituent Assembly, the National Party announced its intention to withdraw from the Government of National Unity.

In a book published at the beginning of 1999, the author argued that ANC dominance seemed likely to grow on the precedent of what had happened in Kenya, Zimbabwe and Namibia after the end of white minority rule:

> The party's status as the country's liberation movement forms the basis of its victory at the first democratic elections, while in the second, it does even better because it has the advantage of being the government with patronage at its disposal, in addition to still being seen as the country's liberator.[37]

This turned out to be the case in South Africa's second democratic elections in June 1999, the conduct of which attracted far fewer complaints or allegations of irregularities than the first (see Table 9.3).[38] Besides the further advance of the ANC, the most significant result of the 1999 election was the collapse in support for the New National Party, as the party now styled itself. The main reason for its decline was the shattering of white illusions about the nature of the deal the National Party had agreed with the ANC in 1993. The principal beneficiary of the party's decline was the Democratic Party. It fought

Table 9.3   General election results, 1994 and 1999*[39]

Party	1994		1999	
	Seats	*% of vote*	*Seats*	*% of vote*
African National Congress	252	62.6	266	66.4
(New) National Party†	82	20.4	28	6.9
Inkatha Freedom Party	43	10.5	34	8.6
Freedom Front	9	2.2	3	0.8
Democratic Party	7	1.7	38	9.6
Pan-Africanist Congress	5	1.2	3	0.7
African Christian Democratic Party	2	0.5	6	1.4
United Democratic Movement	N/A		14	3.4
United Christian Democratic Party	N/A		3	0.8
Federal Alliance	N/A		2	0.5
Minority Front	0	0.1	1	0.3
Afrikaner Einheids Beweging	N/A		1	0.3
Azanian People's Organisation	N/A		1	0.2

Notes:
* Only parties winning seats in the National Assembly in 1994 and/or 1999.
† Competed as the National Party in 1994; the New National Party in 1999.
N/A – Party did not contest 1994 election.

the election under the slogan 'Fight Back' (prompting the telling retort 'Don't fight blacks'). The Democratic Party's slogan prompts a question. Why did the National Party government not put up more resistance to the coming of the majority rule in the mid-1990s? This chapter has provided a partial answer to that question. A further dimension of the puzzle is addressed in the next chapter on the transnational dimension of the demise of apartheid.

10

The Worldwide Anti-Apartheid Movement: Peripheral or Crucial?

The absence of international involvement in the negotiations that led to South Africa's political settlement has been touted by some of the participants as one of the ingredients of the success of the process. They present an attractive picture of the problems of South Africa being solved by South Africans themselves. The National Party's chief negotiator, Roelf Meyer, has argued that this is an important lesson of the South African case that is applicable to other conflicts.[1] In particular, he has argued that what Northern Ireland needs is a new agreement negotiated among the parties in Northern Ireland themselves without the involvement of the British, Irish or American governments. The evident advantage of such an approach is that greater legitimacy would accrue to an agreement achieved without external intervention. In fact, it is partly because few wish to detract from the legitimacy of the South African settlement that the myth of external exclusion from South Africa's transition is not more vigorously challenged. A strong case can be made that external pressures played an important role not only in creating the conditions for negotiations but also in influencing their outcome. The role of external pressures, more widely from the sports boycotts that began in the 1960s to the economic sanctions of the 1980s, forms the subject of this chapter.

The defeat of the Nazis discredited biologically based theories of racism. However, it did not immediately lead to the acceptance of a norm of racial equality. This change only came about with the civil rights movement in the United States and the completion of the process of decolonisation in the 1960s. The change did not take place overnight and for many years it continued to be resisted by conservative elements within Western societies and indeed is continuing to be resisted in some quarters. Nevertheless, the change had a far stronger impact on domestic attitudes towards apartheid within Western societies than on the foreign policies of the major Western states towards South Africa. The difference between the two levels can somewhat simplistically be explained as a difference between interests and values. That is to say, foreign policy was based on the perception of policymakers as to the national interest. In the context of the Cold War, apartheid South Africa was regarded for many years as a reliable bulwark against Communism precisely because of its hostility towards notions of human equality. Governments of the major Western states, such as the Carter Administration in the United States, which based their policies on hostility towards apartheid, inevitably ran into criticism that their approach was needlessly jeopardising the West's geo-strategic interests.

By contrast, domestic opinion did not regard South Africa's anti-Communism as a factor in mitigation of the offensive character of apartheid. Further, governments could not afford to ignore the strength of public condemnation of apartheid altogether. In addition to the influence of their own domestic public opinion on the issue, Western governments were also under pressure from Third World states to take action over apartheid. The consequence was a wide difference between the rhetoric of governments on the subject of apartheid and their behaviour in practice. In the introduction to a book published in 1979 on the British government's deceit over the application of oil sanctions to Rhodesia after UDI, Anthony Sampson described American and British policy towards the region as characterised by 'institutionalised hypocrisy'.[2] Calls for the application of economic sanctions against South Africa because of the policy of apartheid were first made in the late 1950s. They gained further impetus as a result of the Sharpeville massacre in 1960.

However, the governments of South Africa's main trading partners were unwilling to impose economic sanctions on the Republic. The furthest Western governments would go in the 1960s was to permit the passage through the United Nations Security Council of a resolution calling for the application of a voluntary arms embargo to South Africa.

The resistance of governments to international action against apartheid meant that those campaigning against apartheid within Western societies eventually sought other transnational avenues that bypassed government to make their opinions heard. The most significant of these was sport. What gave further weight to sport in the struggle against apartheid was the influence within the realm of sport of a very wide range of states, most of which had strong domestic reasons for disapproving of the policy of apartheid. But the story of South Africa's sporting isolation also illustrates how late the shift in attitudes on race occurred in a number of societies that maintained links with South Africa.

The Role of Sport

The team sport in which South Africa excelled was rugby union and the country's main rival in the sport was New Zealand. The relationship between the two countries was complicated by the fact that rugby was a passion of New Zealand's Maori population. On South Africa's first tour of New Zealand, controversy was engendered when a South African journalist covering the tour reported on the team's negative reaction to the inclusion of a fixture against a Maori side in their itinerary. It led to the fixture being dropped during the next tour in 1937. At South Africa's insistence Maoris were excluded from tours by the New Zealand All Blacks to South Africa in 1928, 1949 and 1960. In 1960 the demand that the All Blacks should be all white prompted opposition to the tour centred on the churches. However, both the New Zealand Labour government and the National Party opposition supported the tour. The Labour Party was damaged in the process and lost the general election later that year partly as a result of the unpopularity of the party's stance among Maori voters.[3] By the mid-1960s, there was a consensus in New Zealand that further tours of South Africa would not take place under such circumstances and only an invitation that placed no racial bar on the selection of the New Zealand team would be accepted.

From the perspective of the early 2000s it seems remarkable that as late as 1960 other countries would be willing to kowtow to apartheid to the extent of accepting racial restrictions on their selection of players for the national team. However, it was not an isolated example. In 1968 England's cricket selectors failed to include Basil

D'Oliviera in the touring team that was due to go to South Africa, despite his scoring a century against Australia in a test match shortly before the touring team was announced. There was an outcry over his exclusion. When the selectors subsequently included D'Oliviera in the touring team when one of those who had originally been selected dropped out, the South African Prime Minister, B.J. Vorster, told a provincial congress of the National Party that the team would not be admitted. He put his objections as follows: 'The team as constituted now is not the team of the MCC but the team of the Anti-Apartheid Movement, the team of SANROC [South African Non-Racial Olympic Committee], and the team of Bishop Reeves.'[4] What made the case of D'Oliviera so difficult for Vorster, who was in fact in the process of relaxing the insistence that touring teams should be all white so as to maintain the country's sporting relations with its traditional partners, was his South African origin.

Before the 1960s South Africa had encountered relatively little opposition to the practice of segregation in sport. Between 1908 and 1960 all-white South African teams had competed in successive summer Olympic Games. So entrenched was the practice of segregation in South African sport when the National Party came to power in 1948 that the new government did not consider it necessary to issue any statement of policy on the issue. The first such statement was made in 1956, making clear the government's opposition to inter-racial sport within South Africa and that visiting teams would have to respect South African customs. The context of the statement was a challenge to South African practices by the International Table Tennis Federation (ITTF), which recognised the non-racial South African Table Tennis Board (SATTB) at the expense of the country's white sporting authority for table tennis. The government took action to prevent the ITTF from creating a precedent for other sports by withdrawing the passports of SATTB players to make it impossible for them to take part in international competition.

One of the first opponents of apartheid to recognise that sport might be a field in which the policy could be undermined was Trevor Huddleston. He wrote the following:

But it may well be that South Africa will soon find herself isolated from the sporting world as completely as it is isolated in its political thinking from the world of both East and West. Already the World Association football body is finding South Africa an embarrassment, for there are more Africans in the Union playing Soccer than Europeans. Already there are questions concerning the Olympic Games. And it is not impossible that in cricket, other countries besides the West Indies will find it hard to accept South African teams. Just because the Union is so good at sport, such isolation would shake its self-assurance very severely. Fantastic though it may sound, it might be an extraordinarily effective blow to the racialism which has brought it into being.[5]

Huddleston's words in many ways proved prophetic, though moves to isolate South Africa in sport did not arise as quickly as he anticipated.

Another pioneer in the struggle against apartheid in and through sport was Dennis Brutus. Brutus was one of the founders of the non-racial South African Sports Association (SASA) formed in October 1958 to promote the formation of non-racial sports bodies. The intention was to secure international recognition for the non-racial bodies and the withdrawal of recognition from the established white sports federations. In October 1962 at the initiative of SASA, the South African Non-Racial Olympic Committee (SANROC) was launched. The intention was that in due course SANROC would apply for recognition from the International Olympic Committee in place of the South African Olympic and National Games Association (SAONGA). The government responded to the threat that SANROC posed by banning its leading members, including Brutus. That effectively ended SANROC's activities in South Africa and forced the organisation into exile. Brutus was jailed for violating the terms of his banning order and then subsequently for escaping from police custody. He left South Africa on an exit permit in 1966.

To begin with, white attitudes were relatively little affected by the international campaign against apartheid in sport. In a book published in 1965, Leo Kuper described attitudes towards the issue as follows:

Generally in sport, a strong, though not absolute color bar is raised between White and non-White. White sports administrators tend to regard this as nonpolitical, simply as one of the customs of the country, and they often characterize attempts to remove the color bar as the intrusion of politics into sport. The more militant non-White sportsmen see apartheid in sport, and the monopoly of national colors by Whites, as obviously political, and part of systematic political discrimination.[6]

South Africa was excluded from the Tokyo Olympics of 1964 after failing to satisfy the IOC's demand that SAONGA dissociate itself from segregation in sport. By the time of the Mexico Olympics government sports policy permitted the selection of a single mixed team, albeit on the basis of segregated trials. Initially, the IOC decided to permit South Africa to participate on this basis but the majority in favour of the invitation was overturned after the threat of an extensive boycott of the Games.

However, a much greater impact was made on white opinion in South Africa by the demonstrations against South African touring teams that followed the D'Oliviera affair. Widespread protests greeted the Springbok rugby tour of Britain and Ireland in 1969–70 prompting the cancellation of a planned South African cricket tour of England in 1970. Disruption of the South African rugby tour of Australia in 1971 led to the cancellation of a cricket tour that had been due to take place later that year. In response to isolation there were successive changes to the government's sports policy. Integration of sporting events was permitted first under the rubric that they were international events and so did not compromise the domestic practice of segregation. In 1976, in a major statement of policy, the government declared that it would even permit integration at club level under the multinational rubric when circumstances justified it. When the extent of integrated sport became a matter of contention within the National Party, there was a further shift in government policy. The autonomy of sports bodies to determine their own policies in this area was accepted. These changes for the most part failed to reverse the country's sporting isolation. At the same time, some contact was maintained with the outside world through unofficial tours by rebel teams, as well as the occasional official tour. As late as 1985, the Springbok rugby team toured New Zealand amid widespread protests and deep divisions over the issue of the tour within the country.[7]

By the 1980s if not earlier, the justification for sporting boycotts was no longer segregationist practices within sport itself but simply apartheid itself, even in its reformist version. In the 1990s the role played by sport in the country's politics was very different, but scarcely less remarkable.[8] An obstacle to South African participation in a number of sports was the existence of competing sports bodies, particularly after the creation of the South African Council on Sport (SACOS) in 1973 as an umbrella organisation for the non-racial sports movement. By the late 1980s SACOS's rigid policy of non-collaboration had begun to alienate black trade unions. They helped to create the National Sports Congress with the aim of creating single non-racial sports bodies for each sporting code. Even before its legalisation the ANC started to play a part in the process of encouraging contacts among sports bodies to this end. Most remarkably of all, a meeting took place in Harare between the ANC and the representatives of South Africa's different rugby bodies in October 1988. At the meeting the sports bodies agreed to establish a single non-racial body to control the sport and the ANC 'undertook to use its good offices to ensure that non-racial South African rugby takes its rightful place in world rugby'.[9]

The ANC's decision to facilitate South Africa's entry or re-entry into international sporting competition made it possible for South Africa's sporting isolation to end ahead of the complete dismantling of apartheid and the transition to democracy. It also meant that sport could be used to promote political change during the transition itself. Thus, when President de Klerk sought white approval in March 1992 to continue negotiations on a settlement with the ANC in a referendum, one of the most effective advertisements of the 'yes' campaign highlighted South Africa's participation in the cricket World Cup then taking place in Australia. It contrasted a photograph of the South African team celebrating victory over Australia with a picture of an overgrown pitch and broken stumps to suggest what the consequences of a 'no' vote might be. The significance of the role of sport in the fall of apartheid was that it was a field in which the role of government was relatively limited. The same applied to the cultural boycott of South Africa. However, the value of isolating South Africa from cultural trends elsewhere in the world was open to question, so applying sanctions in this field never generated the same level of support as the sports boycotts.

Embargoes and Sanctions

The main form that government action against apartheid took in the 1960s and the 1970s was an arms embargo. In August 1963 the

United Nations Security Council passed a resolution calling on all states to cease the sale and shipment of arms to South Africa. However, it was left to states whether they wished to follow this advice or not and it was ignored by a number of leading arms-exporting states. In November 1977 the Security Council turned its voluntary arms embargo into a mandatory one by passing a resolution under Chapter 7 of the UN Charter that proclaimed South Africa's acquisition of arms to be a threat to the maintenance of international peace and security. The somewhat ironic effect of the mandatory arms embargo was to facilitate the development within South Africa of a large, arms-manufacturing industry that ultimately became an important source of the country's exports. This was the context of the passage in December 1984 of a Security Council resolution calling on states not to import arms, ammunition or military vehicles from South Africa.

Neta Crawford accepts that the arms embargo had little immediate effect on South Africa.[10] In particular, it did not deter South Africa from pursuing an aggressive military strategy of regional destabilisation in the early 1980s. It was only in the late 1980s that the embargo had a significant impact on the balance of power in the region. Deliveries of advanced fighter aircraft to Angola by the Soviet Union in the mid-1980s resulted in South Africa's losing air superiority over Southern Angola. South African efforts to overcome this change included the establishment of links with Loyalist paramilitaries in Northern Ireland, including supplying them with weapons, in a bid to secure surface-to-air missiles to counter the impact of Angola's new MiGs on the conflict. The loss of air superiority contributed to a series of military reverses for the South African forces intervening in the Angolan civil war. These setbacks played a role in the South African government's agreement in 1988 to a political settlement in Namibia. It is arguable that the Namibian settlement was significant as a precursor to the South African government's decision to enter into negotiations with the ANC on the future of South Africa. To that extent, it can be claimed that the arms embargo made a contribution to South Africa's transition to democracy.

Of the various forms of sanctions, economic sanctions tended to be seen as the most important. Calls for a boycott of South African goods were made by the ANC as early as 1958. Boycotts did not depend completely on action by governments in so far as individuals could decide themselves not to purchase South African products. At this level, the individual actions of consumers had little impact until the mid-1980s, by which time the climate of opinion was sufficiently hostile to apartheid as to affect the sale and availability of products such as wine in most Western countries. However, before the era of people's sanctions in the mid-1980s, anti-apartheid campaigners concentrated their efforts almost entirely on persuading governments to adopt sanctions. They did so in the belief that only far-reaching action by governments was likely to have a sufficient impact on South Africa's economic ties with the rest of the world to force the South African government to abandon apartheid. This continued to be a widely held assumption even in the 1980s. Thus, the SACP leader, Joe Slovo, declared in September 1988:

> I am convinced that if comprehensive and obligatory sanctions would be introduced, the ruling circles in the RSA [Republic of South Africa] would be forced to negotiate with the national liberation movement even on the most vital problems within the next six months.[11]

Despite numerous international declarations in support of economic sanctions, throughout the 1960s and 1970s the campaign for economic sanctions was largely a failure where it mattered most in economic terms, that is among South Africa's major economic trading partners. South Africa's crisis of governability in the mid-1980s led to the adoption by Western government of the first significant tranche of economic sanctions against South Africa. The most far-reaching measure was the Comprehensive Anti-Apartheid Act (CAAA) of 1986, which was adopted by Congress by a two-thirds majority that overrode President Reagan's veto:

> The act banned certain imports into the United States from South Africa, such as gold Krugerrands, iron and steel, uranium, coal, agricultural products, textiles, and military articles. It prohibited a number of U.S. exports to South Africa, including petroleum, nuclear materials, and technology, and computers for 'apartheid-enforcing agencies'. In addition to sanctions on trade, the CAAA imposed a variety of sanctions on capital, with perhaps a greater long-term impact. It barred virtually all new U.S. loans to South Africa and virtually all new investment in South Africa.[12]

The emphasis Davis places on the financial measures in the CAAA was due to the recognition by anti-apartheid campaigners of the effectiveness of such sanctions in the 1980s.[13] The fact that the refusal of a number of banks to roll over South African loans caused a sharp fall in the value of South Africa's currency in 1985 provided a striking demonstration of South Africa's vulnerability in this area. The Commonwealth and the European Community (EC) also recommended that their members adopt a variety of economic sanctions. These were not as extensive as the American measures, owing in large part, to the strong opposition to sanctions of the British government under Thatcher.

There continued to be opposition to sanctions from a variety of sources in the 1980s that extended far beyond apologists for white minority rule in South Africa. Opponents of economic sanctions stressed that huge damage might be done to the South African economy in the process. For example, Merle Lipton painted a cataclysmic picture of the possible consequences of sanctions:

> If sanctions have their intended effects, economic decline could erode those economic bonds that have drawn together the diverse people of (what has become) South Africa, and strengthen the fissiparous tendencies, thus making more possible partition, against a background of growing violence throughout the region.[14]

In the event, economic sanctions were in place for no longer than five years in most cases and their impact on the South African economy is very hard to measure. By contrast, it is far easier to connect the short history of economic sanctions to political developments. Thus, the South African government's repeal of the remaining so-called pillars of apartheid in 1991 was clearly designed to meet the precise requirements of the Comprehensive Anti-Apartheid Act for the lifting of American sanctions.

Not surprisingly, many writers reviewing the use of sanctions in the South African case have concluded that it presents a striking example of the successful employment of sanctions. For example, Audie Klotz concludes perfectly reasonably: 'On balance, the South African experience demonstrates that international sanctions can play a constructive role in domestic political change.'[15] However, the South African case is by no means as straightforward as it appears. Sanctions were far from being the only reason, or even the principal reason, why the government of De Klerk committed itself in 1990 to negotiations with the ANC on the future of South Africa. Further, it is dangerous to generalise about the utility of economic sanctions in other situations from the South African case. They were far less successful in the case of Rhodesia and in the case of Iraq in the 1990s they caused a humanitarian catastrophe, demonstrating that the collateral effects of sanctions could indeed be devastating.

Codes of Conduct

Sanctions were by no means the only means by which the outside world sought to influence South Africa's racial policies. One of the most influential initiatives of the 1970s was the drawing up of a code of conduct for American firms operating in South Africa. The Reverend Leon Sullivan, a significant figure in the American civil rights movement and a colleague of Martin Luther King, was appointed to the board of General Motors (GM) in 1971. His appointment was part of corporate America's efforts to address civil rights in the United States in the wake of the ghetto riots of the late 1960s. From the outset, Sullivan asked questions about GM's involvement in apartheid through its presence in South Africa. His engagement with the issue deepened when he visited Lesotho in 1975. The trip gave him the opportunity to experience conditions in South Africa on his way to and from Lesotho. His brief presence in Johannesburg did not go unnoticed and he was strip-searched at Jan Smuts Airport as he was about to leave the country.

On his return to the United States, Sullivan proposed a first draft of his principles, entitled 'Principles of Equal Rights for American Firms in the Republic of South Africa'. On 1 April 1977, the public launch of the principles took place, with the support of 12 companies including GM, IBM, Mobil, Ford, Caltex and Citibank, among others. What became universally known as the Sullivan principles set the following guidelines:

(1) Nonsegregation of the races in all eating, comfort, and work facilities.
(2) Equal and fair employment practices for all employees.
(3) Equal pay for all employees doing equal or comparable work for the same period of time.

(4) Initiation of and development of training programs that will prepare, in substantial numbers, blacks and other nonwhites for supervisory, administrative, clerical, and technical jobs.

(5) Increasing the number of blacks and other nonwhites in management and supervisory positions.

(6) Improving the quality of employees' lives outside the work environment in such areas as housing, transportation, schooling, recreation, and health facilities.[16]

The implementation of the principles was secured through regular monitoring of the performance of individual firms. In subsequent years there were further amplifications of the principles and the addition of a seventh principle: 'Working to eliminate laws and customs which impede social, economic and political justice'.[17] The approach taken by Sullivan was copied by others, including the EC, which adopted a similar code of conduct for the firms of its member states. Citing the progress made during the decade of the operation of the principles between 1977 and 1987, Sullivan argues that the principles 'created a revolution not only in job opportunities but also in the way black workers were viewed by white people in South Africa'.[18]

The incremental approach of the principles was ultimately abandoned by Sullivan himself. After setting a deadline for South Africa to end statutory apartheid that the government failed to meet, Sullivan called on American companies to withdraw from South Africa. By this time, a campaign for South African divestment was in full swing at American universities and his call chimed in with the prevailing mood in the United States. Many companies heeded Sullivan's call and sold their operations in South Africa to local owners. Whether or not the withdrawal of American companies in these circumstances made a constructive contribution to change in the country remains a debatable point. But what this history does demonstrate was South Africa's susceptibility to transnational pressures. One of the most remarkable aspects of Sullivan's campaigns to change South Africa was their lack of dependence on the American government. The fact that South African society could be so influenced by these campaigns was testimony to the extent of South Africa's integration in the West.

Another indication of South Africa's integration into the West was that debate within most Western societies on how to get rid of apartheid was limited to non-violent methods. The language of liberation movements and armed struggle to describe the use of violence to overthrow apartheid was accepted in the Third World, but remained contested in Western societies, where references to the ANC as terrorists by rightwing conservatives was not uncommon. The focus on sanctions by anti-apartheid campaigners recognised that there was a taboo against the employment of violent means against South Africa. Indeed, part of the impetus for action to persuade the South African government to abandon apartheid came from the fear, intensified by the country's crisis of the mid-1980s, that the whites of South Africa were heading for self-destruction. In promoting his principles in Europe, Sullivan enlisted the aid of a former British Prime Minister, Edward Heath, to organise meetings with business leaders. In raising the spectre of a race war in the absence of far-reaching change in South Africa, Sullivan prompted (according to Sullivan) the following response from Heath: 'This means that it is more urgent than ever that these meetings succeed because the world will not stand by and see four million white people go down.'[19] This was in 1986.

Deon Geldenhuys identifies four different approaches by the international community to the pursuit of change in South Africa: intervention, isolation, conditional engagement and mediation.[20] South Africa was never subject to direct military intervention. A naval blockade to enforce sanctions was mooted as a possibility in certain circumstances, such as the defeat of De Klerk in the referendum on negotiations in 1992. The threat that such action might be considered by the major powers was the closest South Africa came to being subject to direct intervention by other states. However, indirect intervention was more prevalent. It generally took the form of support for MK, the ANC's armed wing. Geldenhuys discusses sanctions under the heading of isolation, while the Sullivan principles provide an example of his third approach of conditional engagement. A further example is provided by the positive measures agreed by the EC in September 1985. These arose out of disagreements among the member states on the imposition of sanctions. Largely because of British opposition, the EC had been unable to agree on a substantial package of sanctions. That had provided the impetus for the adoption of another approach to signal how seriously the EC viewed the crisis in South Africa. This was the context of the launch by the EC of a special programme to assist the victims of apartheid. The programme channelled aid to non-governmental organisations in five sectors: education and training; health; rural and agricultural development; good governance; and democratisation. Aid to organisations monitoring the observance of human rights was included under the last of these categories. The South African case was an early example of an approach that became increasingly influential in the 1990s, of seeking to promote liberal democracy through strengthening civil society.

Mediation

Since mediation presupposes a situation in which the parties to a conflict can be persuaded to enter into negotiations, the fourth of Geldenhuys's approaches only arose as a possibility in the final years of the apartheid era.[21] The first major effort at external mediation arose without prior consultation with the parties. As in the case of the European Community's positive measures, it arose out of disagreement over sanctions. At the Commonwealth Heads of Government meeting in Nassau, the Bahamas, in October 1985, Thatcher's strong opposition to a comprehensive package of measures, particularly in the economic field, frustrated the adoption of such a package. As a compromise, it was agreed that a mission of eminent persons should be established to explore the possibility of dialogue between the South African parties, before consideration was given to the adoption of more restrictive measures against South Africa. The membership of the Eminent Persons Group (EPG), as it became known, was announced in November 1985. The co-chairmen of the group were the former Australian Prime Minister, Malcolm Fraser, and a former military ruler of Nigeria, General Olusegun Obasanjo.

The Commonwealth Accord on Southern Africa adopted at Nassau effectively placed parameters on the EPG's mission. The Accord called on the authorities in Pretoria to take five steps as a matter of urgency:

(a) Declare that the system of apartheid will be dismantled and specific and meaningful action taken in fulfilment of that intent.

(b) Terminate the existing state of emergency.

(c)   Release immediately and unconditionally Nelson Mandela and all others imprisoned and detained for their opposition to apartheid.

(d)   Establish political freedom and specifically lift the existing ban on the African National Congress and other political parties.

(e)   Initiate, in the context of a suspension of violence on all sides, a process of dialogue across lines of colour, politics and religion, with a view to establishing a non-racial and representative government.[22]

Nevertheless, the South African government decided, at least initially, to cooperate with the EPG mission. It was mindful that its refusal would have prompted the automatic intensification of sanctions by most of the Commonwealth. There was also a possibility the ANC would respond negatively to the requirement of a suspension of violence, allowing blame for the political *impasse* to be shifted away from the government.

The EPG visited South Africa in March 1986, its engagements including a meeting with Nelson Mandela in Pollsmoor prison. A second visit of the group to South Africa and Zambia took place in May. This visit was cut short on 19 May when the South African Air Force launched a series of bombing attacks on the neighbouring states of Botswana, Zambia and Zimbabwe. By this time the EPG's mission had led to a white backlash in South Africa. That was reflected in the disruption of public meetings organised by the National Party by the extreme rightwing Afrikaner Weerstands Beweging (AWB). It was evident at this point that Pretoria had decided that the continuation of the mission was no longer in its interest. That was underlined by a letter sent to the EPG by the South African foreign minister on 29 May. This made it clear that the South African government sought a termination of violence, not simply its suspension by its adversaries. Further, it asserted that the government's own measures to maintain law and order lay outside the scope of steps needed to create an environment free of violence and intimidation. Finally, Pik Botha also declared that the government was only prepared to negotiate about a new constitutional dispensation that would provide for power-sharing.[23]

The report of the EPG's mission to South Africa was published in June. It formed the basis of the decisions taken by a special summit of the Commonwealth on the issue of South Africa in August 1986.

Its powerful indictment of the South African government provided the basis for all members of the Commonwealth, except Britain, agreeing to the intensification of sanctions. A particularly significant aspect of the EPG's report was its approach to the question of violence in South Africa, especially in the light of the politically diverse membership of the group. Its starting point was that apartheid was an inherently violent system, while it laid most of the responsibility for current political violence in the country at the door of the government, including so-called 'black on black' violence which it argued was partly encouraged and fomented by the government.[24] This assessment went hand in hand with the report's judgement that the ANC would be likely to win an election held on the basis of universal franchise.

President de Klerk's dramatic initiative of February 1990 appeared to leave little scope or need for external mediation. However, the deterioration of relations between the government and the ANC over the issue of violence reopened the question of the need for external involvement. In April 1991, the ANC sent the government an ultimatum over the violence, threatening to suspend all negotiations. The ANC's stance on the issue of political violence was strengthened in July 1991 by revelations that the government had been financing the IFP. Progress towards the resolution of the issue of violence was made in September 1991 when the government, the ANC and the IFP signed the National Peace Accord. This led to the appointment of Judge Richard Goldstone at the head of a standing Commission of Inquiry Regarding the Prevention of Public Violence and Intimidation and to the setting up of a National Peace Committee supported by regional and local committees. However, these measures failed to stem the tide of violence, leading to concerted pressure during 1992 for greater international involvement in efforts to end the violence.

At the end of March 1992 the report of a fact-finding mission from the International Commission of Jurists (ICJ) was published. It was based on two visits to South Africa by a team of five lawyers, the first in September 1991 and the second in March 1992. The report was strongly critical of the IFP leader, Chief Mangosuthu Buthelezi, whom it described as bearing 'a heavy responsibility for the escalation of the violence'.[25] It called for international monitoring of the violence. The ICJ's proposal was taken up inside South Africa. When Nelson Mandela visited Alexandra following an upsurge of violence between the residents and hostel-dwellers in the township after the white referendum in March, he called for the establishment of an independent international monitoring team as 'the only way we can stop the violence'.[26] In June, Amnesty International issued a highly critical report on South Africa alleging complicity of the security forces in political killings.[27] That was followed by the Boipatong massacre and the shooting of unarmed demonstrators during De Klerk's ill-judged visit to the squatter camp.

After Boipatong the ANC suspended its bilateral negotiations with the government and demanded an international inquiry into the violence. A sharp fall in the value of the financial rand underlined the reaction of foreign investors to the crisis. The government's response was to appoint a number of foreign experts to assist the Goldstone Commission. However, that proved insufficient to quieten international concern, which culminated in a debate on 15 and 16 July in the UN Security Council on the crisis in South Africa. At the end of the debate the Security Council adopted Resolution 765 of 1992. It expressed concern at the breakdown of negotiations, condemned the escalation of violence, making particular reference to the events in Boipatong, called for effective implementation of the National Peace Accord, and underlined the importance of all parties cooperating in the resumption of negotiations. In effect, the resolution balanced criticism of the failure of the South African authorities to deal effectively with the issue of violence and pressure on the ANC to return to the negotiations. But the most important element of the resolution was the invitation to the UN Secretary-General to appoint a special representative to advise on measures to end the violence.[28]

Following the passage of the resolution, the Secretary-General, Boutros Boutros-Ghali, appointed the former US Secretary of State, Cyrus Vance, as his special representative. After Vance visited South Africa, a team of UN observers was sent to South Africa to monitor the ANC's campaign of rolling mass action. At the climax of the mass action in early August the team was credited with ensuring restraint on all sides. The success of Vance's efforts prompted suggestions that he would make an ideal mediator in constitutional negotiations between the government and the ANC. In the event the Secretary-General put forward a more modest proposal to the Security Council as a result of the Vance mission. The number of UN observers was increased. It was also supplemented by the addition of observers from other appropriate external sources, including the

Commonwealth, the OAU and the EC. However, the intensification of international monitoring of the violence did not prove a panacea. Further serious episodes of violence occurred, including a massacre of ANC demonstrators by members of the Ciskei Defence Forces in Bisho on 7 September 1992. But the presence of monitors did affect the interpretation of the violence and in the case of the Bisho massacre added to the pressures on the government to reach an accommodation with the ANC. On 26 September, President de Klerk and Nelson Mandela signed the Record of Understanding, ending the suspension of formal negotiations between the two sides. With negotiations back on track, external mediation lost its high visibility.

Impact on the Settlement

International involvement in the transition was not confined to assisting the process through monitoring of the violence. It also had an influence on the substance of the negotiations. In particular, the South African government was unable to muster international support for a consociational settlement. The position of the Bush Administration in the midst of the crisis following the Boipatong massacre was particularly striking. Giving evidence before the Africa subcommittee of the House of Representatives, the Assistant Secretary of State for African Affairs, Herman Cohen, stated the following:

> All sides must recognise the right of the majority to govern, while assuring that all South Africans have a stake in their government... [But no side could insist on] overly complex arrangements intended to guarantee a share of power to particular groups which will frustrate effective governance. Minorities have the right to safe-guards; they cannot expect a veto.[29]

European diplomats played their part by discouraging the notion that the Swiss system of cantons provided a viable model for demo-cratisation in South Africa.[30]

In the final phase of the transition, after the installation of the Transitional Executive Council in December 1993, the main concern of foreign governments was that the elections in April 1994 should be as inclusive as possible. Their efforts were directed towards achieving an accommodation between the ANC and the IFP that would persuade the latter to participate in the elections. International mediation was offered to Buthelezi by Mandela at the beginning of March 1994, but only finally taken up in the second week of April. The team of seven mediators headed by the former American Secretary of State, Henry Kissinger, and the former British Foreign Secretary, Lord Carrington, arrived in South Africa on 12 April. In the event, their services were not employed as the ANC and the IFP could not even agree on terms of reference for the mediators. However, this effort did not prove entirely fruitless. A Kenyan academic appointed as an adviser to the team, Washington Okumu, stayed on in South Africa after the departure of Carrington and Kissinger and was credited with influencing Buthelezi's eleventh-hour decision to participate in the elections.

It remains true that the international community did not play a direct role in the negotiations that led to a settlement between the National Party government and the ANC in December 1993. This mattered, as clearly an externally imposed settlement would have enjoyed far less legitimacy than one freely arrived at by the principal parties. Nevertheless, the role that the international community played on the sidelines was of crucial importance in determining the outcome. Giliomee suggests that the outcome of the negotiations might have been different if De Klerk had been willing to use the force at his disposal. He quotes the Chief of the Defence Force, George Meiring, as telling De Klerk on the day of Mandela's inauguration as President: 'You never used your strong base to negotiate from, you never used the military as a base for strength, which you had available to you, you never wanted to use it.'[31] The implication of Giliomee's analysis is that by being more forceful De Klerk might have achieved the balanced political settlement based on group rights that he had sought at the outset.

However, what external mediation during the transition demonstrated was that more forceful action by De Klerk would have detracted even further from the South African government's depleted international legitimacy. At the same time, the international community would not have countenanced as a balanced political settlement one in which the whites as a group retained a veto over the decisions of government. In this context, it is notable that the Western policy-makers of the day showed a better understanding of the change necessary to create the basis for legitimate government in South Africa than did some of the theorists of consociationalism. South Africa was far too unequal a society in terms of the distribution of its resources to justify special protection for groups who were already privileged in terms of their share of the country's wealth. Indeed, even the ANC's success in securing white acquiescence to the transition to majority rule was a sufficient source of suspicion for some that real change had not occurred.

The nature of South Africa's transition makes the notion that South Africa owed the peculiarity of its political development to its isolation from other countries impossible to sustain. On the contrary, the extent of South Africa's penetration by transnational influences at the start of the age of globalisation suggests just the opposite. It also suggests the need for external influences to be more fully woven into the story of South Africa's development, not just at its culmination in majority rule, but from its creation as a political entity. Admittedly, the interweaving of governmental and non-governmental influences, whereby governments took their cue from the reports of non-governmental agencies, was a particular feature of the last decade of minority rule. At the same time, the success of the transition made South Africa something of a special case among societies where the West attempted to shape the course of political development in the 1990s.

11
Conclusion: Taking the Long View on Apartheid's Demise

In *Small World*, David Lodge's novel about academic conferences and pretensions, the hero, Persse McGarrigle, impresses a publisher by proposing to write a book on the subject of the influence of T.S. Eliot on William Shakespeare. Since Shakespeare died hundreds of years before Eliot was born, his subject is on the face of it absurd. However, as the hero explains, his point is that modern audiences cannot engage with Shakespeare as if in total ignorance of the subsequent history of English literature, including, obviously, the work of T.S. Eliot.[1] This is a nice conceit and points to a fundamental truism. People's views of the past are greatly influenced by the times in which they live. As the world constantly changes, historians will never ever be out of business since they can rely on a virtually limitless demand to reinterpret the past in the light of current events. The point has particular relevance to the interpretation of the rise and fall of apartheid, as it seems inevitable that perceptions of apartheid in this century will be fundamentally shaped by South Africa's political development during the course of the next decades.

Of course, current events cannot change facts of the past, but as E.H. Carr pointed out very eloquently, history cannot consist, and has never consisted, of a literal recitation of facts about the past.[2] Such facts are virtually infinite, so inevitably even the most detailed, empirical accounts of particular events consist of the interpretation of a very tiny selection of what seem to the historian the most significant facts about the past. The consensus on what is significant tends to change with the passage of time. Accounts of South Africa's transition to democracy published in the 1990s understandably focused on the detail of what appeared at the time to be a miraculous escape from the catastrophe that had been predicted even before the National Party came to power in 1948.[3] The emphasis on the way in which South Africa changed as opposed to why South Africa changed has tended to direct attention away from the long-term factors that underpinned the country's transformation. Five broad sources of change can be identified: demographic, economic, ideological or normative, external and political.

Sources of Change

The demographic pressure for change can best be illustrated by examining the shift in the racial composition of South Africa's population (see Table 11.1). Up until 1960 whites constituted over a fifth of the population, while up to 1970 Africans constituted less than 70 per cent of the population. These two facts helped to underpin minority rule. They made it possible for the government to ensure that the control of the state machinery was for the most part in white hands and that the representation of Africans in the machinery of the state was not such as to threaten white control. A further dimension of South Africa's demography not conveyed by the totals in Table 11.1 was the urban – rural divide in the population. In 1921, only a third of the total urban population was African and even by the end of the century urban Africans constituted a minority of South Africa's African population.[4] By contrast, large majorities of whites, Coloureds and Indians lived in the urban areas by 1921.[5] Consequently, as late as the 1970 census, Africans constituted a minority of the urban population of South Africa.

This book has not dwelt at any length on the economic dimension of the rise and fall of apartheid. The best account of the structural economic factors that in the long run undermined the economic viability of apartheid as envisaged by Verwoerd remains Merle

Table 11.1 Population of South Africa by race in census years, 1911–96[6]

Year	Africans %	Whites %	Coloureds %	Indians %	Others/ Unclassified	Total
1911	67.3	21.4	8.8	2.5	N/A	5,972,757
1921	67.5	22.0	7.9	2.4	N/A	6,927,403
1936	68.8	20.9	7.8	2.3	N/A	9,587,863
1946	68.6	20.8	8.1	2.5	N/A	11,415,925
1951	67.6	20.8	8.7	2.9	N/A	12,671,482
1960	68.3	19.3	9.4	3.0	N/A	16,002,797
1970	70.4	17.1	9.4	2.9	N/A	21,794,000
1980	N/A	N/A	N/A	N/A	N/A	28,978,510
1985	74.1	14.8	8.6	2.6	N/A	33,621,863
1991	N/A	N/A	N/A	N/A	N/A	37,737,620
1996	76.7	10.9	8.9	2.6	0.9	40,583,574

Note: N/A = not available or not applicable.

Lipton's book, *Capitalism and Apartheid*.[7] The treatment of Africans as temporary sojourners in white areas by means of influx control was geared to an economy based on cheap labour. The growth of manufacturing and the service sector of the economy increased the demand of employers for a more differentiated labour force. Further, the sectors that had traditionally depended on cheap labour, mining and agriculture, themselves underwent change. With mechanisation, they also wanted more skilled or semi-skilled workers. The labour bureaux provided an effective mechanism for the allocation of cheap labour, but they were ill-equipped to provide a trained workforce. The consequence was that employers turned against the migrant labour system at the heart of Verwoerd's vision of apartheid.

The record of the South African economy from apartheid's formative years to its collapse is summarised by Terreblanche as follows:

> South Africa's economy grew at the relatively high rate of at least 5 per cent a year in the post-war period from 1947 to 1974. This high rate of growth was attained by means of a large inflow of foreign investment, foreign entrepreneurship, and foreign technology. Measured in 2000 prices, FDI [foreign direct investment] in 1974 totalled almost R175 billion. Many of the foreign companies that invested in South Africa exploited cheap and docile African labour to make very big profits. When the oil crisis of 1973 slowed

down economic growth elsewhere, South Africa also experienced a severe recession. But, in contrast with most other countries, the recession deteriorated into chronic stagflation that coincided with a period of political instability and black unrest, culminating in the collapse of white political domination in the early 1990s.[8]

Terreblanche acknowledges that what he calls the Verwoerdian accumulation strategy based on effective control of cheap labour and an industrialisation policy of import substitution reached its limits in the 1970s. Nevertheless, he attributes the poor performance of the economy thereafter primarily to political factors. In so far as political instability discouraged foreign investment it is possible to argue that South Africa's successive political crises from the Soweto uprising onwards contributed to the weak performance of the economy. However, political mobilisation was itself a response to the weakness of the economy and the failure of the government's policy in the economic realm was attributable at least as much to economic as to political factors, as Terreblanche's own analysis of its limits suggests. Like the Soviet system, apartheid did not prove adaptable as an economic system after the oil shocks of the 1970s.

A striking indicator of the economy's poor performance was the stagnation in real terms of per capita incomes (see Table 11.2). In the

Table 11.2   Gross domestic product per capita, 1960–96, at constant 1990 prices[9]

Year	GDP pc	Year	GDP pc	Year	GDP pc
1960	R5717	1973	R7765	1986	R7517
1961	R5780	1974	R8033	1987	R7495
1962	R5974	1975	R7969	1988	R7631
1963	R6245	1976	R7946	1989	R7633
1964	R6559	1977	R7733	1990	R7434
1965	R6770	1978	R7755	1991	R7192
1966	R6876	1979	R7848	1992	R6879
1967	R7171	1980	R8163	1993	R6816
1968	R7270	1981	R8380	1994	R6854
1969	R7408	1982	R8138	1995	R6938
1970	R7587	1983	R7790	1996	R7007
1971	R7704	1984	R7987		
1972	R7625	1985	R7700		

year Mandela became President per capita incomes in real terms remained below what they had been in 1966 near the zenith of the boom of the 1960s when South Africa had one of the highest economic growth rates in the world. White incomes in the 1980s were adversely affected both by the general stagnation in incomes and by a decline in the white share of total incomes as a result of the modest racial redistribution brought about by reform apartheid. In other situations, such conditions have fuelled support for parties of the extreme right. Support for the Conservative Party in South Africa fits the pattern. It also explains why there was a measure of anxiety among some liberal analysts that economic sanctions could prove counterproductive. One reason why economic conditions helped to persuade whites of the need for change rather than the reverse was the readiness of the ANC to assuage white fears about their economic future.

A third factor explaining South Africa's transformation is ideological or normative change. The self-identification of white South Africans as members of Western, Christian civilisation meant that ultimately the West's own abandonment of racism as a basis for dividing up humanity and its formal commitment to racial equality had an effect on the belief of white South Africans in racism. While racial prejudice did not disappear (as was also the case elsewhere), it was less and less rooted in dogmatic belief in the division of humanity into races with fixed and different characteristics. The consequence was that from the 1970s even at an official level, white South Africans ceased to espouse the racism of previous generations. Rather, government representatives attempted the impossible, to justify apartheid in terms of contemporary international norms. An early example was a statement made by South Africa's representative at the United Nations, Pik Botha, to the Security Council in 1974. Botha proclaimed that 'the S.A. Government did not condone discrimination purely on the grounds of race or colour'.[10]

The fourth factor of external pressures was discussed at length in Chapter 10 and does not require further elaboration here beyond making the point that the effectiveness of external pressures was facilitated by the existence of normative change. The fifth factor encompasses the history of African nationalism and more specifically that of the ANC. The story of the fall of apartheid is also that of the rise of the ANC. Part of the reason for the ANC's success was its ability to project a different conception of South Africa's future to the dismal one offered by the National Party government based on discredited theories of racial/ethnic difference. The point is well made by Rupert Taylor in his discussion of the role that a particular segment of civil society, peace and conflict resolution non-governmental organisations played in South Africa's transition to democracy:

> Nonracialism, premised upon a discourse of equality and the principled rejection of race, provided an alternative understanding of South African society that increasingly enabled activists to comprehend their social worlds outside the warped logic of apartheid.[11]

But a note of caution about the political factor is in order. The ANC's current hegemony inevitably colours contemporary views of its role in South Africa's history. Those who wrote about African nationalism in South Africa before 1994 typically referred to both the ANC and the PAC. The almost complete disappearance of the PAC in post-apartheid South Africa has been as surprising as the remaking of the liberal Democratic Party as a party of the right.

The Triumph of the ANC

In the decade after the banning of the ANC and the PAC it appeared that the government had succeeded in crushing opposition to its policies among the African population. Revival came through the Black Consciousness Movement of the late 1960s. Although it was ultimately subjected to the same persecution as the ANC and the PAC had been, the government failed to re-establish full control of the society, even after the death of the inspirational Black Consciousness leader, Steve Biko, in 1977. The main rival to the Black Consciousness Movement in the 1970s was Inkatha, an organisation formed by the Zulu leader, Chief Mangosutho Buthelezi in March 1975. The Black Consciousness Movement paved the way to the revival of ANC-aligned organisations within South Africa in the 1980s, by far the most important of which was the United Democratic Front (UDF). In retrospect, it seems that the seeds were sown for the ANC's long march to power by the formation of the ANC Youth

League in 1944 by a remarkable group of leaders, which included Nelson Mandela, Oliver Tambo and Walter Sisulu. They were responsible for the transformation of the ANC into a mass movement that retained a large measure of legitimacy among the population at large even during the long period of its effective suppression within the country.

At the same time, the new political dispensation has cast a fresh light on political structures of the apartheid era. Critics of the apartheid system during the National Party's rule rarely accorded any measure of credibility to the system of homeland governments created by Pretoria. They were vindicated by the outcome of the 1994 election in so far as it demonstrated the political irrelevance of ethno-nationalism, except in the case of the Zulus. However, from the perspective of the governance of South Africa, the homeland structures have been far from irrelevant. Their legacy is to be found in the regional governments established in 1994 which 'spend about two-thirds of the national budget (after repayment of the national debt) and employ the vast majority – about 750,000 – of the country's 1.1 million public servants'.[12] As Tom Lodge points out, a majority of these, 400,000, are 'the former functionaries of the old apartheid homelands'.[13] If the ANC had treated this sizeable constituency of people as collaborators with apartheid, it could easily have alienated a significant segment of African opinion in the process. Instead, with the exception of KwaZulu which has remained a stronghold of the IFP, they were incorporated into the ranks of the ANC, thanks to Mandela's espousal of a policy of reconciliation.

This is far from the only example of continuity between the old regime and the new that was a consequence of the nature of South Africa's transition to majority rule, the 'how' of South Africa's transformation as opposed to the 'why'. By far the most significant aspect of continuity in South Africa's political development is that the country made the change from one order to another by constitutional means. Giliomee treats it as a by-product of De Klerk's caving in to ANC in the negotiations:

> After the balance of power had tipped against it in mid-1992, the De Klerk government spent much of its energy on avoiding the symbolism of defeat in the transition to a new system. There would be no guerrilla army parading through the streets in a victory march; no toppling of statues and no multi-party control of the

security forces in the run-up to the election. The government got its way on constitutional continuity.[14]

Consequently, the new dispensation required formal endorsement by the old institutions and the judges kept their positions. Giliomee suggests that the ANC conceded on what he describes as symbolism so as to gain the substance of what it wanted.

But far more significant than symbolism was that the transition from minority to majority rule by constitutional means sustained a long-running tradition of constitutional government in the country. This tradition was stretched to the limit during apartheid's 'golden age', but even then placed a constraint on the government's actions inside the country. Ultimately the tradition of constitutionalism can be traced all the way back to the establishment of the Union of South Africa in 1910. It was a legacy of British imperialism, as was racism, though that is not to say that imperialism was the sole source of either. Nevertheless, paradoxically, the very fact that the Union constitution was so accommodating to racism probably contributed to the survival of constitutionalism in the first half of the century. While the case of Chile shows that a long tradition of constitutional order may not necessarily safeguard a society against the overthrow of a demo-cratically elected government, it does make it more probable that once established, democratic institutions will survive.

Consequences of Continuity

The value of constitutional government to post-apartheid South Africa has been demonstrated in the first years of the twenty first century by the role that the Constitutional Court has played in ensur-ing a rational response by government to the AIDS pandemic.[15] It broke the government's resistance, which was based on President Mbeki's personal scepticism as to the causes of AIDS, to ensuring the wide availability of anti-retroviral drugs to people who were HIV-positive. AIDS emerged after the transition as by far the greatest threat the country has ever faced to the well-being of the population. This book has scarcely touched on the issue. The main reason for that is that it does not form a part of the story of the rise and fall of apartheid. Admittedly, the argument might fairly be made that the migrant labour system that was so central to apartheid has been a major factor in South Africa's susceptibility to the spread of the virus. However, this is not especially illuminating, as most of the country's current social ills can be seen in one way or another as a legacy of apartheid.

Another major consequence of continuity between the old order and the new is that South Africa has remained a very unequal society in terms of the distribution of incomes and wealth. For some writers, the current scale of inequality in South Africa provides grounds for casting doubt on the authenticity or completeness of the transition. For example, Terreblanche characterises South Africa's transformation as incomplete, its version of neoliberal democratic capitalism as apparently dysfunctional, and argues:

> The viability of the new democracy is threatened by bureaucratic incapacity, the inability of the state to make meaningful progress in deracialising the economic system, and its failure to alleviate the widespread poverty and social deprivation inherited from apartheid.[16]

Not merely has the new dispensation failed to make inroads into the overall level of inequality, but inequality has actually increased slightly, with the Gini coefficient rising from 0.68 in 1971 to 0.69 in 1996.[17] At the same time, there has been quite substantial change in the racial distribution of incomes. While the white share of incomes has fallen from 71 per cent in 1970 to 52 per cent in 1996, the African share has risen from 20 per cent in 1970 to 36 per cent in 1996.[18]

Further, unequal as South Africa is as a society, it is not as unequal as the global economy in its distribution of incomes. It may be reasonable to pose the question as to whether democracy can survive in the conditions of inequality that prevail in South Africa. But that also begs the question as to whether liberal-democracy is sustainable as a universal basis for legitimate governance in a world that remains as unequal as it is today. The two problems not only mirror each other, but are arguably interdependent. If it is reasonable to characterise the operation of the world economy as a form of global apartheid, then it might also be reasonable to characterise the new divide in South Africa between a multiracial top layer and a poor black or African base as a kind of neo-apartheid. Yet one can hardly blame whites in South Africa for wanting to retain First

World living standards and lifestyles or those who were oppressed and discriminated against under apartheid for wishing to enjoy the full fruits of deracialisation. In addition, a strong case can be made that the implementation of radical policies of redistribution would damage the economy because of their impact on the capacity of the country to retain its most highly skilled members in the most productive sectors of the economy.

In the medium term, inequality seems unlikely to threaten the ANC's hegemony. However, the government has little reason for complacency. Some of post-apartheid South Africa's most serious social problems, such as crime, are clearly connected both to the scale of economic inequality and to the related extent of unemployment. In this context, the land question is a particularly difficult problem for the government. White retention of their large farms, another consequence of constitutional continuity, is seen by many in African communities as the product of their own conquest in earlier times and no more legitimate now than it was in the past. Resentment at the seeming incapacity and unwillingness of the government to effect change in this area has been reflected in the destabilising phenomenon of the murder of white farmers.[19] This issue also explains in part the government's cautious approach to the problem created by the catastrophic breakdown of the Zimbabwean economy and Mugabe's violations of constitutional and democratic norms in his efforts to cling on to power. The South African government's irritation at the British government's pronouncements over the question of Mugabe's misdeeds is also understandable.[20] Both the British and American governments signally failed to honour the promises they made in 1979 to provide Zimbabwe with the resources to bring about an orderly redistribution through the purchase of land from white farmers, as was done in Kenya. Further, Western governments also bear a measure of responsibility for the disastrous Economic Structural Adjustment Programme (ESAP) that was imposed on Zimbabwe in the 1990s and started the downward spiral of the economy.

While inequality has formed the basis of leftwing criticism of the South African miracle, rightwing critics have tended to focus on issues such as crime and corruption. But overriding rightwingers' current concerns has been their gloomy expectation that South Africa is unlikely to have a rosy future under majority rule. Since the end of the twentieth century, this has most commonly been put in the form of the question: will South Africa follow the path of Zimbabwe? It would be easy to respond to this question by listing all the differences between South Africa's evolution and Zimbabwe's historical development, including, for that matter, the issue of constitutional continuity. However, what is most wrong with the question is that it is generally asked as if what happens to the rest of the world has no bearing on the answer. The message of this book is that South Africa's political development during the course of the twentieth century was intimately bound up with what happened in the rest of the world. Indeed, the major failing of much of the literature on South Africa has been its inward-looking character, starting with the once widely believed contention that the origins of South African racism lay on the frontier. There seems little reason to suppose that South Africa's future will be any less bound up with international developments than its past. In the circumstances, to make any predictions about South Africa would be folly, since it is evident that the world itself is in flux. What can perhaps be safely predicted is that the word apartheid is not about to disappear from the political lexicon.

Notes

Chapter 1

1. Andrew Kenny, 'How Apartheid Saved South Africa', *The Spectator* (London), 27 November 1999.
2. *New Oxford English Dictionary*, Oxford: Clarendon Press, 1998, p. 75.
3. Edgar H.Brookes, *Apartheid: A Documentary Study of Modern South Africa*, London: Routledge and Kegan Paul, 1968, p. 1.
4. Dan O'Meara, *Forty Lost Years: The Apartheid State and the Politics of the National Party 1948–1994*, Randburg: Ravan Press, 1996, p. 64.
5. Hermann Giliomee, *The Afrikaners: Biography of a People*, Cape Town: Tafelberg, 2003, p. 454.
6. *Ibid.*, p. 463.
7. Quoted in Bernard Friedman, *Smuts: A Reappraisal*, London: George Allen and Unwin Ltd, 1975, p. 164.
8. James Barber, *South Africa's Foreign Policy 1945–1970*, London: Oxford University Press, 1973, p. 40.
9. Frank Welsh, *A History of South Africa*, London: HarperCollins, 2000, p. xxvi.
10. J.E. Spence, 'The Most Popular Corpse in History', *Optima*, 34 (1) (March 1986).
11. *Environment News Service* at http://www.ens-news.com/aug2002.
12. *Cable Network News* web-site at http://www.cnn.com for 28 August 2002.
13. Patrick Bond, *Against Global Apartheid: South Africa Meets the World Bank, IMF and International Finance*, Lansdowne: University of Cape Town Press, 2001, p. 286.
14. Anthony H. Richmond, *Global Apartheid: Refugees, Racism and the New World Order*, Toronto: Oxford University Press, 1995.
15. Titus Alexander, *Unravelling Global Apartheid: An Overview of World Politics*. Cambridge: Polity Press, 1996.
16. Fidel Castro, *War, Racism and Economic Justice: Global Apartheid and the World Economic Order*, Melbourne: Ocean Press, 2001.
17. Thomas Schelling, 'The Global Dimension' in Graham Allison and Gregory F. Treverton (eds), *Rethinking America's Security*, New York: Norton, 1992, p. 200.
18. See http://www.twnside.org.sg/title/just-cn.htm. The Third World Network is based in Penang in Malaysia.
19. Marwan Bishara, *Palestine/Israel: Peace or Apartheid? Prospects for Resolving the Conflict*, London: Zed Books, 2001 and Uri Davis's

Apartheid Israel: Possibilities for the Struggle Within, London: Zed Books, 2003.

20. See, for example, Henry Siegman, 'Israel: The Threat from Within', *New York Review of Books*, 51 (3) (26 February 2004).

21. George Hicks, *Japan's Hidden Apartheid: The Korean Minority and the Japanese*, Aldershot: Ashgate, 1997.

Chapter 2

1. See David Welsh, *The Roots of Segregation: Native Policy in Colonial Natal, 1845–1910*, London: Oxford University Press, 1971.

2. Province of Transvaal, *Report of the Local Government Commission*, Pretoria, TP1/1922, paras 42 and 265.

3. See Martin West, 'Population Group' in Emile Boonzaier and John Sharp (eds), *South African Keyword: The Uses and Abuses of Political Concepts*, Cape Town and Johannesburg: David Philip, 1988, p. 104.

4. Carole Cooper, Jennifer Schindler, Colleen McCaul, Robin Hamilton, Mary Beale, Alison Clemans, Lou-Marie Kruger, Isabelle Delvare and John Gary Moonsamy, *Race Relations Survey 1988/89*, Johannesburg: South African Institute of Race Relations, 1989, p. 152.

5. Quoted in Muriel Horrell, *A Survey of Race Relations in South Africa 1965*, Johannesburg: South African Institute of Race Relations, 1966, p. 303.

6. Union Government, *Report of the Department of Bantu Administration and Development for 1958–9*, Pretoria: UG51/1960, p. 23.

7. See Horrell, *A Survey of Race Relations in South Africa 1970*, Johannesburg: South African Institute of Race Relations, 1971, p. 164.

8. Florence Elliott and Michael Summerskill, *A Dictionary of Politics*, Harmondsworth: Penguin, 1957, pp. 314–5.

9. John Kane-Berman, 'Beware the Culture of Silence', *Fast Facts* (Johannesburg, South African Institute of Race Relations) No.6 (June 2001).

10. See Hermann Giliomee and Lawrence Schlemmer, *From Apartheid to Nation-building*, Cape Town: Oxford University Press, 1989, pp. 139–45.

11. Kader Asmal, Louise Asmal and Ronald Suresh Roberts, *Reconciliation through Truth: A Reckoning of Apartheid's Criminal Governance*, Cape Town: David Philip, 1996, p. 132.

12. *Ibid.*, p. 182.

13. Hermann Giliomee, 'Asmal Offers No Fresh View, No Ground-Breaking Synthesis of Truth', *Cape Times*, 23 October 1996.

14. Antjie Krog, *Country of My Skull*, London: Jonathan Cape, 1998, p. 58.

15. The book was first published in 1964. A revised edition was published in 1969, which is the edition used here. The details are as follows: Brian Bunting, *The Rise of the South African Reich*, Harmondsworth: Penguin, 1969.

16. Patrick Laurence, 'Playing the Nazi Card', *Focus* (Parklands, Helen Suzman Foundation) No.20 (December 2000).

17. Hermann Giliomee, *The Afrikaners*, Cape Town: Tafelberg, 2003, p. 442.
18. *Ibid.*, p. 418.
19. *Ibid.*, p. 495.
20. Allister Sparks, *The Mind of South Africa: The Story of the Rise and Fall of Apartheid*, London: Mandarin, 1991, pp. 162–3.
21. James Barber, *South Africa in the Twentieth Century: A Political History – In Search of a Nation State*, Oxford: Blackwell, 1999, p. 140.
22. Sparks, *The Mind of South Africa*, p. 185.
23. William Beinart, *Twentieth-Century South Africa*, Cape Town: Oxford University Press, 1994, p. 138.
24. Julian Barnes, 'Holy Hysteria', *New York Review of Books*, 1 (6) (10 April 2003), p. 32.
25. Hannah Arendt, *The Origins of Totalitarianism*, New York: Meridian, 1958, pp. 93–4.
26. See Daniel Jonah Goldhagen, *Hitler's Willing Executioners: Ordinary Germans and the Holocaust*, London: Abacus, 1997, pp. 416–54.
27. Arendt, *Origins of Totalitarianism*, p. 151.
28. *Ibid.*, p. 155.
29. *Ibid.*, p. 204.
30. *Ibid.*, p. 206.
31. *Ibid.*, p. 202.
32. *Ibid.*, p. 158.
33. Laurence, 'Playing the Nazi Card'.

Chapter 3

1. Frank Welsh, *A History of South Africa*, London: HarperCollins, 2000, p. 325
2. Sampie Terreblanche, *A History of Inequality in South Africa, 1652–2002*, Pietermaritzburg: University of Natal Press, 2002, p. 243.
3. Hermann Giliomee, *The Afrikaners, Biography of a People*, Cape Town: Tafelberg, 2003, p. 246.
4. Ronald Robinson and John Gallagher with Alice Denny, *Africa and the Victorians: The Official Mind of Imperialism*, London: Macmillan, 1961, p. 53.
5. J.A. Hobson, *The War in South Africa: Its Causes and Effects*, London: J. Nisbet, 1900, p. 313.
6. *Ibid.*, p. 292.
7. Quoted in J.A. Hobson, *Imperialism: A Study*, London: George Allen and Unwin, 1938, p. 5.
8. *Ibid.*, p. 6.
9. *Ibid.*
10. *Ibid.*, p. 7.
11. *Ibid.*, pp. 6–7.
12. D.W. Krüger, 'The British Imperial Factor in South Africa from 1870 to 1910', in L.H. Gann and Peter Duignan (eds), *Colonialism in Africa: Volume 1*, London: Cambridge University Press, 1969, p. 341.

13. Hannah Arendt, *The Origins of Totalitarianism*, New York: Meridian, 1958, p. 133.
14. Hobson, *Imperialism*, p. 46.
15. *Ibid.*, p. 48.
16. *Ibid.*, p. 51.
17. J.A. Hobson, *Problems of a New World*, London: G. Allen and Unwin, 1921, p. 28.
18. *Ibid.*, p. 85.
19. See J.A. Hobson, *The Psychology of Jingoism*, London: G. Richards, 1901.
20. See, for example, A.J.P. Taylor, 'Hobson's Misapplication of the Theory' in D.K. Fieldhouse, *The Theory of Capitalist Imperialism*, London: Longman, 1967.
21. Hobson, *Imperialism*, p. 223.
22. See, for example, L.H. Gann and Peter Duignan, 'Reflections on Imperialism and the Scramble for Africa', in Gann and Duignan (1969), p. 102.
23. Hobson, *The War in South Africa*, pp. 232–3.
24. *Ibid.*, p. 231 and p. 286.
25. Quoted in Hobson, *The War in South Africa*, p. 233.
26. *Ibid.*, p. 197.
27. Thomas Pakenham, *The Boer War*, London: Futura Publications, 1982, pp. xvi–xvii.
28. *Ibid.*, p. xvi.
29. Monica Wilson and Leonard Thompson (eds), *The Oxford History of South Africa: Volume 2*, London: Oxford University Press, 1971, p. 320.
30. Robinson and Gallagher, *Africa and the Victorians*, p. 461.
31. Annexed to the Cape Colony in 1865 to save money despite the colonists' objections.
32. CO 48/444, Note by Buckingham, July 1868.
33. C.F. Goodfellow, *Great Britain and South African Confederation*, Cape Town: Oxford University Press, 1966, p. 15.
34. S. Herbert Frankel, *The Tyranny of Economic Paternalism in Africa*, supplement to *Optima* (Johannesburg), December 1960, p. 5.
35. CO 48/389 D 116, Grey to Stanley, 5 July 1858.
36. CO 48/390, Bulwer-Lytton to Grey, 6 September 1858.
37. CO 48/390, Grey to Bulwer-Lytton, 19 November 1858.
38. *Ibid.* Minute by Carnarvon, 7 January 1859.
39. Frankel, *Tyranny of Economic Pateralism*, p. 5.
40. See Goodfellow, *Confederation* p. 4. The first line to Wellington was completed in 1863.
41. CO 48/441, D 33, May 1868.
42. Annexed by the Cape in the 1870s, it was soon returned to Britain under whose jurisdiction it remained until independence in 1966.
43. CO 48/441, D 62, Dispatch from Wodehouse, 18 July 1868.
44. CO 48/444, Minute by Buckingham, 8 November 1868.
45. *Handbook to South Africa*, London: S.W.Silver and Co., 1875, p. 3.
46. John Angove, *In the Early Days: Pioneer Life on the South African Diamond Fields*, Kimberley: Handel, 1910, p. 199.

47. Mr Gilpin, *Hansard Vol. CCXI*, Third Series, Col.814, 28 May 1872.
48. Mr W.M. Torrens, *ibid.*, Col.815.
49. Mr R.N. Fowler, *Hansard Vol. CCIV*, Third Series, Col.1278, 3 March 1871.
50. Mr Kinnaird, *ibid.*, Col.1282.
51. *Carnarvon Papers*, Public Record Office files, London. 30/6/4, 12 December 1876. See Goodfellow, *Confederation*, p. 117.
52. John Benyon, *Proconsul and Paramountcy in South Africa: The High Commission, British Supremacy and the Sub-Continent 1806–1910*, Pietermaritzburg: University of Natal Press, 1980, p. 342.
53. Timothy Keegan, *Colonial South Africa and the Origins of the Racial Order*, Cape Town and Johannesburg: David Philip, 1996, p. 293.
54. Heribert Adam, *Modernizing Racial Domination: The Dynamics of South African Politics*, Berkeley: University of California Press, 1971, p. 14.
55. D.C. Watt, *A History of the World in the Twentieth Century: Part 1 1899–1918*, London: Pan Books, 1970, p. 104.
56. Hobson, *Imperialism*, p. 345.
57. Anthony Atmore and Shula Marks, 'The Imperial Factor in South Africa in the Nineteenth Century: Towards a Reassessment' in E.F.Penrose (ed.), *European Imperialism and the Partition of Africa*, London: Frank Cass, 1975, p. 132.
58. Pakenham, *The Boer War*, p. 572.
59. *Ibid.*, p. xvii and Kenneth O. Morgan, 'Britain's Vietnam? Lloyd George, Keir Hardie, and the Importance of the "Pro-Boers"', in Wm Roger Louis (ed.), *Still More Adventures with Britannia*, London: I.B. Tauris, 2003, pp. 51–74.

Chapter 4

1. John W. Cell, *The Highest Stage of White Supremacy: The Origins of Segregation in South Africa and the American South*, Cambridge: Cambridge University Press, 1982, p.3.
2. *Ibid.*, pp. 192–5.
3. Saul Dubow, *Racial Segregation and the Origins of Apartheid in South Africa, 1919–36*, Basingstoke: Macmillan, 1989, p. 23.
4. *Report of the South African Native Affairs Commission*, London: HMSO, 1905 (Cd 2399), p. 58.
5. *Ibid.*, pp. 67–70.
6. Quoted in David Welsh, *The Roots of Segregation: Native Policy in Colonial Natal, 1845–1910*, Cape Town: Oxford University Press, 1971, p. 208.
7. Julius Lewin, *Politics and Law in South Africa*, London: Merlin Press, 1963, p. 91.
8. Sampie Terreblanche, *A History of Inequality in South Africa, 1652–2002*, Pietermaritzburg: University of Natal Press, 2002, pp. 260–1.
9. D. Hobart Houghton, *The South African Economy*, London: Oxford University Press, 1973, p. 146.
10. Terreblanche, *History of Inequality*, p. 239.

11. C.W. de Kiewiet, *A History of South Africa – Social and Economic*, London: Oxford University Press, 1941, pp. 150–1.
12. Derived from T.R.H. Davenport, *South Africa: A Modern History* (4th edn), Basingstoke: Macmillan, 1991, pp. 564–5.
13. James Barber, *South Africa in the Twentieth Century*, Oxford: Blackwell, 1999, p. 76.
14. Ronald Hyam, *The Failure of South African Expansion, 1908–1948*, London: Macmillan, 1972, p. 31.
15. *Ibid.*, p. 32.
16. Quoted in Hyam, *Failure of South African Expansion*, p. 66.
17. Quoted in Freda Troup, *South Africa: An Historical Introduction*, London: Eyre Methuen, 1972, p. 233.
18. David Yudelman, *The Emergence of Modern South Africa: State, Capital, and the Incorporation of Organized Labor on the South African Gold Fields, 1902–1939*, Westport, CT: Greenwood Press, 1983, pp. 24–9.
19. Prime Minister's Circular No. 5 of 1924, Union Government, *Official Yearbook No.9*, Pretoria, 1927, p. 203.
20. Hermann Giliomee, *The Afrikaners*, Cape Town: Tafelburg, 2003, p. 323.
21. Union Government, *Annual Report for the Department of Labour for 1934*, Pretoria, UG 11/1936, p. 80.
22. Union Government, *Report of the Industrial Legislation Commission*, Pretoria UG 37/1935, para 1075.
23. Allister Sparks, *The Mind of South Africa: The Story of the Rise and Fall of Apartheid*, London: Mandarin, 1991, p. 171.
24. Frank Welsh, *A History of South Africa*, London: Harper Collins, 2000, p. 418.
25. Hermann Giliomee, 'The Growth of Afrikaner Identity', in Heribert Adam and Hermann Giliomee, *Ethnic Power Mobilized: Can South Africa Change?*, New Haven, CT and London: Yale University Press, 1979, pp. 114–15.
26. Giliomee, *The Afrikaners*, p. 481.
27. Paul Rich, *State Power and Black Politics in South Africa, 1912–51*, Basingstoke: Macmillan, 1996, p. 158.
28. Kenneth A. Heard, *General Elections in South Africa 1943–1970*, London: Oxford University Press, 1974, p. 31.
29. Giliomee, *The Afrikaners*, p. 447. Chapter 13 is entitled, 'The Making of a Radical Survival Plan'.

Chapter 5

1. Deborah Posel, *The Making of Apartheid 1948–1961: Conflict and Compromise*, Oxford: Clarendon Press, 1991, p. 1.
2. *Ibid.*
3. *Ibid.*, p. 3.
4. Hermann Giliomee, *The Afrikaners, Biography of a People*, Cape Town: Tafelberg, 2003, p. 477.

5. Posel (1991), p. 5.
6. Dan O'Meara, *Forty Lost Years: The Apartheid State and the Politics of the National Party, 1948–1994*, Randburg: Ravan Press, 1996, p. 35.
7. *Ibid.*, pp. 65–6.
8. Posel, *Making of Apartheid*, p. 6.
9. See graph in Stan Siebert and Adrian Guelke, *Is State Control of Labour in South Africa Effective?*, London: Mandate Trust, 1973, p. 2.
10. Posel, *Making of Apartheid*, p. 258.
11. *Ibid.*, p. 97.
12. Republic of South Africa, *Report of the Department of Bantu Administration and Development for 1970*, Pretoria, RP 44/1972, p. 50.
13. Lawrence Schlemmer, *Employment Opportunity and Race in South Africa*, Johannesburg: South African Institute of Race Relations, 1973, p. 13.
14. Hermann Giliomee and Lawrence Schlemmer, *From Apartheid to Nation-Building*, Cape Town: Oxford University Press, 1989, p. 69
15. *Ibid.*, p. 72.
16. Quoted in Edgar H. Brookes, *Apartheid: A Documentary Study of South Africa*, London: Routledge and Kegan Paul, 1968, p. 6.
17. Colin de B. Webb, 'The Foreign Policy of the Union of South Africa' in J.E. Black and K.W. Thompson (eds), *Foreign Policies in a World of Change*, New York: Harper and Row, 1963, p. 426.
18. Quoted in T.R.H. Davenport, *South Africa: A Modern History*, Basingstoke: Macmillan, 1991, p. 333.
19. *State of South Africa: Economic, Financial and Statistical Year-Book for the Republic of South Africa*, Johannesburg: Da Gama, 1970, pp. 39 and 43.
20. Giliomee, *The Afrikaness*, p. 519.
21. *Ibid.*, p. 515.
22. For example, O'Meara writes, 'The years between 1964 and 1972 are sometimes described as "the golden age of apartheid".' O'Meara, *Forty Lost Years*, p. 116.
23. James Barber, *South Africa's Foreign Policy 1945–1970*, London: Oxford University Press, 1973, p. 47.
24. *Ibid.*, p. 75.
25. Peter Calvocoressi, *South Africa and World Opinion*, London: Oxford University Press, 1961, pp. 9–10.
26. *Ibid.*, p. 11.
27. J.E. Spence, *Republic under Pressure*, London: Oxford University Press, 1965, p. 47.
28. Quoted in Freda Troup, *South Africa: An Historical Introduction*, London: Eyre Methuen, 1972, p. 348.
29. E. Munger, *Afrikaner and African Nationalism*, London: Oxford University Press, 1967, p. 80.
30. The phrase is Heard's. Kenneth A. Heard, *General Elections in South Africa 1943–1970*, London: Oxford University Press, 1974, p. 158.

Chapter 6

1. Heribert Adam, *Modernizing Racial Domination: The Dynamics of South African Politics*, Berkeley and Los Angeles: University of California Press, 1971, p. 15.
2. *Ibid.*, p. 16.
3. *Ibid.*, p. 61.
4. *Ibid.*, p. 65.
5. *Ibid.*, p. 97.
6. *Ibid.*, p. 145.
7. *Ibid.*, p. 153.
8. Back cover of Pierre van den Berghe, *South Africa: A Study in Conflict*, Berkeley and Los Angeles: University of California Press, 1970.
9. *Ibid.*, pp. 263–4.
10. *Ibid.*, page unnumbered.
11. Quoted in Colin Legum and John Drysdale (eds), *Africa Contemporary Record 1968–9*, London: Africa Research Ltd, 1969, p. 317.
12. Hyam (1972), pp. 193–4.
13. See the discussion in Hermann Giliomee, *The Afrikaners: Biography of a People*, Cape Town: Tafelberg, 2003, pp. 531–2.
14. Quoted in Jack Halpern, *South Africa's Hostages: Basutoland, Bechuanaland, and Swaziland*, Harmondsworth: Penguin, 1965, p. 432.
15. H.F. Verwoerd, *The Road to Freedom for Basutoland, Bechuanaland, Swaziland* (Fact Paper No.107), Pretoria: Department of Information, 1963, p. 14.
16. *Ibid.*
17. Giliomee, *The Afrikaners*, p. 284.
18. *Africa Confidential*, No.9 (28 April 1967), p. 5.
19. They included the Upper Volta, Niger, Dahomey, Togo and Gabon, according to *The Guardian*, 9 November 1970.
20. Henry A. Kissinger, *National Security Study Memorandum 39*, quoted in B. Cohen and M.A.El-Khawas (eds), *The Kissinger Study of Southern Africa*, Nottingham: Spokesman Books, 1975, p. 37. The book reproduced the NSC study in full.
21. *Ibid.*, p. 63.
22. *Ibid.*
23. *Ibid.*, p. 70.
24. *Ibid.*, p. 94.
25. *Ibid.*, p. 86.
26. *Ibid.*, p. 84.
27. *Ibid.*, p. 89.
28. James Mayall, *Africa: The Cold War and After*, London: Elek, 1971, p. 149.
29. Eschel Rhoodie, *The Third Africa*, Cape Town: Nasionale Boekhandel, 1968, p. 162.
30. J.H.P. Serfontein, *Die Verkrampte Aanslag*, Kaapstad en Pretoria: Human and Rousseau, 1970, p. 75.

31. The episode is referred to in passing in Kenneth A. Heard, *General Elections in South Africa 1943–1970*, Oxford University Press, (1974), p. 201.
32. For further details see Muriel Horrell, *A Survey of Race Relations in South Africa 1970*, Johannesburg: South African Institute of Race Relations, 1971, pp. 4–5 and Muriel Horrell, *A Survey of Race Relations in South Africa 1974*, Johannesburg: South African Institute of Race Relations, 1975, pp. 6–8.
33. *Financial Mail* (Johannesburg), 27 April 1973.
34. James Barber and John Barratt, *South Africa's Foreign Policy: The Search for Status and Security 1945–1988*, Cambridge: Cambridge University Press, 1990, p. 105.
35. Sampie Terreblanche, *A History of Inequality in South Africa, 1652–2002*, Pietermaritzburg: University of Natal Press, 2002, p. 327.

Chapter 7

1. R.W. Johnson, *How Long Will South Africa Survive?*, London and Basingstoke: Macmillan, 1977.
2. *Ibid.*, p. 290.
3. *Ibid.*, p. 303.
4. *Ibid.*, p. 15.
5. *Ibid.*, pp. 15–16.
6. *Ibid.*, p. 17.
7. *Ibid.*, p. 16.
8. *Ibid.*, p. 294.
9. *Ibid.*, p. 314.
10. Pierre van den Berghe, *South Africa: A Study in Conflict*, Berkeley and Los Angeles: University of California Press, 1970, p. 262.
11. James Barber and John Barratt, *South Africa's Foreign Policy: The Search for Status and Security 1945–1988*, Cambridge: Cambridge University Press, 1990, p. 181.
12. On the South African government's substantiation of its claims of American involvement in the intervention, see *The Star Weekly* (Johannesburg), 22 April 1978.
13. See Muriel Horrell (ed.), *Survey of Race Relations in South Africa 1981*, Johannesburg: South African Institute of Race Relations, 1982, p. 1.
14. Dan O'Meara, *Forty Lost Years: The Apartheid State and the Politics of the National Party, 1948–1994*, Randburg: Ravan Press, 1996, p. 224.
15. Barber and Barratt, *South Africa's Foreign Policy*, p. 247.
16. L.H. Gann and Peter Duignan, *Why South Africa Will Survive*, London: Croom Helm, 1981.
17. *Ibid.*, p. 290.
18. *Ibid.*
19. *Ibid.*, p. 291.
20. *Ibid.*, p. 288.

21. *South Africa: Time Running Out* (The Report of the Study Commission on US Policy Toward Southern Africa), Berkeley and Los Angeles: University of California Press, 1981.
22. *Ibid.*, p. 408.
23. *Ibid.*, pp. 407–8.
24. Richard Leonard, *South Africa at War: White Power and the Crisis in Southern Africa*, Westport, CT: Lawrence Hill and Company, 1983; Joseph Hanlon, *Apartheid's Second Front: South Africa's War against Its Neighbours*, Harmondsworth: Penguin Books, 1986; Joseph Hanlon, *Beggar Your Neighbours: Apartheid Power in Southern Africa*, London: James Currey (for the Catholic Institute for International Relations), 1986; and Phyllis Johnson and David Martin, *Apartheid Terrorism: The Destabilization Report*, London: James Currey (for the Commonwealth Secretariat), 1989.
25. Stephen Chan (ed.), *Exporting Apartheid: Foreign Policies in Southern Africa 1978–88*, London and Basingstoke: Macmillan, 1990; Chris Alden, *Apartheid's Last Stand: The Rise and Fall of the South African Security State, 1978–1990*, Basingstoke: Palgrave, 1996; and William Minter, *Apartheid's Contras: An Inquiry into the Roots of War in Angola and Mozambique*, Johannesburg: Witwatersrand University Press, 1994.
26. The term predated the Reagan Administration. In particular, it had been used in a different context by Merle Lipton. See Merle Lipton, 'British Investment in South Africa: Is Constructive Engagement Possible?', *South African Labour Bulletin*, October 1976.
27. Quoted in Leonard, *South Africa at War*, p. 258.
28. Hanlon, *Apartheid's Second Front* (1986), p. 1.
29. *Ibid.*
30. M. Horrell, T. Hodgson, S. Blignaut and S. Moroney, *A Survey of Race Relations in South Africa 1976*, Johannesburg: South African Institute of Race Relations, 1977, p. 12.
31. O'Meara, *Forty Lost Years*, p. 323.
32. Loraine Gordon (ed.), *Survey of Race Relations in South Africa 1979*, Johannesburg: South African Institute of Race Relations, 1980, p. 386.
33. Merle Lipton, *Capitalism and Apartheid: South Africa, 1910–86*, Aldershot: Wildwood House, 1986.
34. *Ibid.*, p. 49.
35. *Ibid.*, p. 82.

Chapter 8

1. Carole Cooper, Jennifer Shindler, Colleen McCaul, Frances Potter and Melanie Cullum, *Race Relations Survey 1984*, Johannesburg: South African Institute of Race Relations, 1985, p. xvii.
2. *Ibid.*
3. Carole Cooper, Jennifer Shindler, Colleen McCaul, Frances Potter, Melanie Cullum, Monty Narsoo and Pierre Brouard, *Race Relations*

Survey 1985, Johannesburg: South African Institute of Race Relations, 1986, p. 534.
4. F.W. de Klerk, *The Last Trek: A New Beginning*, London and Basingstoke: Macmillan, 1998, p. 103.
5. *Ibid.*
6. Cooper *et al. Survey 1985*, p. 116.
7. Carole Cooper, Jennifer Shindler, Colleen McCaul, Pierre Brouard, Cosmas Mareka, Jon-Marc Seimon, Michael Markovitz, Harry Mashabela and Claire Pickard-Cambridge, *Race Relations Survey 1986*, Johannesburg: South African Institute of Race Relations, 1987 (Part 2), p. 520.
8. Quoted in Neta C. Crawford and Audie Klotz (eds), *How Sanctions Work: Lessons from South Africa*, Basingstoke: Macmillan, 1999, p. 11.
9. Mark A.Uhlig (ed.), *Apartheid in Crisis*, Harmondsworth: Penguin, 1986; Jesmond Blumenfeld (ed.), *South Africa in Crisis*, London: Croom Helm, 1987; John Saul and Stephen Gelb, *The Crisis in South Africa*, London: Zed Press, 1986; and Robin Cohen, *Endgame in South Africa?*, London: James Currey, 1986.
10. Cohen, *Endgame*, p. 95.
11. *Ibid.*
12. Uhlig (ed.), *Apartheid in Crisis*, p. 7.
13. *Ibid.*, p. 9.
14. Blumenfeld (ed.), *South Africa in Crisis* p. 14.
15. John D. Brewer (ed.), *Can South Africa Survive?: Five Minutes to Midnight*, Basingstoke: Macmillan, 1989, p. 343.
16. Bernard Crick, 'The High Price of Peace' in Hermann Giliomee and Jannie Gagiano (eds), *The Elusive Search for Peace: South Africa, Israel and Northern Ireland*, Cape Town: Oxford University Press, 1990, p. 265.
17. Quoted in Nelson Mandela, *Long Walk to Freedom*, Randburg: Macdonald Purnell, 1994, p. 536.
18. D.J. van Vuuren, L. Schlemmer, H.C. Marais and J. Latakgomo (eds), *South African Election 1987: Context, Process and Prospect*, Pinetown: Owen Burgess Publishers, 1987, p. 1.
19. *Ibid.*, p. 98.
20. Carole Cooper *et al.*, *Race Relations Survey 1989/90*, Johannesburg: South African Institute of Race Relations, 1990, pp. 548–50.
21. O'Meara, *Forty Lost Years*, p. 349.
22. *Ibid.*, p. 391.
23. De Klerk, *The Last Trek* pp. 160–1.
24. Mandela, *Long Walk to Freedom* p. 546.
25. *Ibid.*, p. 542.
26. *Proceedings of Joint Sitting, 2 February 1990, Debates of Parliament* (Republic of South Africa) second session – ninth parliament.
27. Willem de Klerk, *F.W. De Klerk: The Man in His Time*, Johannesburg: Jonathan Ball Publishers, 1991, p. 55.
28. Frederik van Zyl Slabbert, 'The basis and challenges of transition in South Africa: a review and a preview' in Robin Lee and Lawrence

Schlemmer (eds), *Transition to Democracy: Policy Perspectives 1991*, Cape Town: Oxford University Press, 1991, pp. 4–10.

29. Lawrence Schlemmer, 'The Turn in the Road: Emerging Conditions in 1990' in Lee and Schlemmer (eds), *Transition to Democracy*, p. 16.
30. *Ibid.*, p. 17
31. *Ibid.*, pp. 17–18.
32. Kathryn A. Manzo (ed.), *Domination, Resistance, and Social Change in South Africa: The Local Effects of Global Power*, Westport, CT: Praeger, 1992, p. 251.
33. *Ibid.*, p. 253.
34. Jeremy Cronin, 'The Boat, the Tap, and the Leipzig Way', *African Communist*, 23, Third Quarter, (1992), p. 45.
35. James Barber, *Forging the New South Africa*, London: Royal Institute of International Affairs, 1994, p. 6.
36. Hermann Giliomee, 'Democratization in South Africa', *Political Science Quarterly*, 110 (1) (Spring 1995), p. 86.
37. South Africa's Administrator-General in Namibia on the eve of the country's independence openly expressed disappointment to a group of visiting UK-based academics that the Democratic Turnhalle Alliance had not insisted on power-sharing after SWAPO's failure to secure a two-thirds majority in the 1989 elections. He argued that the implication for South Africa was that the government should not place reliance on the mechanism of a constituent assembly to draw up an acceptable constitution.
38. Giliomee, 'Democratization in South Africa', p. 91.
39. *Ibid.*
40. Allister Sparks, *Tomorrow is Another Country: The Inside Story of South Africa's Negotiated Revolution*, Sandton: Struik Book Distributors, 1994, p. 98.
41. *Ibid.*, p. 12.
42. Adrian Guelke, 'The Impact of the End of the Cold War on the South African Transition', *Journal of Contemporary African Studies*, 14 (1) (January 1996). This chapter draws freely on that article as well as on Chapter 2 of Adrian Guelke, *South Africa in Transition: The Misunderstood Miracle*, London: I.B.Tauris, 1999. Daniel's reply appeared as John Daniel, 'A Response to Guelke: The Cold War Factor in the South African Transition', *Journal of Contemporary Studies*, 14 (1) (January 1996).

Chapter 9

1. Arend Lijphart, 'Prospects for Power-Sharing in the New South Africa' in Andrew Reynolds (ed.), *Election '94 South Africa: The Campaigns, Results and Future Prospects*, Cape Town and Johannesburg: David Philip, 1994, p. 222.
2. Giliomee, *The Afrikaners: Biography of a People*, Cape Town: Tafelberg, 2003, p. 643.

3. *Ibid.*
4. This issue is discussed further in Chapters 10 and 11.
5. Allister Sparks, *Tomorrow is Another Country: The Inside Story of South Africa's Negotiated Revolution*, Sandton: Struik Book Distributors, 1994; Richard Spitz with Matthew Chaskalson, *The Politics of Transition: A Hidden History of South Africa's Negotiated Settlement*, Oxford: Hart Publishing, 2000; Robert Harvey, *The Fall of Apartheid: The Inside Story from Smuts to Mbeki*, Basingstoke: Palgrave, 2001; and Patti Waldmeir, *Anatomy of a Miracle: The End of Apartheid and the Birth of the New South Africa*, London: Viking, 1997.
6. Harvey, *Fall of Apartheid*, p. xv.
7. Timothy D.Sisk, *Democratization in South Africa: The Elusive Social Contract*, Princeton, NJ: Princeton University Press, 1995; Steven Friedman and Doreen Atkinson (eds), *The Small Miracle: South Africa's Negotiated Settlement*, Johannesburg: Ravan Press, 1994: Murray Faure and Jan-Erik Lane, *South Africa: Designing New Political Institutions*, London: Sage Publications, 1996 and Siri Gloppen, *South Africa: The Battle over the Constitution*, Aldershot: Ashgate, 1997.
8. Sisk, *Democratization*, p. 13.
9. Friedman and Atkinson (eds), *The Small Miracle*, pp. xii-xiii.
10. *Ibid.*, p. xiii.
11. Faure and Lane (eds), *South Africa* p. 9.
12. *Ibid.*, back cover.
13. Gloppen, *Battle over the Constitution*, p. 247.
14. Spitz, *The Politics of Transition*, p. 421.
15. *Ibid.*, p. 422.
16. Lijphart in Reynolds (ed.), *Election '94* p. 222.
17. *Ibid.*, p. 223.
18. *Ibid.*, p. 227. The description was coined by Theodor Hanf.
19. Hermann Giliomee and Charles Simkins (eds), *The Awkward Embrace: One-Party Domination and Democracy*, Cape Town: Tafelberg, 1999, p. 338.
20. Heribert Adam, Frederik van Zyl Slabbert and Kogila Moodley, *Comrades in Business: Post-Liberation Politics in South Africa*, Cape Town: Tafelberg, 1997, pp. 158–9.
21. Hein Marais, *South Africa: Limits to Change – The Political Economy of the Transition*, Cape Town: University of Cape Town Press, 2001; Patrick Bond, *Elite Transition: From Apartheid to Neoliberalism in South Africa*, Pietermaritzburg: University of Natal Press, 2000; and Dale T. McKinley, *The ANC and the Liberation Struggle: A Critical Political Biography*, London: Pluto Press, 1997.
22. Sampie Terreblanche, *A History of Inequality in South Africa, 1652–2002*, Pietermaritzburg: University of Natal Press, 2002.
23. Marais, *Limits to Change*, p. 4.
24. Bond, *Elite Transition* p. 17.
25. *Ibid.*
26. *Ibid.*, p. 55.
27. McKinley, *ANC and the Liberation Struggle* p. 132.

28. Terreblanche, *Inequality* pp. 97–8.
29. Giliomee and Simkins (eds), *The Awkward Embrace*, p. 339.
30. Elizabeth Sidiropoulos *et al., South Africa Survey 1996/97*, Johannesburg: South African Institute of Race Relations, 1997, p. 600.
31. Daniel Reed, *Beloved Country: South Africa's Silent Wars*, Johannesburg: Jonathan Ball Publishers, 1994 and Anthea J.Jeffery, *The Natal Story: 16 Years of Conflict*, Johannesburg: South African Institute of Race Relations, 1997.
32. Adrian Guelke, 'Interpretations of Political Violence during South Africa's Transition', *Politikon*, 27 (2) (2000), p. 243.
33. Stephen Ellis, 'The Historical Significance of South Africa's Third Force', *Journal of Southern African Studies*, 24 (2) (1998), pp. 283–5.
34. Giliomee, *The Afrikaners*, p. 642.
35. Reynolds (ed.), *Election '94*, p. 193.
36. Adam, Slabbert and Moodley, *Comrades in Business*, p. 54.
37. Adrian Guelke, *South Africa in Transition: The Misunderstood Miracle*, London: I.B. Tauris, 1999, p. 198.
38. See Andrew Reynolds's comments in Andrew Reynolds (ed.), *Election '99: South Africa – From Mandela to Mbeki*, New York: St. Martin's Press, 1999, p. 174.
39. For further details, see Herma Forgey *et al.*, *South Africa Survey 1999/2000: Millennium Edition*, Johannesburg: South African Institute of Race Relations, 1999, p. 326.

Chapter 10

1. See, for example, Roelf Meyer, *Paradigm Shift: The Essence of Successful Change*, Londonderry: INCORE, 2003, p. 17.
2. Anthony Sampson, 'Introduction' in Martin Bailey, *Oilgate: The Sanctions Scandal*, London: Coronet Books, 1979, p. 8.
3. Richard Thompson, *Retreat from Apartheid: New Zealand's Sporting Contacts with South Africa*, Wellington: Oxford University Press, 1975, p. 93.
4. Quoted in R.E. Lapchick, *The Politics of Race and International Sport: The Case of South Africa*, Westport, CT: Greenwood Press, 1975, p. 128.
5. Trevor Huddleston, *Naught for Your Comfort*, London: Fontana Books, 1957, pp. 149–50.
6. Leo Kuper, *An African Bourgeoisie*, New Haven, CT: Yale University Press, 1965, p. 357.
7. For a fuller account, see Adrian Guelke, 'The Politicisation of South African Sport' in Lincoln Allison (ed.), *The Politics of Sport*, Manchester: Manchester University Press, 1986.
8. See, for example, Adrian Guelke, 'Sport and the End of *Apartheid*' in Lincoln Allison (ed.), *The Changing Politics of Sport*, Manchester: Manchester University Press, 1993.
9. *The Times*, 17 October 1988.

10. Neta C. Crawford, 'How Arms Embargoes Work' in Neta C. Crawford and Audie Klotz (eds), *How Sanctions Work: Lessons from South Africa*, Basingstoke: Macmillan, 1999, pp. 45–6.
11. Quoted in Stephen P. Davis, 'Economic Pressure on South Africa: Does It Work?' in George W. Shepherd, Jr (ed.), *Effective Sanctions on South Africa: The Cutting Edge of Economic Intervention*, Westport, CT: Greenwood Press, 1991, p. 66.
12. *Ibid.*, pp. 70–1.
13. See, for example, Keith Ovenden and Tony Cole, *Apartheid and International Finance: A Program for Change*, Ringwood: Penguin, 1989.
14. Merle Lipton, *Sanctions and South Africa: The Dynamics of Economic Isolation*, London: Economist Intelligence Unit, 1988, p. 122. Quoted in Neta C. Crawford, 'Trump Card or Theater? An Introduction to Two Sanctions Debates' in Crawford and Klotz (eds), *How Sanctions Work*, p. 18.
15. Audie Klotz, 'Making Sanctions Work: Comparative Lessons' in Crawford and Klotz (eds), *How Sanctions Work*, p. 280.
16. Quoted in Leon H. Sullivan, *Moving Mountains: The Principles and Purposes of Leon Sullivan*, Valley Forge: Judson Press, 1998, p. 52.
17. *Ibid.*, p. 196.
18. *Ibid.*, p. 57.
19. *Ibid.*, p. 82.
20. Deon Geldenhuys, 'International Involvement in South Africa's Political Transformation' in Walter Carlsnaes and Marie Muller (eds), *Change and South African External Relations*, Johannesburg: International Thomson Publishing, 1997, pp. 37–9.
21. A fuller account of this section of this chapter can be found in Guelke, *South Africa in Transition*, pp. 143–58.
22. The Commonwealth Group of Eminent Persons (CGEP), *Mission to South Africa: The Commonwealth Report*, Harmondsworth: Penguin Books for the Commonwealth Secretariat, 1986, p. 142.
23. Botha's letter is reproduced in Stephen Chan, 'British and Commonwealth Actors in the 1980s' in Stephen Chan and Vivienne Jabri (eds), *Mediation in Southern Africa*, London and Basingstoke: Macmillan, 1993, pp. 34–5.
24. CGEP, *Mission to South Africa* (1986), pp. 61–2.
25. ICJ, *Agenda for Peace: An Independent Survey of the Violence in South Africa by the International Commission of Jurists*, Geneva: International Commission of Jurists, 1992, p. 22.
26. Quoted in *Anti-Apartheid News* (London), May/June 1992.
27. *South Africa: State of Fear – Security Force Complicity in Torture and Political Killings, 1990–1992*, London: Amnesty International, 1992.
28. See paragraph 1 of Boutros Boutros-Ghali, *Report of the Secretary-General on the Question of South Africa*, United Nations S/24389, New York (7 August) 1992.
29. Quoted in Steven Friedman (ed.), *The Long Journey: South Africa's Quest for a Negotiated Settlement*, Johannesburg: Ravan Press, 1993, p. 157.

30. Chris Landsberg, 'Directing from the Stalls? The International Community and the South African Negotiation Forum' in Steven Friedman and Doreen Atkinson (eds), *The Small Miracle: South Africa's Negotiated Settlement*, Johannesburg: Ravan Press, 1994, p. 289.
31. Hermann Giliomee, *The Afrikaners: Biography of a People*, Cape Town: Tafelberg, 2003, p. 641.

Chapter 11

1. David Lodge, *Small World*, London: Penguin, 1985, p. 52.
2. E.H. Carr, *What is History?*, Harmondsworth: Penguin, 1964, pp. 7–30.
3. Most notably in the fictional history by Arthur Keppel-Jones, *When Smuts Goes: A History of South Africa from 1952 to 2010 First Published in 2015*, London: Victor Gollancz, 1947.
4. John Kane-Berman (ed.), *South Africa Survey 2001/2002*, Johannesburg: South African Institute of Race Relations, 2001, p. 128.
5. John Kane-Berman (ed.), *South Africa Survey 2002/2003*, South African Institute of Race Relations, Johannesburg 2003, p. 10.
6. Table put together from information in Herma Forgey *et al.*, *South Africa Survey 2000/01*, Johannesburg: South African Institute of Race Relations, 2001, p. 48.
7. This was first published in hardback in 1985. I have used the paperback edition with the additional epilogue on the crisis of the mid-1980s that was published in 1986.
8. Sampie Terreblanche, *A History of Inequality in South Africa, 1652–2002*, Pietermaritzburg: University of Natal Press, 2002, pp. 374–5.
9. See Elizabeth Sidiropoulus, Anthea Jeffery, Shaun MacKay, Herma Forgey, Cheryl Chipps and Terence Corrigan, *South Africa Survey 1996/97*, Johannesburg: South African Institute of Race Relations, 1997, p. 654.
10. Muriel Horrell, Dudley Horner and Jane Hudson, *A Survey of Race Relations in South Africa*, Johannesburg: South African Institute of Race Relations, 1975, pp. 120–1.
11. Rupert Taylor, 'South Africa: The Role of Peace and Conflict Resolution Organizations in the Struggle against Apartheid', in Benjamin Gidron, Stanley N. Katz and Yeheskel Hasenfeld, *Mobilizing for Peace: Conflict Resolution in Northern Ireland, Israel/Palestine, and South Africa*, New York: Oxford University Press, 2002, p. 87
12. Tom Lodge, *Politics in South Africa: From Mandela to Mbeki*, Cape Town: David Philip, 2002, p. 32.
13. *Ibid.*
14. Hermann Giliomee, *The Afrikaners: Biography of a People*, Cape Town: Tafelberg, 2003, p. 645.
15. John Kane-Berman (ed.), *South Africa Survey 2002/2003*, Johannesburg: South African Institute of Race Relations, 2003, p. 293.
16. Sampie Terreblanche, *A History of Inequality in South Africa, 1652–2002*, Pietermaritzburg, University of Natal Press, 2002, p. 419.

17. John Kane-Berman (ed.), *South Africa Survey 2001/2002*, Johannesburg: South African Institute of Race Relations, 2001, p. 374.
18. *Ibid.*, p. 376.
19. An excellent account of the issue centred on one case is Jonny Steinberg, *Midlands*, Johannesburg: Jonathan Ball, 2002.
20. See 'Mbeki Criticises Commonwealth over Zimbabwe', *Financial Times*, 13/14 December 2003.

Concise Bibliography

What follows is a small selection of the books which I think the reader would find of value in extending his or her consideration of the rise and fall of apartheid. I have not assumed that the reader would have access to a massive library of South African books. I have therefore restricted the list for the most part to books that are currently available. I have also generally avoided the inclusion of texts of historical interest that have been overtaken by events or require prior understanding of the period in which they were written to be comprehended.

Barber, James (1999) *South Africa in the Twentieth Century: A Political History – In Search of a Nation State*, Oxford: Blackwell.

Barber, James and John Barratt (1990) *South Africa's Foreign Policy: The Search for Status and Security 1945–1988*, Cambridge: Cambridge University Press.

Beinart, William (1994) *Twentieth-Century South Africa*, Cape Town: Oxford University Press.

Dubow, Saul (1989) *Racial Segregation and the Origins of Apartheid in South Africa, 1919–36*, Basingstoke: Macmillan.

Friedman, Steven and Doreen Atkinson (eds) (1994) *The Small Miracle: South Africa's Negotiated Settlement*, Johannesburg: Ravan Press.

Giliomee, Hermann (2003) *The Afrikaners: Biography of a People*, Cape Town: Tafelberg.

Guelke, Adrian (1999) *South Africa in Transition: The Misunderstood Miracle*, London: I.B. Tauris.

Harvey, Robert (2001) *The Fall of Apartheid: The Inside Story from Smuts to Mbeki*, Basingstoke: Palgrave.

Keegan, Timothy (1996) *Colonial South Africa and the Origins of the Racial Order*, David Philip, Cape Town and Johannesburg.

Krog, Antjie (1998) *Country of My Skull*, London: Jonathan Cape.

Lipton, Merle (1986) *Capitalism and Apartheid: South Africa, 1910–86*, Aldershot: Wildwood House.

Lodge, Tom (2002) *Politics in South Africa: From Mandela to Mbeki*, Cape Town: David Philip.

Mandela, Nelson (1994) *Long Walk to Freedom*, Randburg: Macdonald Purnell.

Minter, William (1994) *Apartheid's Contras: An Inquiry into the Roots of War in Angola and Mozambique*, Johannesburg: Witwatersrand University Press.

O'Meara, Dan (1996) *Forty Lost Years: The Apartheid State and the Politics of the National Party 1948–1994*, Randburg: Ravan Press.
Pakenham, Thomas (1982) *The Boer War*, London: Futura Publications.
Posel, Deborah (1991) *The Making of Apartheid 1948–1961: Conflict and Compromise*, Oxford: Clarendon Press.
Rich, Paul (1996) *State Power and Black Politics in South Africa, 1912–51*, Basingstoke: Macmillan.
Sisk, Timothy D. (1995) *Democratization in South Africa: The Elusive Social Contract*, Princeton, NJ: Princeton University Press.
Sparks, Allister (1991) *The Mind of South Africa: The Story of the Rise and Fall of Apartheid*, London: Mandarin.
Sparks, Allister (1994) *Tomorrow is Another Country: The Inside Story of South Africa's Negotiated Revolution*, Sandton: Struik Book Distributors.
Spitz, Richard with Matthew Chaskalson (2002) *The Politics of Transition: A Hidden History of South Africa's Negotiated Settlement*, Oxford: Hart Publishing.
Terreblanche, Sampie (2002) *A History of Inequality in South Africa, 1652–2002*, Pietermaritzburg: University of Natal Press.
Waldmeir, Patti (1997) *Anatomy of a Miracle: The End of Apartheid and the Birth of the New South Africa*, London: Viking.
Welsh, Frank (2000) *A History of South Africa*, London: HarperCollins.

Index